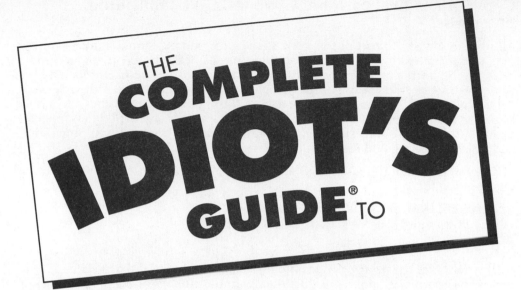

THE COMPLETE IDIOT'S GUIDE® TO

Knowledge Management

by Melissie Clemmons Rumizen, Ph.D.

ALPHA

A member of Penguin Group (USA) Inc.

International Standard Book Number: 0-02-864177-9
Library of Congress Catalog Card Number: 2001092308

12 11 10   12 11 10 9

Interpretation of the printing code: The rightmost number of the first series of numbers is the year of the book's printing; the rightmost number of the second series of numbers is the number of the book's printing. For example, a printing code of 02-1 shows that the first printing occurred in 2002.

Printed in the United States of America

This is a CWL Publishing Enterprises Book, developed by John A. Woods for Penguin Group (USA) Inc./Alpha Books. For more information, contact CWL Publishing Enterprises, 3010 Irvington Way, Madison, WI 53713-3414 (608)273-3710.

Publisher
Marie Butler-Knight

Product Manager
Phil Kitchel

Managing Editor
Jennifer Chisholm

Senior Acquisitions Editor
Renee Wilmeth

Development Editor
Joan D. Paterson

Production Editor
Katherin Bidwell

Copy Editor
Amy Borrelli

Illustrator
Jody Schaeffer

Cover Designers
Mike Freeland
Kevin Spear

Book Designers
Scott Cook and Amy Adams of DesignLab

Indexer
Amy Lawrence

Layout/Proofreading
Mary Hunt
Kimberly Tucker

Contents at a Glance

Contents

Foreword

Knowledge management has been easily dismissed by some as just the latest management fad. Dilbert has lampooned it. Untold software vendors slap the label of KM on their packages and tout miraculous cures for all our knowledge failings. Yet, behind all the jargon and the hype, we find companies engaged in serious efforts to manage their most precious asset—their working knowledge.

Managing knowledge is clearly one of the new fundamentals for success in the new economy. It is a tough job and few organizations do it well. Knowledge management involves many complex organizational issues; simplistic approaches will not work, nor will throwing technologies at people somehow magically make knowledge happen.

Written by an expert practitioner, this book cuts through the lingo that has littered the knowledge management field. Drawing upon years of experience, Melissie Clemmons Rumizen debunks some widely held beliefs and puts into perspective those that hold true under fire. She provides a solid review of the knowledge-based ideas and practices that have most influenced how companies function. Both those new to the questions and those seeking to improve their current efforts will enjoy this practical, savvy guided tour through the eclectic mix of disciplines, concepts, methods, and approaches that form the field of knowledge management.

Far too many people working in KM obsess over creating the perfect approach. The important thing is to start asking the knowledge questions and be willing to experiment in various ways. Rumizen shows us how to do this by focusing on commonsense principles and sharpening our senses to sniff out the knowledge value to the business.

Rumizen covers a wide range of related topics, ranging from how to work with information technology to the fine points of a communications strategy. The most important of these topics is dealing with an organizational culture and managing change. She quite rightly assesses that challenge is the biggest potential barrier and offers practical tips for meeting that challenge.

This is not an unwieldy academic tome; Rumizen follows the dictum of Oscar Wilde to treat unimportant things seriously and important things lightly. It is good to remember that humor and humility serve any change effort well, including becoming more knowledge-focused.

Leading a knowledge management effort within an organization is a sometimes thankless job and it requires a jack-of-all-trades. Rumizen zeroes in on the skills needed, the expertise required, and above all the mind-set demanded. Successful initiatives in KM require imagination, daring, persistence, an entrepreneurial spirit, and a willingness to occasionally be outrageous and outspoken. You must be prepared to win big—or fail greatly. But the potential prize for your organization matches the size of the challenge.

Managing knowledge must become part of how every organization does business. Those who fail to manage what they know simply cannot be serious players in the new business environment.

—Laurence Prusak

Executive Director, IBM Institute for Knowledge Management

Mr. Prusak is the co-author of several books on knowledge management: *In Good Company: How Social Capital Makes Organizations Work* (with Don Cohen), Harvard Business School Press, 2001; *Working Knowledge: How Organizations Manage What They Know* (with Thomas H. Davenport), Harvard Business School Press, 1997; and *Information Ecology: Mastering the Information and Knowledge Environment* (with Thomas H. Davenport), Oxford University Press, 1997. He is also the editor of *Knowledge in Organizations,* Butterworth-Heinemann, 1997.

Introduction

Decades ago, Peter Drucker began writing about the knowledge worker. Over the last decade, however, more and more attention has been paid to the true engine of today's organizations: the brainpower of employees.

Saying that is simple, but managing an organization so that it best taps the knowledge of its employees isn't so simple. For one thing, employees must be given what they need to do a good job: leadership, processes, a supporting organizational culture, information technology, measurement, and leadership. In addition to the leadership of the organization, a new role has emerged in many organizations to lead the knowledge management charge: the Chief Knowledge Officer.

The purpose of this book is to look at the various components needed to manage knowledge in an organization. Doing knowledge management right is much like juggling many balls in the air at the same time. It requires a good bit of skill, not to mention aplomb. But it can be done, and those that do it well see the payoff as they begin to take advantage of the vast store of know-how possessed by employees. This book will help you to learn how to do it.

Part 1, "Exploring the Oxymoron," gives you the foundation you need to understand knowledge management and what people are doing in the field. It explains the rationale for knowledge management, covers popular theoretical models, gives some basic definitions, and details case studies of two successful knowledge implementations. It also explains the new role in many organizations to lead knowledge management, the Chief Knowledge Officer.

Part 2, "Getting Started," looks at how to begin implementing knowledge management. This process includes selecting a strategy, a strong suggestion to start with a pilot, and how to build an infrastructure to support the implementation. Several chapters also look at specific approaches to include what I call "the killer application," *communities of practice*.

Part 3, "Can't Live with IT; Can't Live Without IT," looks at another critical success factor for knowledge management—information technology. The first chapter explores a critical partner and ally, the Chief Information Officer. Other chapters give some fundamentals such as intranets, collaborative technology, and portals.

Part 4, "The Showstopper of Culture," looks at what knowledge management tries to change—how "we do things around here." It also includes several chapters on change management, a discipline for successfully bringing about organizational change.

Part 5, "Keeping Score," focuses on what is often the Achilles heel of knowledge management—measurement. This part opens with a chapter looking at some general guidelines for measures and then moves to three chapters giving specific methodologies.

Part 6, "Settling In for the Long Haul," looks at some pitfalls you might encounter along the way and how to scale up. The last chapter looks at personal knowledge management, knowledge management for you on your own.

There's also a glossary with all of the key definitions in the book.

Special Features

In addition to the regular text, this book contains four extra features designed to help you learn about knowledge management.

Didn't Know

Didn't Know boxes give a little more in-depth background. They may be a story, a reference, or some information you might find interesting.

Know Nos

These boxes give you traps to avoid, like common misassumptions and missteps. I've made some of these mistakes myself, so I can vouch for them!

Know These

These boxes define terms in more depth than they're explained in the regular narrative of the chapter. Like any other field, knowledge management has its own jargon. To learn more about the field you need to speak the language.

Know How

Know How boxes give you additional tips that supplement the text. They are meant to be practical and to the point.

Acknowledgments

My thanks to John Woods of CWL Publishing Enterprises, who invited me to write this book and shepherded me through the process. I applaud his editing skills, his knowledge of the field, and his patience. I'd also like to thank Bob Magnan of CWL Publishing Enterprises whose humor and support was helpful.

I am more grateful than I can say to Chuck Seeley of Intel Corporation, who served as my personal technical editor. Chuck is a rare bird, someone who knows a great deal and takes the time to document and share his knowledge. Having Chuck as my technical editor was a constant spur to do my very best. Also thanks to my technical editor for the information technology section, Jeff Stemke, for both his technical expertise and his humor, which I enjoy tremendously and hope one day to understand. And a thank you to Alicia Hill, who provided much needed accounting expertise.

I also owe thanks to many in the knowledge management community. First I must mention Carla O'Dell, Jack Grayson Jr., and the staff and members of the American Productivity and Quality Center. They inspired me to enter this field, and they were also my first teachers.

Finally, I owe thanks to many in the closely-knit and generous knowledge management community. We are all learning together. I'd like to thank those that taught me and directly helped with this book (in alphabetical order):

Verna Allee, the American Red Cross, Bill Baker, Steve Barth, Lucinda Berlew, Mary Bernhard, Susan Biggs, Patrick Bresnan, Mike Burtha, Celemi, Mark Clare, Bill and Laura Clemmons, Don Cohen, Mick Cope, David Coleman, Chris Collison, Rob Cross of University of Virginia, Jane Davis, Steve Denning, The Delphi Group, Arthur Detore, Bill Dietrick, Nancy Dixon, Keith Dompier, Lynette Freese, Carol Gorelick, Kevin Hans, Hewlett-Packard Consulting, Dan Holtshouse, Cindy Hubert, Paula Jacobs, Knowledge Management Review, Knowledge Transformation International, Jerry Landon, Eric Lesser, Marilyn Martiny, Richard McDermott, Jim McKeen, Nick Milton, RS Moorthy, Fred Nickols, Ann Noles, John Old, Geoff Parcell, Peggy Parskey, Larry Prusak, Judi Sandrock, SAP America, Lisa Sasson, John Smith, Dave Snowden, Bill Snyder, Bill Spencer, Sandy Staples, Belinda Stinson, Karl-Erik Sveiby, Erick Thompson, Etienne Wenger, Rowan Wilson, and Tom Young.

Special Thanks to the Technical Reviewer

The Complete Idiot's Guide to Knowledge Management was reviewed by experts who double-checked the accuracy of what you'll learn here, to help us ensure that this book gives you everything you need to know about knowledge management. Special thanks are extended to Chuck Seeley, Jeff Stemke, Alicia Hill, and Verna Allee.

Trademarks

All terms mentioned in this book that are known to be or are suspected of being trademarks or service marks have been appropriately capitalized. Alpha Books and Penguin Group (USA) Inc. cannot attest to the accuracy of this information. Use of a term in this book should not be regarded as affecting the validity of any trademark or service mark.

Part 1

Exploring the Oxymoron

It was September 11, 1995. Along with almost 500 other people, I was attending the Knowledge Imperative Symposium sponsored by the American Productivity and Quality Center and Arthur Andersen. The conference brochure had said the symposium was about something called knowledge management. It sounded weird to me. How do you manage knowledge? Isn't that impossible?

One of the first speakers was Ken Derr, then CEO of Chevron. He told us that "managing knowledge is something all companies will have to master if they expect to compete in the global economy. Those that can learn quickly and then leverage and use that knowledge within the company will have a big advantage over those that can't. And this will be true whether knowledge is developed internally or acquired elsewhere."

In this section, we'll explore what knowledge management is, look at some of the theoretical thinking behind it, and discuss a new leadership role that often supports it. Additionally, we'll look at two case studies of organizations that successfully implemented a KM program.

What's in a Name?

You had hoped that after the reengineering craze mercifully faded out, the flood of conference brochures would stop—but then another wave of brochures for knowledge management started showing up. Although all of these conferences say they are about knowledge management, the focus seems to be all over the map. Some concentrate on information technology, like data warehousing; some are about e-business; and some target specific industries, like pharmaceuticals and oil and petroleum. Some have titles with strange terms not in your dictionary, like intellectual capital, tacit knowledge, and communities of practice. But the titles of the conferences are tame compared with the titles of the speakers: Leader of Learning and Change, Director of Knowledge Networking, Knowledge Architect, and Knowledge Sorceress. (I'm not making any of these up.)

Like used car commercials, though, the various conferences do have some aggravating characteristics in common. None of them explain why this "knowledge management" seems to have become important to a lot of people who pay good money for conferences.

None of them give you an idea of why you should bother to pay any attention to it. Worst of all, none of them actually define what the heck knowledge management is.

In this chapter, we describe knowledge management and how it got started. We also look at the reasons why so many companies have started knowledge management programs. Finally, we look at who's doing this and why it's worth their while.

The Publisher and the Krona

Let's start with a story about what unleashed this flurry of interest in the first place. You probably know the story of the delicate princess who couldn't sleep because of the pesky pea under the mountain of mattresses she slept on. One Swedish krona similarly befuddled the founding father of knowledge management, Karl-Erik Sveiby. (A *krona* is a small coin, about the equivalent of a dime in U.S. dollars today—the financial equivalent of a very small pea indeed.)

In 1979 Sveiby took a big leap, leaving a job at giant conglomerate Unilever to join nine friends in Stockholm in publishing a new business weekly. He soon felt as if he had beamed down to a different planet—and he wasn't sure if his new planet could sustain human life. Since the company had only 10 employees, Sveiby turned his hand to whatever needed to be done. As he had been an accountant at Unilever for two years, this included looking at the books.

Know These

Intangible assets have value to a company, but no physical existence. Some intangible assets have been recognized for years: patents, copyright, and trademarks. However, relatively few organizations make any attempt to put a dollar value on them. In contrast, physical assets (such as land, buildings, and equipment) can be sold, used, and depreciated.

Every year at his new company he grew quite annoyed. One inactive account was valued at just one krona—the value of their well-known brand. He couldn't believe it was given such a measly value. It was one of the most important assets his new company had—and it didn't have many.

That wasn't the only thing that was out of whack. Upon digging deeper, he found an important asset not even on the books—the competence of the few employees the company had. These employees formed an eccentric miniature brain trust, including some of Sweden's most respected financial analysts. Also not on the books was the enormous amount of goodwill they had amassed from a large network of friends and well-wishers. In fact, nothing that seemed to matter for their survival, let alone future prosperity, was considered an asset. Instead, the balance sheet listed typewriters and desks!

Sveiby then decided he had to give up, unlearn everything he knew, and start all over again. Business people like himself seemed to know quite a bit about managing tangible assets, but not beans (or peas) about what he began calling *intangible assets*. He began to talk to leaders of companies like his and discovered that those leaders saw their businesses in a different way from the people he had left behind in the manufacturing environment of Unilever. They viewed their intangible assets as real. As good managers, they also understood that since their job was to manage the assets of a company, some of the assets to manage were the intangible ones.

Didn't Know

Karl-Erik Sveiby wanted to share the intangible assets work in Sweden globally and sent an article to the *Harvard Business Review*. An HBR editor, as Sveiby puts it, "politely refused" the article. She commented, "I am sure these ideas are very interesting for your native Sweden. However, they are not new to our U.S. managers and you have no U.S. companies as cases." He now self-publishes, sharing much of his work freely on his Web site, www.sveiby.com.au.

What Sveiby and others quickly realized is that what really counts is knowledge. The articles, the books, the conferences, and the knowledge management programs in company after company stem from this radically different view: The intangibles are the most important things to manage for success.

So Sveiby began suggesting to business leaders in Sweden that they had to think differently. He became part of a working group of business people from different organizations, Konrad, and in 1986 published their work in a book, *The Invisible Balance Sheet*. Soon a number of people in Scandinavia began to pick up on his ideas at companies like WM Data, Celemi, and Skandia AFS, one of the largest financial services corporations in Europe.

Meanwhile, back on the U.S. ranch, people were asking the same questions. Peter Drucker—management authority, writer, and self-titled "insultant"—had started raising the flag in 1959. Tom Stewart wrote his first piece about *intellectual capital* in a 1991 issue of *Fortune*. Portions of the balanced-scorecard approach to corporate

Know These

Intellectual capital includes everything an organization knows. That can be ideas, different kinds of knowledge, and innovations. The bottom line, though, is that it's knowledge that an organization can turn into profit.

measures—a concept originated by Robert Kaplan and David Norton in their article, "The Balanced Scorecard: Measures that Drive Performance" (*Harvard Business Review*, February 1992)—included areas that were intangible, like renewal and development.

The conferences also had started. Ernst & Young and the Strategic Leadership Forum sponsored the first knowledge management conference in 1994, the Knowledge Advantage Colloquium. The seminal event, however, was the 1995 Knowledge Imperative Symposium. Held by Arthur Andersen and the American Productivity and Quality Center (APQC), it attracted about 500 people. The halls of the conference hotel were so crowded that it was hard to walk.

Around the world an explosion of experimentation, discovery, learning, and success had started.

Exploring Knowledge Management

First of all, if you think the name "knowledge management" sounds silly, relax. No one else likes this name either. A few terms I've heard suggested to replace it are "knowledge sharing," "knowledge focus," and "knowledge creation."

The sticking point is the word "management." It evokes an image of someone in a smart business suit sitting in an office with an M.B.A. diploma hung on the wall, reaching into people's brains for knowledge, rifling through the contents, and somehow managing the knowledge found there as easily as if it were auto parts—but knowledge is not a thing. To many people, management also means control, as if knowledge were something static and unchanging—but knowledge is constantly changing.

Many specialists in the field shudder at the term "knowledge management" because it fails to name even one of the activities associated with knowledge—creating, identifying, sharing, capturing, acquiring, and leveraging knowledge, to name a few. But at this point the name has become so well known that we're stuck with it.

Know These

Knowledge is information in context to produce an action-able understanding.

Now that you may be thoroughly confused by the term "knowledge management," let's define some terms relating to knowledge. Then we'll move on to knowledge management itself.

Defining Knowledge

We often hear the terms "data" and "information" and "knowledge" tossed around. Usually, they are considered to form a hierarchy, from data to information to *knowledge*.

Data are just bits and numbers. They are discrete, self-contained, and in isolation have no meaning. Data are like Legos we collect and use to build information. Usually, the purpose for which we need the information helps us to decide what to do with the Legos. For example, as a researcher I collected data in the form of test scores for students and put them into a database. I usually followed this process to look at the data:

1. First, I scanned for bad data, perhaps a test score I had entered incorrectly or one I had missed altogether. Only when I was sure that the data were spotlessly clean would I go any further. Information technology has brought this home to us; otherwise it is garbage in, garbage out.

2. My next step was to get a thumbnail sketch of the test scores: the average score, the range of scores, and how much variation there was among the scores. This gave me an overall description.

3. I then grouped the test scores in various categories, such as by the groups of students who had taken the test or the types of questions.

4. Next, I could use statistics to analyze whether or not there were any significant differences among the categories.

5. If I wanted to look at just one part of the test, I would select the data for the subset of questions for that part.

Once I arranged and assembled the data, they had meaning, something I could communicate to other people. The data Legos had become information. But I still didn't know what to do next with my Legos. The information needed a context.

The teacher knew what the test was intended to measure, how well the students had been expected to do, and where the class was in the course. This was a context that made the information actionable for the teacher. If most students miss the questions covering a specific topic, the teacher could decide to review those points before going on. Of course, students had their own context. They knew that they needed to pass the course and how well they had done up until that test. Within that context, the information could lead to action. A student with a bad grade could swear to study harder next time, drop the course as quickly as possible, or just swear. The key point is that the combination of information and context enabled both teacher and students to decide what, if anything, they needed to do.

Know Nos

Don't fall into the trap of trying to categorize everything as data, information, or knowledge. Everyone provides his or her own context and decides which is which. My information can be your knowledge. Your knowledge can be my information.

Notice that key word: actionable. Forget about "nice to have," the knowledge you don't need for any action. It piles up in stacks of paper nobody reads, databases nobody uses, and archives nobody ever visits.

Do you have any "data junkyards" in your organization? If you're lucky, you're only wasting resources that could have been used on something else. But you're probably losing something more important. When the amount of data grows too large, it can bury what's valuable. You can't find what you need from what you don't need.

Action, or the ability to take action, is what makes knowledge valuable. This is the most important criterion for knowledge within an organization. What knowledge do you need for what actions? How will you use knowledge for actions? Will the actions be the right ones? In short, what critical capability does knowledge give you?

This criterion also forces you to focus on what is vital. I've rarely heard anyone complain about having too little data or information. Instead, I've spent many hours trying to get people to define what an organization needs to know to achieve its goals. Be ruthless. Put knowledge to the test: How useful is it?

Tacit and Explicit Knowledge

Two more important terms are tacit knowledge and explicit knowledge. This is a key distinction in knowledge management.

Explicit knowledge can be said, written down, and transmitted. It is objective, lending itself to rules and definitions. It is easily captured, stored, and transmitted electronically. Most of all, it is what we know that we can put into words.

Know These

Explicit knowledge encompasses the things we know that we can write down, share with others, and put into a database. One example is the steps used to perform CPR. Those steps can be described in a detailed, exact sequence of actions you can teach to someone. **Tacit knowledge** is what we do not know that we know. It includes know-how, rules of thumb, experience, insights, and intuition. Let's take the example of CPR again. If your mother was in cardiac arrest, who would you want to treat her: someone who knows the steps of CPR but lacks experience, or an emergency room doctor with years of experience treating cardiac arrests?

Tacit knowledge includes know-how, judgment, experience, insights, rules of thumb, and skills. It exists within context. But it is silent. As Michael Polyani, author of *The Tacit Dimension,* puts it, "We know more than we can tell." Beyond that, we don't even know what we know until we need to know it. Accordingly, it is hard to express, process, capture, or transmit in any systematic or logical manner. The distinction between tacit and explicit knowledge is critical; we'll come back to it a number of times later in the book.

Defining Knowledge Management

This brings us to the main attraction: *knowledge management (KM),* which is the systematic processes by which knowledge needed for an organization to succeed is created, captured, shared, and leveraged.

Know These

Knowledge management (KM) focuses on how an organization identifies, creates, captures, acquires, shares, and leverages knowledge. Systematic processes support these activities, also enabling replication of successes. All of these are specific actions organizations take to manage their knowledge.

Organizational Drivers for Knowledge Management

Do any of these scenarios sound familiar to you?

➤ You're part of a large, global organization. You've got a serious problem at work with no solution. You're sure someone somewhere knows the answer, but you don't know who. You don't even know which continent!

➤ You're on top of the world. After months of working nights and weekends, your team has finished the big project. This one is really going to make a difference regarding an ongoing problem your organization has encountered. Then, before your meeting to present your recommendations, you find out that another team in Brazil had already solved it six months before. Not only that—their solution is better than the one you planned to propose because they had additional information.

➤ You've got something that has to be done right now for a big customer who's as important as he is angry. You call the office that's responsible for handling it. Somebody there tells you that only one person can do the job and that she'll take care of it first thing—when she gets back from vacation in two weeks.

➤ You survived the merger. Before you can breathe a sigh of relief, you pick up the phone to call Joe for some information. Then, you stop dialing as you realize that Joe is gone as a result of the merger. You don't know who else to call for the information.

➤ You need some specific information for a report that's due in a few hours. You try searching on the corporate intranet. After 1,139 hits, you give up. There's too much to plow through and you have no idea of what's important.

➤ You're a top-level manager looking at the performance of four plants. All have roughly the same equipment. All of the employees have roughly the same type and level of training. One plant is doing better by far than the other three. One is abysmal. The other two are somewhere in the middle. How can there be such differences? What can you do to bring the other three up to the level of the top performer?

Maybe your organization is one of many that has gotten big, the corporate equivalents of a sprawling metropolis. As expanding organizations reach across the country and around the globe, it's no longer possible for one person to know where critical knowledge is located within the organization.

Or maybe your company has shrunk, losing people through downsizing and restructuring. Or maybe through an acquisition or merger you lost some employees even as you gained others. Each person lost represents a unique body of knowledge lost to the organization.

Didn't Know

From the days when someone else would pump your gas, some of us remember the road maps that oil companies had. Chevron built on this concept to create a road map to expertise that even folded up like a real map. For different knowledge areas, the map included names, phone numbers, locations, and other information for people to contact. Chevron soon realized a paper version had fatal limitations. It was hard to keep up-to-date. It was hard to make changes in which knowledge areas were listed. Quickly, they moved to a Web-based version.

Prior to a planned merger in 2000, a large U.S.-based company vested all of its senior managers, who immediately left in droves. The merger did not go through, and now the company is struggling to replace the knowledge lost. It's not as simple as hiring new managers, even if you find people with the necessary managerial skills and experience. The managers lost also knew "how things are done around here" and who to call. No newcomer comes on board with that type of company-specific knowledge. And once the knowledge walks out the door, it's too late to do anything about it.

The cry to increase efficiency and cut costs is constant. For example, the requirement for enormous capital investments has driven the oil industry to do the best, cheapest, and smartest job possible. Leveraging knowledge can make a crucial difference. As employees in a company share and reuse knowledge, big savings in one location rapidly multiply to impressive numbers across continents. Read a list of the players in knowledge management and you will see many oil companies.

"Faster, faster, faster" is another constant cry. In 1981 FedEx introduced overnight delivery of letters, which forever changed my expectations as a customer for speed of service. Now any major player in the delivery business must be able to get it there overnight.

Pharmaceutical companies continually try to increase their new product development speed. The drug pipeline of development, testing, and obtaining government approval and marketing takes years. A company that can shorten that time will start the profits rolling in sooner and outpace its competitors.

In the semiconductor industry, every player works feverishly to put out the next new chip, as Moore's law continues to hold true: Each new chip doubles the capacity of its predecessor and is released within 18–24 months of the previous chip. At that pace, no company can afford not to work as hard and as smart as possible, or a competitor will eat them for lunch.

Maybe you're not in the delivery business or pharmaceuticals or semiconductors, where the need for speed is particularly great. The fact remains that the need to innovate and deliver services faster is a growing concern in any industry. No matter how fast you are today, you have to get faster.

The bottom line is that knowledge is our most important asset. Knowledge—what we know, how well we use it, and how quickly we can learn new things—makes us competitive. It can give us an advantage that makes the difference.

And the Winners Are ...

Although not everyone has caught on yet, many companies in diverse industries have knowledge management programs. In fact, there are too many to list all of them. A few are

Intel	Johnson & Johnson
Siemens	World Bank Group
IBM	Motorola

11

British Petroleum	Best Buy
The United States Navy	Citibank
British Telecom	Gateway
Eli Lilly	Hewlett-Packard
Ford Motor Company	Clarica
The Saint Paul Companies	Cap Gemini Ernst & Young
Xerox	Phillips Petroleum

Coming up with the numbers, though, is harder. Just as it's hard to quantify the value of information technology, it's tough to assign numbers to knowledge management programs. Many companies report the benefits in anecdotes.

However, the good news is that it doesn't take long to get a return on investments in the millions once a company starts looking. A few examples are as follows:

➤ By sharing a method to reduce time installing brakes on the assembly line, Ford Motor Company recorded cycle-time savings of more than $160,000 for that process in one year.

Know How

In many organizations, communities of practice are an essential component of knowledge management. These are groups of practitioners who share a common interest in a specific area of competence and are willing to share their experiences. Communities of practice are sometimes known by other names, such as learning communities or networks (Hewlett-Packard), best practice teams (Chevron), family groups (Xerox), and thematic groups (World Bank).

➤ Before the annual meeting of its communities of practice, American Management Systems would collect anecdotes showing ROI. Usually after four or five stories, the total would reach millions. At this point the knowledge management office would stop asking for stories for another year.

➤ At US West, the threshold for beginning any project was that it must return a tenfold ROI. According to Sherman Woo, senior development director for US West's Global Village Development group, meeting that requirement was easy.

➤ Texas Instruments noticed huge differences in the performance of various semiconductor plants. They launched an effort to bring the level of all plants up to that of the star performers. The first iteration gained $500,000 in savings. Two successive iterations also netted $500,000 in savings each. The savings were so large that Texas Instruments in effect gained production equal to adding several plants at that time.

But perhaps the most impressive story to date of the payoff on an organizational level is that of Chevron. In 1992 Chevron launched an effort to reduce operating costs. Then-CEO Ken Derr stated, "The key to progress will be the way we behave. We all need to share our successes and be willing to learn from others." Initially, Chevron set up 13 teams to identify knowledge that could be leveraged across Chevron to cut costs. In the first year alone, one team generated savings of $150,000. By 2000, the reduction in annual operating costs was estimated at $2 billion.

All of these success stories show the immense financial potential of knowledge management.

The Least You Need to Know

➤ Knowledge is the most important asset for organizations today. Knowledge is information in context to produce an actionable understanding.

➤ Knowledge management is the systematic processes by which knowledge needed for an organization to succeed is created, captured, shared, and leveraged.

➤ There are many drivers for organizations to effectively manage their knowledge.

➤ Barriers to managing knowledge can be overcome.

➤ Managing knowledge pays off well.

Chapter 2

More Models Than a Car Show

In This Chapter

➤ A world of knowledge workers

➤ The components of intangible assets

➤ The spiral of knowledge creation

➤ Creating a learning organization

➤ How value is created

You did it. You picked a conference brochure out of the bunch and decided to attend. Now that you're going to sessions, it's still confusing. You're expecting people to start out by talking about the things they're doing, the great results they're getting, and their plans for the future. Instead, people begin by quoting Drucker, Sveiby, Nonaka, Senge, and Allee. At least you may know who Peter Drucker is—you can't get through Management 101 without acknowledging this guru. But those other people are strangers.

Do you need to know about those people? No. It's perfectly possible to work miracles, to live long and prosper without reading the work of these thinkers. Not everyone working in knowledge management has been inspired by their work. Not everyone knows all of the theories. However, many of us find it extremely useful to use the work of the leading thinkers in the field. It gives us new ways of framing knowledge management in the business context.

If you're a manager, these frameworks help you talk to your fellow managers about why this is important for the business. If you're working with management, this gives you the language to put knowledge management into their context. Then, once they have an actionable understanding, you can begin to get their commitment.

Didn't Know

At the beginning of his career, Peter Drucker published a paper on the New York stock market in a prestigious economic journal. In this paper, he predicted that the market was only capable of going up. The paper was published in September 1929. Although this experience cured him of making financial prophecies, his other predictions have proved that it was the exception to the rule. He's kept ahead of the rest of the world for three-quarters of a century.

The World Has Changed, Says Peter Drucker

If you've avoided reading Drucker before now, this may inspire you to look him up. If so, expect to be overwhelmed by an embarrassment of riches. He's written more than three dozen books and more than 75 articles just in the past 10 years on a wide range of topics. If you want to focus on some of the ones relevant to knowledge management, I've given a short list in the bibliography at the end of this book.

Know How

There's nothing more practical than a good theory. Inside your organization, it will help you in many ways—thinking about what's important, picking your strategy, and explaining to other people what you want to accomplish. Externally, it will help understand the thinking behind what other people are doing.

How has the world changed, according to Drucker? A song popular just after World War I asked the musical question, "How 'ya gonna keep 'em down on the farm after they've seen Paree?" It was an important question, because until World War I farmers were the largest group of workers in every country. But even before World War I, the emergence of manufacturing prompted the beginning of a shift to the blue-collar worker. Farmers started heading off to the factories for jobs. Around 1900 these blue-collar workers in the manufacturing industries had become a notable force in society. Their numbers grew rapidly: By the 1950s blue-collar workers were the single largest group in every developed country.

But the situation shifted again. In the closing decades of the twentieth century, the industrial workforce shrunk. Increasingly, work has become knowledge-based and workers have become *knowledge workers*. Chances are that's what you are.

The result is a lot of headaches for managers, who wind up herding cats. The dirty secret is that managers of knowledge workers don't know what their employees know and what they can do. Only the knowledge worker himself can describe his expertise, what his tasks could be, and what information he needs to do his job.

I encountered this myself, forcefully, for the first time in 1988 when I started a new job. I was greeted warmly and told to decide what my job would be, since they had never had anyone like me before. I thought they were nice people—but nuts! In about six months I learned about what we did and came up with a project. They also learned what I could do. I realized they were right. And ever since then I've had a major say in defining my my job.

Chances are your boss can't define your job to the nth degree, either. However, the prospect of defining our own jobs puts the bell on us knowledge worker cats to be accountable. Figuring out what to produce, how much, what the quality will be, and how much it will cost is tough. Thinking through what the results should be often makes you realize that your goals are unclear. Clarifying goals is another tough job that requires you to accept responsibility for your results.

Know These

Knowledge workers are minds, not hands. They are educated and have experience. They're hired for what they know. At work they need information and knowledge as they apply theoretical and analytical knowledge. They see work as a source of satisfaction, a place to create and produce. They must continuously learn and they'll probably have several careers over the course of their lives.

Congratulations! This makes you a capitalist. You now own the most important means of production for your organization—the knowledge in your brain. It's what you know that matters to the organization. You even take that knowledge with you wherever you go, which may be to a competitor.

So what can your boss do to make you effective? In a presentation I attended in 1998, Drucker gave a short list of ways to do this:

➤ Make demands on knowledge workers. Work with them to make sure they have goals to reach.

➤ Give them responsibility for achieving those goals in the way they think is best.

➤ Make sure the organization provides them with education and training—both for their current jobs and their future development.

➤ Place them where they can be productive. Sometimes a square peg must be moved from a round hole to a square one.

➤ Ensure that they have rewards and recognition of a kind that has meaning for them. This means you will have to know them well enough to know what matters to them or ask them.

If you are a manager, this tells you what you must do for the knowledge workers you lead. On the other hand, if you are a knowledge worker, this is what you should expect from your boss so that both you and the organization get what you need.

Know How

When you discuss Sveiby's framework, the key question to ask is this: "How can we maximize leverage of all our intangible assets for our customers?" This leads you to your current investments and identification of any gaps. From there you move to what needs to be done.

What the Krona Started

The intellectual capital framework of Karl-Erik Sveiby is a stealth strategy for talking to management about knowledge management. It goes straight to the heart of a manager's job, which is growing the assets of a firm. I've found this an easy way to start a discussion with managers at all levels. That "intellectual capital" stuff sounds weird, but "resources and investment" they understand. The framework has three elements:

➤ Employee competence (human capital)

➤ Internal structure (structural or organizational capital)

➤ External structure (customer or relationship capital)

Employee Competence

Employee competence is the capabilities of the people within an organization. When they leave, either for the day or permanently, it goes with them.

Know These

The capabilities of people in an organization are the **employee competence.** Writing computer programs, selecting sites to drill for oil, and conducting pharmaceutical research are all employee competences.

➤ Employee competence grows when more people know more that is useful to the organization and the organization uses more of what people know. Two key issues are creating environments where people willingly transfer tacit knowledge and improving trust among people.

➤ As employee competence grows, there is better performance, more innovation, a higher concentration of skills in what's important, and more people working in areas critical for organizational success.

➤ Employee competence creates internal and external structure.

Internal Structure

Internal structure is the organizational capabilities to meet customer requirements. It includes the business strategy and vision, knowledge of processes, patents, and information in information technology (IT) systems. It is left behind when people go home. It also gives the people in an organization the support continuity they need to perform.

➤ Internal structure grows when leadership provides vision, policy, strategy, and systems. Another critical role of leadership is to develop and nurture organizational culture.

➤ Documenting and managing processes will grow internal structure as well. Information technology systems also can help increase it.

➤ As internal structure grows, what one person knows becomes available for others. There's less dependence on individuals, less of the infamous "but nobody else knows what to do."

➤ It doesn't matter how good people are if they don't have the internal structure they need.

➤ Supported people who have what they need to do their jobs, know what the goals are, and live in a good culture do better work.

Know These

Internal structure belongs to the organization. It includes patents, documented processes, and information carried on computer systems. Leadership produces much of internal structure, such as vision, strategy, and policies. People may come and go, but internal structure remains.

External Structure

External structure is your relationships with your suppliers, stakeholders, partners, and customers. Customers judge and value our products and services.

➤ External structure grows when you deliver customized solutions. You also provide feedback and influence processes for your customers. You involve your partners in planning and phases of product development.

➤ As external structure grows, you have more open communications with your customers. There's more trust. There's an open exchange of knowledge. You gain customer loyalty. Your products and services have more value.

Know These

External structure is the value of your relationships with the people with whom you do business.

➤ There's always a degree of uncertainty here. Reputations and relationships change over time, sometimes in a flash. Remember the outrage over the flawed Intel chip?

Know How

Internal structure confused me at first. If the term confuses you, too, I'd suggest thinking about what it's like when you go into work on the weekends. With no people around, there's no one to call, no one to ask. All you have is internal structure.

Know These

The **knowledge spiral** is a model proposed by Ikujiro Nonaka to represent how tacit knowledge and explicit knowledge interact to create knowledge in an organization, through four conversion processes or patterns—*socialization* (tacit to tacit), *externalization* (tacit to explicit), *combination* (explicit to explicit), and *internalization* (explicit to tacit).

From Making Bread to the Knowledge Spiral

Okay, time for a test. Remember tacit and explicit knowledge? This will be just the first of several times we revisit those concepts. Here, the context is the *knowledge spiral*.

The purpose of the knowledge spiral is to create knowledge that your organization needs. At the heart of the knowledge spiral is the difference between tacit knowledge and explicit knowledge, because the interactions between these two types of knowledge create knowledge. But before we get into the knowledge spiral, we should understand the difference between tacit and explicit.

To illustrate the difference in their book *The Knowledge-Creating Company,* Ikujiro Nonaka and Hirotaka Takeuchi use the example of a bread machine. In 1985, the Matsushita Electric Industrial Company could not get its bread machine to work. The crust of the bread would come out overcooked while the inside would be almost raw. Volumes of data later, they still were clueless.

Finally, a Matsushita software developer named Ikuko Tanaka suggested working side by side with a baker at the Osaka International Hotel, reputed to make the best bread in Osaka. She trained with the head baker learning that he had a special way of stretching the dough. She went back to the engineers, who added special ribs inside the bread machine to stretch the dough. Success! The machine broke sales records for a new kitchen appliance its first year.

This framework shows how Tanaka created knowledge. It's best shown as a 2x2 matrix. In each quadrant, knowledge is either tacit or explicit. There are also four modes of transfer from quadrant to quadrant: socialization, externalization, combination, and internalization.

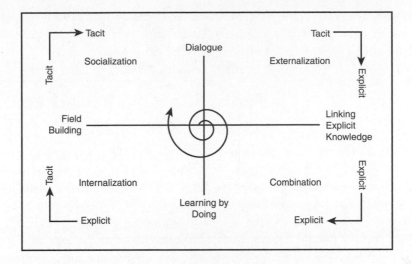

Framework for a learning organization

Socialization involves transferring tacit knowledge from one person to another, as Tanaka did with the head baker. Think of on-the-job training, someone new to a job learning from an old hand. It results in new skills and common ways of looking at things. This is people to people, usually two at a time.

Externalization makes tacit knowledge explicit. One way is for someone to talk about their tacit knowledge in words, metaphors, and analogies. Another way is to bring out the tacit knowledge of people like customers and experts and translate it into a readily understandable form. Dialogue is an important means for both ways of externalizing. Talking together face-to-face, people share beliefs and learn how to better explain their thinking through instant feedback and exchange of ideas. This is *people to people*, usually individuals within a group. Tanaka did this when she was able to articulate her knowledge to share it with the engineers.

Combination transfers explicit knowledge to explicit knowledge. This is where IT shines. You can put explicit knowledge into documents, e-mail, and databases. You can share it through meetings and briefings. The key steps are getting the relevant knowledge, editing and processing it to make it usable, and disseminating it. This is *machine to machine,* usually involving transfer among groups across organizations.

Internalization is when one person magically transforms explicit knowledge into tacit knowledge. An example for me is cooking from a new recipe. Initially, all I know is the recipe. Over time I learn quirks, things not to do, and perhaps ways to make it better. I know much more than when I first tried the recipe. This is *one person learning through experience*, either by actually doing or by simulation.

So, that's how the knowledge spiral works. That's how knowledge is created.

Didn't Know

Shout this to the skies: Three out of the four quadrants for knowledge creation are centered on people. In only one does IT shine. Think about this when you see software packages touted as "knowledge management," when databases are equated to knowledge, and when vendors tell you that their IT systems will create knowledge. Focus on IT and you miss three-quarters of your possibilities for knowledge creation. I always ask, "Where are the people? How are they involved in creating knowledge?"

Creating a Learning Organization

In 1990, Peter Senge kicked off the learning organization movement by publishing *The Fifth Discipline*. In that book he lays out five core concepts an organization and the individuals in it need to follow to be a *learning organization*.

Senge defines a learning organization as a place "where people continually expand their capacity to create the results they truly desire, where new and expansive patterns of thinking are nurtured, where collective aspiration is set free, and where people are continually learning how to learn together."

Know These

A **learning organization** creates, acquires, transfers, and retains knowledge. It's particularly good at changing its behavior to reflect new knowledge and insights. A learning organization rarely makes the same mistake twice.

Here are Senge's five core concepts or disciplines of learning organizations:

➤ **Personal Mastery:** This discipline urges people to continually clarify what's important to them—their personal vision. At the same time, they must continually reassess where they are today—the current reality. The tension between the vision and reality creates energy. This energy drives personal growth.

➤ **Building Shared Vision:** This concept focuses on shared purpose, not dictated purpose. It explores the skills needed for groups or organizations to develop a common future. Shared vision fosters genuine commitment rather than sullen compliance.

➤ **Team Learning:** This is the discipline of the delicate dance of group interaction. By using dialogue and skillful discussion, teams mesh. They think collectively. The whole becomes more than the sum of the parts.

➤ **Mental Models:** Without knowing it, all of us have hidden assumptions and beliefs that color our thinking. These assumptions are powerful and, unfortunately, they can stop us from learning. Bringing them out into the open can make room for change.

➤ **Systems Thinking:** This is the fifth discipline, the one that integrates all of the others. It's a body of knowledge and tools that help people see the patterns in complex systems.

Didn't Know

Some people have accused Senge of not giving a plan of action in *The Fifth Discipline.* There's truth in that accusation: It's a book of principles, not a blueprint for action. However, since then other books have come out that address the actions needed to create a learning organization. Two are from Peter Senge and his associates, *The Fifth Discipline Fieldbook* and *The Dance of Change.* Both of these were meant to give the concrete how-to's not covered in *The Fifth Discipline.* A favorite of mine is *Learning in Action: A Guide to Putting the Learning Organization to Work* by David Garvin.

Mapping How Value Is Created

Verna Allee, the author of *The Knowledge Evolution: Expanding Organizational Intelligence,* combines key concepts from Sveiby's framework of intangible assets and the discipline of systems thinking. The question she asks is: "How is value created?"

The standard methodology is the value chain, which is fatally flawed and outdated. Like a good production line, in a value chain a thingamajig chunks through a linear progression until completed. Goods and services are exchanged for revenues.

Not so fast! Sure, buyers and sellers exchange goods, services, and revenues. This is the standard "you make it and I pay you for it." All of these exchanges are tangible. Other tangible exchanges include all transactions, invoices, requests for proposals, confirmations, and receipts. Knowledge products—such as reports or package inserts that generate revenue or are expected as part of the service—fit into this category as well.

But there's more to creating value than just goods, services, and revenues. You also exchange knowledge and benefits.

Knowledge and benefits are intangible values. Strategic information, planning knowledge, process knowledge, and collaborative design are examples of knowledge exchanges between buyer and seller. Knowing what your customer plans to do in the future is immensely valuable to you. You may need to retool and revamp. Knowing in advance gives you an advantage.

Intangible benefits are advantages or favors that one person can offer to another. You might agree to support someone politically. You might make a critical introduction for someone, vouching for them. We do this all the time socially and in business. People trade favors to build relationships.

Value chains ignore the intangibles. They focus on only part of the picture—looking only at tangible assets ignores the value of intangible assets. But the intangibles of knowledge and benefits are real deliverables that help build healthy business relationships.

This brings us to another key concept in Allee's work: It's all about relationships. By looking at both the tangibles and intangibles exchanged, we look at the entire relationship, not just at the traditional subset of the tangibles—goods, services and revenues. A web of relationships that delivers economic value through complex exchanges of both tangible and intangible assets is a *value network*.

Know These

A **value network** is a web of relationships that generates economic value through complex exchanges of both tangibles and intangibles. Tangibles are goods, services and revenues. Intangible exchanges include knowledge and other benefits.

The traditional relationship is between buyer and seller, but this approach also can be used to map value exchanges in the public sector as well. All that's needed is two organizations working together whose goal is to generate value for the participants.

When these value exchanges are mapped, what emerges are the patterns of exchanges, the impact of the exchanges and flows, and the dynamics of creating value. It's a telling picture, far more complex than mapping a process. It's a snapshot of a system.

Some startling truths can come out using this approach. Allee tells of mapping the value exchanges for an HMO. To its surprise and dismay, the HMO reluctantly realized that its rue customer was the insurance companies, not its patients. Patients didn't pay the bills. Patients didn't dictate how the HMO should operate. It was a painful, but enlightening revelation.

I'm just scratching the surface of this complex methodology of value mapping, but I hope this gives you a taste of how beneficial it can be.

The Least You Need to Know

➤ Most workers today are knowledge workers who must define their own jobs.

➤ Intangible assets consist of employee competence, internal structure, and external structure.

➤ Knowledge creation is a spiral of converting tacit knowledge to explicit knowledge and then back again.

➤ A learning organization has the capability to learn new things and change the way it behaves.

➤ Buyers and sellers exchange more than goods, services, and revenues. They also exchange intangibles—knowledge and benefits.

Chapter 3

What's a Chief Knowledge Officer?

In This Chapter

➤ Why CEOs need CKOs

➤ Initiating the search for a CKO

➤ Establishing qualifications for a CKO

➤ What do CKOs do?

➤ Locating the CKO in the organization

Despite the funky titles, the folks you are meeting at the conference are great. They are open, frank, and willing to share with you what they're doing. They remind you of people involved in start-ups who are excited about their work. But they also spend time listening to what it's like back home for you and your organization. They connect with you.

More than anything else, they really believe in knowledge management. They talk about how things could be different. They're convinced they can bring a huge competitive advantage to their business. These aren't dreamers talking pie in the sky stuff, though. They are firmly grounded in the business drivers and needs of their organization. They tell you exactly how what they are doing links directly to the organizational goals. They talk about returns, sometimes giving numbers, sometimes telling stories.

In this chapter, we'll take a closer look at people with new and strange titles. Being a formal knowledge manager is a new role in many organizations. So we will look at where these corporate newcomers come from, what they do, and what they're like.

Know These

A **chief knowledge officer** is a senior corporate executive whose role is to leverage knowledge, usually by leading a knowledge management program. Sometimes a CEO appoints someone to the position. The level is equal to that of the chief information officer, head of Human Resources, and other functional roles.

Know These

You also may have seen the title **chief learning officer** (CLO). A CLO is also a senior corporate executive. In contrast to a CKO, though, the role usually focuses more on leveraging learning and on education and training. For example, the former CLO of General Electric, Steve Kerr, was head of GE's education center.

Somebody Has to Do It

Some *chief knowledge officers* (CKO) are self-made. James McKeen and Sandy Staples of the Centre for Knowledge-Based Enterprises at Queen's University in Canada found that about 25 percent of CKOs they studied created their own jobs. These CKOs even write their own job descriptions, although most don't even have one. However, for the most part, chief executive officers (CEOs) create chief knowledge officer positions.

Such CEOs are plagued by internal problems. Knowledge is not being widely captured or shared across a corporation. Lew Platt, formerly CEO of Hewlett-Packard, bemoaned the fact that his organization didn't know what it knew. Or the corporation may have been reorganized, merged, or acquired. The people left after the dust settles don't know what the organization still knows or how to find out what it knows.

Externally, it isn't any better for these CEOs. Their customers get more demanding every day. However, while customers get more demanding, the organization becomes less able to use what the organization knows about customers to meet those demands and develop more business. Despite databases of customer complaints, nothing gets fixed.

And so it goes. Poor knowledge management is the underlying cause of a never-ending list of problems bedeviling CEOs. They become convinced that effectively using their knowledge is the answer, but the organization can't seem to get its act together. It's at this point that organizations start calling for a knowledge management doctor.

You may say that your organization is already doing knowledge management. I'd be surprised if you weren't in some way. Explain the concepts of KM, and people start to recognize they've been doing it before it was cool. Unfortunately, that doesn't mean that there aren't critical gaps or significant opportunities being missed. And this is what drives CEOs in every kind of organization to call for a CKO.

Some of you might argue about the CEO appointing a CKO. Making knowledge the job of a CKO lets everyone else off the hook, you might say. It draws borders around knowledge, which should be everyone's concern. Some also point out it could lead to the dreaded evils of bureaucracy: fossilized thinking, overcentralization, and the building of fiefdoms.

In fact, in an ideal world, everyone should be doing knowledge management. However, it is not an ideal world. Creating the position of CKO, giving it to someone, and holding that person accountable is a time-honored way of putting teeth into a decision. (Not to mention arms and legs.) At least at first, having a honcho in charge can draw attention to knowledge issues. More importantly, a CKO can get an executive mandate and thus the resources that result in the organization's taking KM seriously.

Some CKOs take a middle path. They say the job is temporary. They will get things rolling, conduct pilots and gradually build up a substantial program. Then the knowledge management team may escape and dissolve back into business units, with those units taking over the effort. Another approach is to position a KM group as an independent think tank, perhaps as a side business.

Later on, it may indeed be possible to declare the war won, dismiss the general and the troops, and celebrate victory. But don't expect a short war. Putting together a substantial program and building an infrastructure can take years, even with the best of nonbureaucratic intentions.

The role of CKO is still so new that it is hard to say what is best overall. Each organization has to decide what is best for it.

Stranger from Outside or Hire Within?

This is a conundrum. Hiring the right someone from the inside has many advantages. Many CKOs are relatively young, usually in their 40s. One study found that the average time within the organization for CKOs was nine years. Despite their relative youth, though, they are seasoned and respected managers within their own corporations. They have credibility, and they also have a breadth of experience. Usually, they've held a number of different jobs, perhaps in different functions, in their organizations. This gives them an in-depth knowledge of the business.

They're well connected and familiar with personality foibles of the higher-ups. They know the culture, all of the unwritten do's and don'ts of the "way we do things around here." Insiders don't need to "come on board," get their feet wet, or settle in. They are positioned to take off running.

On the downside, insiders have the faults of their culture. They may be as blind as everyone else to the emperor's lack of knickers. Their connections may include enemies resulting from years of internal skirmishing. Past failures as well as successes are common knowledge. They can start running, but do so burdened with a well-known past.

A stranger lacks the baggage. Clear-eyed, they can survey the corporate landscape and point out the mountains invisible to everyone else. They start with a clean slate, with any luck. They also may come with previous experience as a CKO. Given that most CKOs are first generation, finding anyone internally with previous experience as a CKO is unlikely. Unfortunately, strangers lack the advantages an insider has.

There is no right or wrong answer to the conundrum of internal or external. I know successful CKOs from both sides of the fence. Some individuals have even been successful as both internal and external hires in different companies. In practice, however, most organizations hire from the inside. Executive search firms will tell you that they maybe handle one or two CKO searches per year. There is a dearth of CKO Wanted ads.

Know Nos

I once talked to an organization that expected an external hire for CKO to be effective from day one. This is unrealistic. External hires need time to learn about the organization and most of all, its culture. They need to build networks and alliances from scratch. Cultivate the patience needed for their learning curve.

In Search of the CKO

Thinking over a few of the former and current CKOs I know, I get the following list of previous occupations:

➤ Anthropologist

➤ Code breaker

➤ Librarian

➤ Chemist

➤ University dean

➤ Chief information officer

➤ Computer engineer

➤ Independent consultant

➤ Owner of small business

➤ Doctor of veterinary medicine, specialist in equine obstetrics

Know How

It is possible to have the best of both worlds. Identify an up-and-comer or fast-tracker inside, someone ripe for a role with high visibility and responsibility. Then hire a partner for this individual from outside who knows the KM ropes. If they work well together as a team, you get the advantages of both.

(To preserve a friendship, I shall not name the last individual. I do feel free to say that this gentleman delivered horses, usually at night, in an unheated barn in Minnesota winters.) However, despite the diverse backgrounds as represented in this list, CKOs do tend to play common roles.

CKOs Are Evangelists

CKOs relentlessly spread the word to the rest of the organization—senior management, middle management, and all of the knowledge workers. They also try to inspire and enlist fellow travelers. It isn't enough that you come to believe. You must join the movement. They want followers, allies, partners, and sponsors.

A journalist once asked me if I could sum up what a CKO does. My answer was that it varies, but there is one common denominator. They have passion. You see it in their faces. You hear it in their voices. You feel it as they pound (gently!) the table. They believe with every ounce of their being that knowledge management is the answer to the organization's questions. This passion drives them to be evangelists.

Didn't Know

Michael Earl and Ian Scott of the London Business School studied 20 CKOs in five different countries. Looking at personality traits, they found that CKOs are more able to deal with stress than the average person, and unlikely to dwell negatively on problems. They enjoy social gatherings, like to build close relationships, and seek excitement. They need to be goal-oriented and high achieving. Overall, Earl and Scott describe the needed qualities for a CKO as rare and distinctive, putting the onus on the CEO to find the right personality.

CKOs Are Entrepreneurs

Self-starters, CKOs are driven to build something new. Since this is still largely uncharted territory, they are visionaries. They translate often-vague generalities from a CEO into a vision anchored in reality. They define what knowledge management is, and design concrete programs.

CKOs are willing to take risks. They gamble for high stakes in the following areas:

➤ Creating new capabilities

➤ Proving the value of untried approaches

➤ Changing the way people think

➤ Changing the way people work

31

Know How

Thinking of hiring a CKO? Thinking of becoming one? The American Society for Training and Development found that salaries for chief knowledge officers and chief learning officers range from $81,000 to $750,000.

They are catholic in their sources of new ideas. They may concoct new ideas themselves. They may look to others in the organization, listening and backing the ideas of others. Often mavericks internally, they often look outside for new approaches. Many CKOs begin by looking at what other companies are doing, and talking to consultants.

To be a CKO is to start a new business. They love being at the forefront of something new and exciting and they thrive on it.

CKOs' failures can be as grand as their successes. With a position of high corporate visibility and the eye of the CEO, it is hard to fail discreetly. While failure is a badge of honor in Silicon Valley, it can be the end of a career in a company. Usually, CKOs are canny enough to pick pilot projects that are guaranteed winners with big returns. But, being entrepreneurial, the shadow of failure is always there.

CKOs Are Persuaders

CKOs do not dictate. They use the arts of influence —reciprocity, commitment, consistency, and gentle deference. They build relationships across the breadth of the organization. One way they do this is by earning a reputation for being someone who is always willing to listen to your woes and tribulations. In discussions with you they listen, not dominate. They are open to the ideas of others, but also contribute their own.

Know How

In the days of the early pioneers there were few signposts to follow. The field has grown enough that there are many books, journals, and Web sites dealing with knowledge management (but none exactly like this book, I'm happy to say). You can learn a lot sitting in your easy chair or at your computer. People also tend to be generous about sharing their expertise and suggestions. As busy as they are, most people in this field take the time to share. You really have unlimited sources of ideas externally.

If you peek at their calendar, it is filled with one-on-one meetings with key people. The purpose of such meetings often is not about evangelizing. The purpose is to build relationships. Building relationships takes time.

Or to put it another way, they are getting to know their internal customers. They are learning what you need, what kind of language you use, and how you think. Once they understand your situation, often they are eager to offer help—and then they follow through.

They also give credit to other people. This is not the role for someone with an ego who demands the entire spotlight. Others can talk about building networks and collaborating. The CKO must live it, and one of the best ways is by cheerfully surrendering the glory.

They know their stuff. If they are weak in certain areas, they consult experts from the outside or the inside. They are not afraid to ask questions. They continuously work on learning more—about the organization and about their own field. They understand the internal business processes. They make good judgments. If they are internal hires, they have a history of past successes.

Didn't Know

To learn more about the qualities a good CKO should possess, I suggest reading the article "The Necessary Art of Persuasion" in the *Harvard Business Review* (May/June 1998) by Jay Conger. In it, he says that persuasion is a process of learning from others and reaching a shared solution. It is not forcing people to see things your way. He also gives four essential elements of persuasion: establishing credibility, finding common ground, giving vivid evidence, and connecting emotionally.

CKOs Are Communicators

They are masters of the elevator speech. Think of how long you normally have to explain something to someone on an elevator—maybe about 30 seconds. During that time you must explain what you plan to accomplish, how you plan to do it, and what the results will be. You don't even have time to draw a breath. CKOs handle this like seasoned salespeople.

They also understand the importance of crafting a communications strategy. They pursue multiple means of communication, all that are available to them. They speak at internal events. They publish in the corporate newsletters. They have Web sites built. They look for every way possible to spread the message.

Know Nos

Don't confuse what a CKO does with what a chief information officer does. The CIO is responsible for both IT strategy and the IT infrastructure. He or she must be able to plan to meet business needs and to implement them. The CIO must also be sensitive to the needs of the CKO to efficiently and effectively institute knowledge management initiatives.

CKOs Are IT Savvy

Although they lack the technical skills and experience of the CIO, they understand the capabilities of information technology. They can identify gaps in the existing infrastructure. They then can help recommend changes needed to support their programs. Or they may find new capabilities, if those are needed. They may even need to tackle IT issues before they are able to begin any KM programs.

Overall, CKOs are IT literate. This doesn't mean that they know every software package and vendor. At the very least, however, they should know about general capabilities for information retrieval, content management, integrated systems, and collaborative work. Since they're usually involved in the procurement of knowledge management IT systems, this helps them cast skeptical eyes upon the wild claims of vendors and their own IT department at times.

Most importantly, they understand the limitations of IT. They know that IT doesn't equate to knowledge management. IT is a tool; it is a tool you have got to have. But the users remain king.

Know How

Listen carefully to the pitches of IT vendors. The good ones understand the importance of the users. They're realistic about what IT can and can't deliver. I was at a conference once where a vendor burbled that portals create trust. The friend next to me said, "I've got better things to do. Shall we leave?" We did.

This knowledge and skepticism means they can talk to the CIO semi-intelligently. The CIO or someone in the IT organization is an ally a CKO desperately needs. To work well with an ally, the CKO must able to talk the language of the CIO. IT savviness is so important that we will devote all of Part 3 of the book to IT (pun intended).

But What Do They Do?

The quick answer is a whole bunch of things. More specifically, most CKOs build programs. Let's look at the CKO job by looking at the types of actions needed for building programs:

➤ Identify gaps in capabilities and performance

➤ *Benchmark* new ideas and performance standards

➤ Integrate needs from different parts of the organization

➤ Align resources such as people, IT, and money

➤ Ensure that the IT infrastructure enables knowledge creation, sharing, capture, and leveraging

➤ Develop new strategies, approaches, and tools

➤ Implement pilots and approaches

➤ Build a broad base of support at all levels of management

➤ Collaborate with key people such as the CIO and head of HR

➤ Leverage the strengths of the culture, using them as a jujitsu move to outmaneuver weaknesses

➤ Create environments for creating and sharing knowledge

➤ Practice change management

➤ Demonstrate results

➤ Celebrate successes

Know These

Benchmarking is a systematic process of learning from the best that originated in the quality movement. It focuses on learning to improve performance. It implies humility, a willingness to acknowledge that others are better, and to learn from them.

In other words, they help everyone in the organization take advantage of what different people and groups know and can do to improve, grow, and better serve customers.

Where Do They Perch?

CKOs usually roost in one of four places: a separate, stand-alone office, with the CIO, the corporate training function, or with human resources. An undeniable rub is that any CKO residing in an IT, training or HR function is part and parcel of a larger group. This group has many other responsibilities, many of which will not involve the CKO. There are many competitors for the always-limited resources in any function. The CKO de facto becomes part of the crowd, jostling for resources and visibility.

Know Nos

You may wonder if it would be a good idea to have a chief information officer take on knowledge management as well. This is impractical. There aren't enough hours in the day for a CIO to build, manage, and sustain an information technology infrastructure while leading a knowledge management program. Don't give the CIO an additional headache.

This also makes the CKO dependent on the CIO, head of training or chief of HR. I have seen this work well, with fervent support by these functional leaders. I also have seen it work poorly, as the CKO is sent to the back of the business bus. Why take the chance of lukewarm support from someone with other things on his or her mind?

Know How

If you have ever been involved in a new program or initiative, you know how difficult it is to get things going. It's like trying to turn a battleship. The field of change management focuses on ways to implement change within an organization despite resistance. Most CKOs regard their ability to master change management as a critical success factor.

Another flaw with this approach is that the CKO's boss hobnobs with the honchos, not the CKO. At the routine meetings of the senior executives, the CKO's boss sits at the table, not the CKO. The CKO loses much of his or her needed access. Since gaining support of senior management is a critical success factor for CKOs, this severely hobbles them.

Putting a CKO in such a function also sends a message that knowledge management is merely part of a traditional function. It is nothing special, just a heretofore-undiscovered aspect of an old friend. It isn't so important.

Stand-alone is the best. "Reports directly to the President or CEO"—now that has impact. It says that knowledge management is more important than people had realized. It says that it will be a major concern for the organization. As marketing folks know, perception is all. It trumps reality.

It also gives the entrepreneur more than a little elbow-room. Unhampered by departmental focus, squabbles, and goals, the CKO can direct his or her energies to starting a brand-new business within the business.

The Least You Need to Know

➤ CEOs usually create the chief knowledge officer position, in order to solve organizational problems and create new capabilities.

➤ CKOs can be hired either internally or from the outside. There are advantages and disadvantages for both.

➤ Chief knowledge officers have many hats: evangelist, entrepreneur, persuader, and IT realist.

➤ CKOs need a good relationship with the CIO or someone in the IT organization.

➤ CKOs may be located in the IT function, the corporate training function, the HR function, or as a stand-alone. Stand-alone is best.

Knowledge Management Success Stories

In This Chapter

➤ The quest to become knowledge masters at Hewlett-Packard Consulting

➤ Becoming a learning organization at British Petroleum

➤ Looking at critical success factors

You've gotten past the funky titles and the models. Now you're listening to the corporate evangelists tell their stories. None of the stories are simple. Nor are they all alike, although you do hear some similar themes. It obviously isn't a case of one size fits all.

Perhaps one thing more than anything else impresses you. Some of the evangelists are from some big, well-respected companies. You might have thought that they could continue to do just fine without knowledge management. But for all of them, big and small, managing their knowledge is their key to survival and success.

In this chapter, you will learn about two companies that have successful knowledge management programs. One effort, that of British Petroleum, has been underway since beginning virtual teaming at the end of 1994. Another effort, that of Hewlett-Packard Consulting, started in 1995. Both offer key points for implementing the management of knowledge in any organization. Both set a high standard for anyone wanting to undertake knowledge management.

Introducing Knowledge Masters at Hewlett-Packard Consulting

These folks knock my socks off. I first learned about their effort during a visit in 1998. I was bowled over then, and I have continued to regard their knowledge management effort as one of the best.

Know These

Carla O'Dell, Jack Grayson Jr., and Nilly Essaides give my favorite definition of a **best practice** in their book *If Only We Knew What We Know*: "Best practices are those that have produced outstanding results in another situation and that could be adapted for our situation. Like all knowledge, it is contextual. A best practice is what is best for you."

It is also award-winning. The American Productivity and Quality Center recognized Hewlett-Packard Consulting (HPC) as a *best practice* company for knowledge management implementation. Hewlett-Packard Consulting is the solution-consulting arm of HP. It helps customers integrate and optimize solutions sold by HP and others. The company is also the winner of the prestigious MAKE (Most Admired Knowledge Enterprises) award three years in a row and in 2000 was the winner of Linkage Inc.'s Vision award.

What We Want to Be

Let me start where they want to end up, their *vision:*

➤ Our consultants feel and act as if they have the knowledge of the entire organization at their fingertips when they consult with customers.

➤ They know exactly where to go to find information.

➤ They are eager to share knowledge as well as leverage others' experience in order to deliver more value to customers.

➤ We will recognize those consultants who share and those who leverage others' knowledge and experience as the most valuable members of the consulting team.

Know These

A **vision** is an idealized view of a desirable and achievable future state—where or what an organization would like to be in the future.

This vision clearly portrays what people are expected to do: share and learn from others. It commits to reward people for those behaviors(usually a weak link in KM programs). It defines the future state in simple language—every single consultant has the knowledge of the entire organization for the benefits of customers.

Getting Started

But this isn't where the senior leadership team started. In 1995, they realized that HPC needed to better leverage its knowledge. Customers demanded innovation and rapid execution. In addition to global consistency, they also expected that they would be able to tap HPC's knowledge. And HPC's competitors, the other consulting firms, had already put KM programs in place.

As a result, HPC focused on developing a business case. They went to the people who could best tell it how well it was doing—its customers. The client interviews were revealing. Although customers were satisfied with HPC's overall performance, they thought they could get more value. In particular, they felt that too much depended upon the consultant they happened to get. What they wanted was the knowledge in all of HPC. Customers also felt that HPC could do a better job of transferring its knowledge to them.

HPC listened. The initial business case for KM stated that knowledge was the currency of HPC's business. HPC's ability to grow depended upon how well it managed knowledge across the entire business. HPC was global; it had to act globally.

However, not all knowledge is valuable. HPC only wanted to manage the most useful knowledge, that which would produce business results. The HPC leadership and their KM team put together a program with three objectives:

➤ Balance the reuse of knowledge with innovation

➤ Promote pervasive leveraging and sharing of knowledge

➤ Integrate the sharing of knowledge into work practices so that it will become part of daily work, not another task

Innovation was and is a business driver for Hewlett-Packard itself, which calls itself the original company of inventors. By doing this, HPC clearly tied its effort to a key business driver. However, the company also recognized that "inventing" knowledge that had already been invented elsewhere in the organization was not productive. At the same time, HPCers recognized that it was valuable to innovate upon a proven base of knowledge where it existed. The balance between innovation and reuse, or building upon a proven base of knowledge, is a *critical success factor* for any KM effort.

HPC didn't stop there. It also came up with three measures of success for the program, usually another weak link for KM programs:

➤ **Sharing knowledge between projects.** HPC does consulting; much of the knowledge is created during client projects. It realized that it needed to share that knowledge as well.

Know These

A **critical success factor** is something that has to work so that the intended goal can be met. In other words, it is one of the few things that must go right.

39

Some knowledge, that which could be made explicit, was documented. Some was shared through communities of practice.

➤ **Learning from successes and mistakes.** Sometimes mistakes, painful though they are, offer more to learn from than successes. However, few organizations have the openness and trust needed to admit failure.

➤ **Capturing reusable material from engagements.** Often during engagements, consultants would develop models, methodologies, and solutions. These often could be made more general so that others could use them. Reuse leverages the initial investment. It also decreases response time for those using it.

Know These

SAP stands for Systems, Applications, and Products in Data Processing. SAP is the world's largest inter-enterprise software company and the world's third-largest independent software supplier overall. Its Web site is www.sap.com.

Know How

Think marketing. How are you going to sell your KM program? Another one of the strengths of the HPC program is its ability to market. The pilot project was given a name that was easy to remember, catchy, and reflective of its goals.

Going for a Trial Run

With the groundwork laid, HPC decided to start with a pilot. It knew it needed to start slow to learn how to manage its knowledge in one area before expanding efforts across the company. It wanted a pilot group that was highly visible, had a business need for sharing and leveraging knowledge, and was led by someone committed to making the pilot succeed. It selected its *SAP* consulting group in North America.

HPC named the pilot Project Owl, for Orchestrating Wisdom and Learning. The goal was to help an ongoing project in the group of SAP consultants. It expected this would produce satisfied customers and generate profitable returns.

Project Owl did help the SAP consultants. The SAP practice expanded its delivery approach. Client implementation cycles fell from 18 down to 6 months. You can bet HPC had happy customers. Senior leadership at HPC was happy as well. They gave the go-ahead for a full-blown global KM program. As is characteristic with this exceptionally well-thought-out effort, the team paused to develop a phased approach.

Phase One

The first phase in expanding the HPC knowledge management program was to build the foundation. The goal was to create key knowledge processes. The KM team focused on three processes:

Know These

HPC defines a **learning community** as informal groups of people that cross organizational boundaries and come together to discuss best practices, issues, or skills that the group wants to learn about. They may meet face-to-face or through conference calls. They define a **project snapshot** as a session designed to collect lessons learned and materials from a project team that can be reused by future project teams. A **knowledge map** is a process for identifying knowledge and skills needed to sell or deliver a solution. Again, HPC only wants to focus on valuable knowledge, the knowledge that helps it do what it needs to do.

➤ **Learning communities.** This is the HPC term for communities of practice. These communities quickly multiplied across HPC. I consider this to be the killer application of KM, and we will devote Chapter 8, "Communities of Practice—The Killer Application," to it later.

➤ **Project snapshots.** The purpose of a *project snapshot* is to review projects and capture the learnings for reuse later. This process also was adopted quickly across HPC. The KM team realized that the key to success for this process was to integrate it into the project management work practice.

➤ **Knowledge mapping.** The purpose of the *knowledge map* is to identify what knowledge is needed and where it resides. HPC used the process to identify the knowledge needed to sell and deliver a particular solution. Several of the solution development groups adopted this approach. The result of a knowledge map is to not only identify the knowledge to be managed, but how that knowledge would be managed (through communities or a document management system). Also, because it is a "living map," it can be updated as the solution matures. Initially, it required a two-day workshop to develop a knowledge map, but the returns continued long after the workshop ended.

Know How

Crafting and implementing a KM program requires patience. HPC understood all along that a desire for quick results could cause its efforts to become misguided. It balanced action with planning.

41

Phase Two

The second phase of the knowledge management program was to build and launch the environment. The goal was to design and implement a knowledge-based system. The scope broadened to include measures, new roles, and enabling technology. We'll look at their measurement framework in Chapter 21, "A Sampler of Measurement Approaches."

As part of the goal to integrate knowledge into the work, the KM team worked with the HPC project management team to make the project snapshot process part of everyday work. The timing was right. HPC was deploying a significant enhancement to its project management methodology. The KM team worked to simplify the project snapshot process and integrate it into training for the rollout of the project snapshot process.

The timing also was right for meeting the second goal of creating new roles. HPC overall was undergoing significant reorganization. It created roles for a central KM group, geographical knowledge roles to facilitate knowledge flow throughout HPC, and roles for specific knowledge processes. One of these specific knowledge roles was the learning community lead, the coordinator for each community. Having a community coordinator is a critical success factor for communities of practice, as further explained in chapter eight.

The goal of adopting an enabling technology helped fill a gap in the information technology needed to support the program. In 1998 HPC launched K-Net, its knowledge technology solution. It is an Internet *portal* that includes structured solution knowledge, project workspaces, project document management, and a discussion forum.

Recognizing the importance of content management, HPC formed a HPC Standards Board. The purpose of this board is to evolve content management capabilities, ensure consistent content management practices, and establish guidelines and standards.

Know Nos

Don't rely solely on your own resources. Your KM program may require you to admit there are things you don't know how to do. HPC adroitly used external consultants to help in a number of ways, including assistance with knowledge mapping.

Know These

A **portal** is the opening page of an Internet site that guides users to various other pages that will have the information and knowledge they may be looking for.

Phase Three

The last phase of any knowledge management program is to permeate the environment. The goal of this phase is pervasive knowledge creation and leverage, not to mention sustaining the program. The KM team doesn't want KM to become a *flavor of the month*. A critical part of this phase is sustaining the momentum of the KM program while evolving it to meet changing business needs.

To sustain the momentum, HPC is working on continued leadership guidance and support, as well as modeling of knowledge-sharing behaviors. Additionally, the KM team realized HPC needed to measure its KM efforts. It developed a maturity model, an approach being used in other parts of HP, which we'll discuss in Chapter 21. It also administered the first of what is to become an annual survey to measure the processes over time. The input from the survey will help teams to plan future KM initiatives.

Keep the Fire Burning

As wonderful as this is, HPC still thinks it has a long way to go yet. Its ultimate goal is to have a culture that routinely creates and leverages knowledge. It will be the way the firm does its business without having to think about it. It is an ambitious goal, but I am sure they will get there.

The Learning Organization at British Petroleum

They don't call it black gold for nothing. Drilling an oil well can cost $25 million a day. But even before that, geologists must determine where the oil might be. The drilling structure has to be built. All the while, the clock ticks and no money comes in ... and it may never come in if the well is a bust. That's a lot of money to invest.

Oil people call this the "upstream" portion of the business. The astronomical capital investments needed for upstream are a driver for every oil company to manage its knowledge—knowledge of how to find oil and not rocks, and how to shorten drilling times. If that wasn't enough, there is always the issue of safety. Human lives and the environment are at stake.

Know These

Flavor of the month: a term for management fads that come and go in organizations. Top management, looking for quick fixes, tries, often in a haphazard manner, some new management idea, only to find that it doesn't work for them (usually because they did not fully commit to its implementation).

Didn't Know

With its acquisitions of Amoco and Arco, British Petroleum is the holding company of the world's largest petroleum and petrochemicals groups. It has well-established operations in Europe, North America, South America, Australia, Asia, and Africa.

If you look at exploration in oil companies all over the world, you will find that's where KM started. British Petroleum (BP) is no exception. But unlike the rest, BP is one of the world's most profitable oil companies.

In 1994, then-Managing Director John Browne (now Sir John) had shepherded the re-organization of BP Exploration into 42 separate business assets. The goal was to allow smaller and more autonomous businesses to be more efficient and creative. However, this created another problem—the need for these 42 independents to share knowledge. They were doing the same types of things—assessing oil deposits, drilling, building platforms. But they were scattered across the globe, and at the time, information technology was not enough to connect everyone for sharing.

BP management decided to invest in an 18-month and $13 million pilot project to develop *virtual teams*. It thought that videoconferencing technology would do the trick. A core team of five people with diverse backgrounds was put together.

The pilot team began by developing the specs for the virtual teams, which included desktop videoconferencing equipment, shared whiteboards, multimedia e-mail, and groupware (programs that facilitate people working together over the Internet). Even a document scanner was included. They called this the virtual teamwork station or client. ISDN lines and satellite links, where needed, provided the communications.

Know These

A **virtual team** is a group of people working in different locations and sometimes in different departments whose work coincides and who work as a team by using electronic technology to communicate and share information and knowledge.

The Virtual Team Pilot

Like HPC, BP then began with a pilot of five different communities. The core team and the participants in each group developed performance agreements. Goals included improving decision making, reducing costs, and working with others to creatively solve problems. BP also brought in outside consultants to measure the results to guarantee objectivity. These consultants helped put together the list of expected results and followed actual results throughout the pilot.

They didn't have long. For some groups it only took days; for others it took weeks. People became enthusiastic about the project. Usage increased.

One group, however, failed. Due to unplanned budget constraints, this group was the only one to get going without coaching on how to use the technology. Technology, though, was only about 20 percent of the

Didn't Know

If you would like a look into the mind of a CEO who believes in KM, take a look at the *Harvard Business Review* interview with Sir John in the September–October 1997 issue. It is aptly titled "Unleashing the Power of Learning: an Interview with British Petroleum's John Browne."

coaching time; the rest dealt with how the teams could best use the system to do a better job. Here is a short list of how the successful teams did a better job:

➤ Reductions in travel expenses

➤ Productivity improvements

➤ Less miscommunication

➤ Reduced cycle times

➤ Reduced costs overall

As you can imagine, this success got management's attention. BP then established a knowledge management task force. The purpose of the task force was to identify and recommend new opportunities and strategies. BP wanted to make continuous learning and knowledge sharing the company norm. Not coincidentally, Sir John became head of BP. A believer in the learning organization, he supplied strong leadership support.

How BP Learns Before, During, and After

A strength of BP is its insistence on setting contracts with clear objectives, then following up. The KM team asked, "How can knowledge management make a difference in this simple process of getting business results from business objectives?" The KM team's answer was to learn before, during, and after everything that was done at BP as part of the way work is done.

Learning before means stopping before you do something to ask if others—either inside or outside the company—have done this before. If the answer is yes, then you need to learn from them.

There are several ways BP employees could learn about previous work. One is a search of the corporate intranet or the Internet. Another is a query to a community of practice, simply called communities within BP. BP also developed *corporate yellow pages* to help people find other people with specific expertise.

BP also developed the *peer assist* process. In their book *Learning to Fly*, Chris Collison and Geoff Parcell define a peer assist as a meeting or workshop

Know These

A **corporate yellow pages** is a directory of the people within an organization. It usually includes expertise, interest, and a little personal information. The purpose is to connect people to each other.

Know These

A **peer assist** is a BP process for getting outsiders with needed expertise to help a team. There is a clear purpose and a clear business need.

where people are invited from other teams to share their experience, insights, and knowledge with a team that has requested some help.

For a successful peer assist there needs to be a compelling business reason, one that can be simply stated. The requesting team selects a diverse group of people; the list of names must be large enough to attain a final group of the right size, given people's prior commitments. The team defines deliverables and the time it needs to achieve them.

It might, however, reframe the originating question during the peer discussion. Sometimes, what's important is learning what question to ask.

Learning during involves stopping after you have done something. Strictly speaking, it is learning immediately after.

For learning during, BP adopted the After Action Review (AAR) used by the U.S. Army. This quick and dirty review looks at four questions:

➤ What was supposed to happen?

➤ What actually happened?

➤ What worked well?

➤ What did not work well?

The power in this simple process is taking the time to reflect on what happened. Only then can the learning surface and drive further action.

Learning after focuses on reviewing projects or other activities that occurred over a longer period of time. As with the AAR, the purpose is to review what happened so it can be done better the next time.

Unlike the AAR, it is neither quick nor dirty. A longer project deserves more time for examination and reflection. The outcome is recommendations for action for either teams that follow-up the project or others in the organization.

Comparing HPC and BP

There are important similarities in the stories at HPC and BP:

➤ Formulation of a vision and strategy

➤ Strong leadership support

➤ Insistence on business results

➤ Clear business demands and drivers

➤ Multiple approaches and tools

➤ Use of communities of practice

➤ Bringing in external consultants as needed

➤ Recognition of information technology as a key enabler

➤ Implementation over several years

➤ KM became part of the way work was done

One critical difference is that HPC started with its vision and strategy. BP tried a pilot in one area, virtual teaming, and then went on to craft a vision and strategy. Which is better? Neither. We'll talk about that in the next chapter.

The Least You Need to Know

➤ A successful KM program usually takes several years.

➤ Formulation of a vision and strategy is important.

➤ You need to market your program internally.

➤ Strong leadership support is critical.

➤ Good programs focus on business results.

➤ It usually is best to use multiple approaches and tools.

Part 2

Getting Started

I once attended a conference where an articulate, dedicated, and forthright gentleman spoke about how he and his cohorts had worked valiantly to get the attention of senior managers and teach them about knowledge management and its importance to their firm. He then admitted ruefully that they had succeeded too well, too fast. Management told them to go ahead and implement. But they hadn't thought through what strategies they should recommend or what sort of supporting infrastructure it would take to implement their plan.

He implored all of us to think about what we would do when we got what we wished for: the go-ahead to implement knowledge management. His advice in short was: Be ready.

Crafting a strategy involves asking tough questions, considering a lot of issues, and applying a considerable amount of creativity. We'll look at this in this section, as well as getting started with a pilot to try out your wings. Lastly, we'll look at some approaches you might want to use.

Developing a Strategy

Knowledge management: The evangelists have sold you on the concept. Now you want to go home and do it. Do what? There are so many options, so many things you could do. They all seem worthwhile. Picking one, two, or even three is impossible.

Crafting a KM strategy is tough. There are a lot of decisions to make. There are a lot of questions without a right answer. You have to be creative. You need to rely on your judgment. If you are new to the field, it may even seem unfair that you have to make such tough decisions before you feel ready.

But there are road maps you can follow to make it easier. A road map won't guarantee that you'll get there, but it will give you a plan to follow. In this chapter, we will look at some of the initial steps in crafting a knowledge management strategy.

Fundamentals of a Good KM Strategy

A good strategy tells you what to do. It gives a plan of action. It says what should be accomplished and how long it will take. A good strategy also looks at what investments are needed and in what areas. To get you started, here are some things to consider:

➤ Supporting KM infrastructure—the people needed

➤ Expanding information technology infrastructure

➤ Describing *corporate culture*

➤ Developing specific approaches for carrying out the strategy, like the learning before/during/after approach at BP

➤ Instituting measures

When considering strategy, keep in mind that one size doesn't fit all. What is the perfect strategy for another company could be disastrous for yours. Like a best practice, a strategy must be best for you. You must tailor your KM strategy to your organization. It needs to fit like a glove.

Know These

A **corporate culture** is defined as the unspoken but shared assumptions that guide the daily behavior of people in organizations. It is not only what we do; it is the beliefs underlying what we do—the whys. It is complex and hard to puzzle out.

Know Nos

One of the never-spoken secrets in knowledge management is that usually there isn't just one single, perfect answer for what the best strategy is for any organization. Don't drive yourself crazy trying to figure out what is the "best" for you. Settle for something *good* with demonstrable results. Learn as you go along, and change the strategy *if* you need to. Don't lock yourself in.

Tailoring KM Strategy for Your Organization

So, whom are you tailoring the strategy for? Ask some key questions about your organization:

➤ What is the nature of your business? What do you do?

➤ What is your vision?

➤ What are your goals?

➤ How do you plan to achieve your goals?

➤ What is your organization's current business environment?

➤ What is your industry? What affects it? What is the environment for your industry?

As nifty as KM is, the job of your KM strategy is to help the organization achieve its strategy and goals. *Never forget that.* Your KM strategy must be firmly rooted in the context of your organizational strategy.

To your surprise, the KM conversation may help uncover a need to change the corporate strategy. Perhaps a lack in strategic capabilities was overlooked. Perhaps the company has some strengths that haven't been considered. You may even wind up helping to reshape the company's strategy and vision. That can happen when you start to figure out what the company and its people actually know how to do.

Developing new capabilities through knowledge management also changes the corporate equation. As new things become possible, this can also motivate the need to change the overall organizational strategy. This happened at McKinsey, where a community of practice recommended a new strategic direction for this major management consulting firm.

If you are below corporate level, in a division or other unit, you need to support both corporate and your level's goals. In the HPC example, innovation is a key driver for HPC. So the HPC knowledge management strategy supports innovation. The HPC strategy also supports the goals of HPC itself.

Know How

Authors Michael Tracey and Fred Wiersma give three ways of describing most organizational strategies, which they call market disciplines:

➤ Operational excellence is giving the best value, produced internally by reducing costs and increasing efficiency. This underlies Chevron's strategic drive to reduce operating costs.

➤ Customer intimacy means delivering tailored products and services. One example is Airborne Express.

➤ Product leadership has a focus on innovation, trusting that the best and newest will dominate the market. This is the strategy of Intel.

In *The Discipline of Market Leaders: Choose Your Customers, Narrow Your Focus, Dominate Your Market* (Addison-Wesley, 1995), they argue that top-performing organizations focus on only one. The question for you is what knowledge is needed for the discipline your organization is following.

Talk to key people throughout your organization about strategy and goals. Look at what various units and functions are doing. Discuss plans for the future. Bring up factors that influence reaching goals. Clearly define the end point, where you want to end up.

Look at Your Starting Point

Bore in on any gaps that could prevent the organization from reaching its strategic or its knowledge management goals. Look for pain as you talk to people. I know that looking for pain may sound ghoulish to you (and a possibility for another funky corporate title: Knowledge Management Ghoul). Okay, you can call it looking for problems instead. But whether you call it looking for organizational pain or problems, it shows there are opportunities for improvement. And that's your chance to provide ideas for taking action that can result in a big win to the organization and a big win for proving the value of KM.

Didn't Know

In July 1988 there was an explosion and fire on an oil platform in the North Sea. A supervisor on the rig, Andy Mochan, woke up when he heard the explosion and the alarms. He ran to the edge of the rig and jumped in the North Sea to water ablaze from oil and debris. The water was so cold that it could have killed him within 20 minutes, but as he later said, "It was jump or fry." In organizations, a burning platform is an issue that dictates change because not changing is unthinkable.

The flip side of the problem coin is a significant opportunity. This isn't a chance to fix something, but a chance to do something new. Some possibilities are

➤ Introduction of a new business line or venture.

➤ A change to open up a new market.

➤ Restructuring of an organizational unit.

➤ Another big program, such as implementing Six Sigma.

➤ Building a new facility like a plant.

➤ Mergers, acquisitions, or joint ventures.

➤ Big changes in senior leadership, perhaps a new CEO.

No matter what they are, opportunities give you an opening to use knowledge to make a difference. HPC did this when it expanded the capabilities of its North American SAP practice.

Another way to look at your starting point is to assess your organization's knowledge, searching for gaps in critical knowledge. HPC did this by asking the ultimate judges, the customers. I also suggest talking to suppliers. They, too, know where knowledge potholes are. They drive into them all the time.

Ask both customers and suppliers what it's like to do business with you. Do they get the knowledge they need from you to partner effectively with you? Can they find the people and information in your organization they need when they need it?

One of the most telling comments I have heard from a customer once was that our organization was like a box with many compartments. The problem was that she didn't know where to look in the box for what she needed. Neither did our associates. In the end it didn't matter what we knew—she couldn't find what she needed. Using knowledge maps can help you find gaps in critical knowledge. They can help you establish a baseline and identify

➤ What information is in your organization.

➤ How it can be found.

➤ What expertise is within your organization and where.

➤ What important expertise is outside your organization and where it is.

➤ How to get access to it.

➤ What the best sources of information are, both internal and external.

Once you have mapped the knowledge, you should understand the following:

➤ What critical actions a unit must take.

➤ What decisions people in that unit must make to do their work.

➤ What information they need to make those decisions and do their work. That information may be explicit, codified in various ways. Or that information may be tacit, coming from other people.

Know How

Looking at internal and external knowledge may run you head-on into difficulties. One way organizations are different is whether or not they value internal or external knowledge. Some can be described as xenophobic, rejecting outside knowledge. Others go the other way, only valuing external knowledge. Some can do both. Be prepared for this as a potential roadblock. But then, insist on looking both ways.

Using knowledge mapping was a key process for the solution groups at HPC, too. It helped them focus on what the important knowledge was, as well as ways of managing it.

Advantages of an Executive Sponsor

Undertaking a knowledge management initiative requires resources. An important question becomes: Where do those resources come from and who will pay for them? The first thing that needs to be paid for is your own salary if you are engaged in this initiative. Most of us do not have the position needed to fund the people and resources involved in a KM project. Find and cherish an executive sponsor. (I used to make chocolate chip cookies for one.)

Funding isn't all your sponsor will provide. A sponsor can open doors for you, getting you in to see other senior managers who otherwise wouldn't give you the time of day. At upper-level meetings a sponsor can fight for the cause, carrying the KM banner. In chance meetings a sponsor can persuade and convince.

Connected at the highest levels and canny in the ways of the organization, they can

➤ Coach you on your communication strategy.

➤ Give you a better understanding of the big picture.

➤ Ease your attempts to get funding.

➤ Help you plan your overall strategy.

➤ Encourage you and tell you that what you are doing is important.

Finding one, though, isn't always easy. I was lucky enough to have one call me up and volunteer. (I then danced down the hallways to tell my partner as if I was a bad actor in a musical.)

Know How

Start as much as you can on strengths. For example, one way HPC could have pitched the SAP project was to praise the formidable expertise already in a small group in HPC. Then it could have moved to the need to expand the strength across North America.

On the other hand, my partner and I helped that luck along. We had lobbied to present to the CEO and the Board a KM award (of sorts) that we had won. It gave us a platform for talking about KM. The eventual executive sponsor was there. Turned out that he already believed in KM. He hadn't known anyone was working on it as he was new in town.

It was the difference between night and day for us. Doors suddenly opened up everywhere. He even got us in the door to present to our CEO's boss. He kept his promise to us that he would not rest until the CEO, too, believed.

Consider the Tinker Bell factor when looking for a sponsor. Remember in the story *Peter Pan* when Tinker Bell is dying and everyone who believes is asked to clap his or her hands? Not everyone out there will clap his or her hands for knowledge management.

Some, often intuitively, do understand that knowledge is the key to success for their organizations. Others demand that you lay out detailed specifications, guaranteed returns, and the exact payoff for their investment. But no matter what numbers you give them, they just don't get it.

Old hands in the KM field look for the Tinker Bell factor. If they clap at least once, you usually have a chance to explain, maybe persuade. If not, you're wasting your time.

This was a hard lesson for me to learn. But I have since heard many of my peers talk about the need to be realistic. A mind may be a terrible thing to waste, but wasting your time on a closed mind is also terrible. Your sponsor has to understand KM and believe in its value. There is no substitute for belief.

Also look for a sponsor who is respected by his or her peers. You don't want the corporate loony sponsoring your cause. You want someone who tackles the tough jobs and delivers the goods, the E.F. Hutton type to whom others listen. Also, you might look for someone who is characterized as innovative, a little bit in front of everyone else. Such people are known for blazing the right trail to follow.

I realize this sounds as tough as finding a date that your parents and your friends approve of, but actually it's worse. Looking for a sponsor is like looking for a spouse. It is critically important to select the right one.

Developing the KM Pitch

Face it, the term "knowledge management" on its lonesome isn't sexy. No advertising company would ever recommend it for a marketing campaign. It does not communicate the concept. You need to put the words with it that will make sense for your organization.

Know Nos

Many think the ideal sponsor is your CEO. Maybe, maybe not. Your CEO may not have the right characteristics to lead change, or might not be the best choice in your culture. The mistake I see most often is people assuming that having the CEO for a sponsor will make everything happen magically. Despite the advantages of CEO support, this is dead wrong.

Know How

People are going to ask you if there is something short they can read. Xerox solved this by putting together a pocket-sized booklet that included a definition of KM, knowledge-sharing principles, and some of the Xerox approaches. I also suggest using the little book *Knowledge Management: A Guide for Your Journey to Best-Practice Processes* from the American Productivity and Quality Center's Passport to Success series.

Many people start is by discussing what knowledge management is and what it is not. I sat in once on a session of senior managers who brainstormed the what is and what isn't. It was time-consuming and illuminating. Granted, it would have been easier for me to prance over to the whiteboard, write down "the" definition, and wait for rapturous agreement (and wait, and wait …). But the value was in the discussion. Then you can move to forming a shared definition that has meaning for your organization.

Know Nos

This goes back to the concept of shared vision from *The Fifth Discipline.* If you are leading or participating in a KM effort, your job isn't to give the perfect, expert definition. Your job is to help build organizational consensus on what KM is and what value it will bring.

Going back to the elevator speech (explaining something in about 30 seconds), you also need to include in the definition a brief synopsis of how you will accomplish KM. Lay out concrete actions you plan to take. Name people who will be involved. Describe the timelines you have. Don't worry about whether or not everything is cast in stone. Emphasize the benefits and deliverables. Doing KM is going to do great things for your organization. Always explain how it will benefit people, how it will make their lives easier.

Once you've come to an agreement on your definition of knowledge management in your organization KM, developed your elevator speech, and come up with your vision, then put together a marketing presentation. If you need to, talk to the marketing people or a salesperson in your organization. Ditch the elaborate charts. Keep lots of white space—in other words, make sure you don't fill your PowerPoint slides with lots of little words. Balance clarity with some pizzazz. You've got to have as much sizzle as your culture allows. You want people to be as excited about how KM will help them as you are.

Know How

One way to deliver pizzazz and help develop a shared vision is a well-done video montage. Recently I watched one created by Erick Thompson of the Saint Paul Companies (a large insurance corporation). It had emotional impact. It made us think. It helped us to talk about what knowledge and knowledge management are. It was a springboard for a knowledge vision.

The process of putting together a presentation will help you to clarify your definition, the elevator speech, and your vision. If you can't explain it simply, you haven't got it yet.

One Big Strategy or Multiple Projects?

I think of this as the "big gorilla" or "lots of monkeys" question. The issue is whether or not you want to put together a strategy that sweeps across your entire organization, impacting many processes. With the use of communities and project snapshots, HPC went for the big gorilla. So did BP with its learning before/during/after approach. Both organizations intended to transform the way the entire organization worked. That's impact.

It's a lot harder to work with a big gorilla. You have a large scope and thus a large implementation. You have more to worry about. However, the payoff is also potentially great. Your other option is identifying smaller, more isolated projects in specific areas. This is a surgical approach. These have fewer headaches. They are easier to manage and easier to focus on.

HPC did this with its knowledge mapping approach. As it turned out, knowledge mapping was best suited for its solutions groups, not all of HPC. It still had good results and a good impact. It just didn't reach across all of HPC as the other approaches did.

The answer for your company depends upon your organizational strategies and gaps. If the payoff is large enough, a little monkey is as good as a big gorilla.

Connecting People or Writing Things Down?

In the early days of the KM frontier, many efforts revolved around capturing "the knowledge." Databases were built—enormous piles of data and information. Computer storage capacity increased to house it. Because information technology was needed for search, data mining, and retrieval, IT became king.

A colleague of mine tells the story of a large, well-respected firm that built a best-practices database. Millions were spent on building the best best-practices database money could buy. The structure was impeccable. The content was a marvel. The goldmine then was made easily accessible to everyone.

And no one used it. No one had stopped to involve the users. Most importantly, no one had asked what knowledge was important for the company to reach its goals. No one had asked what value customers expected.

This mania to codify explicit knowledge has happened over and over again in different companies. It isn't necessarily a bad idea. If you have processes that are repeated over and over again across the globe, codifying best practices can have a big payoff. If the work in your organization largely depends upon explicit knowledge, by all means write it down and make it available.

The key issue here is use and reuse of explicit knowledge. If that's important for your organization, then by all means go after it. It will require a heavy investment in information technology to codify, store, and disseminate the explicit knowledge. If this is important to you, then you will live or die by your information technology as well as the goodness of the content. Also expect to invest heavily in the publishing process—writing, coordinating, editing, and maintaining the content. You are developing the equivalent of books for a huge library.

So think carefully about it. Dorothy Leonard-Barton, author of *Wellsprings of Knowledge* (Harvard Business School Press, 1998), believes that 80 percent of the important knowledge in an organization is tacit, and that beast resists codification. I believe that as well.

In contrast, a personalization strategy focuses on linking the source of tacit knowledge: people. You see approaches like networks, communities of practice, and yellow pages. The key word in this approach is "connecting."

You will still need to invest in information technology, but the emphasis will be on technology that connects people to people. The goal is to facilitate exchanges through technologies like threaded discussion and videoconferencing.

Know How

Hansen, Nohria, and Tierney detailed their study findings and conclusions in a *Harvard Business Review* article titled "What's Your Strategy for Managing Knowledge?" It was published in the March–April 1999 issue. It sparked debate in the KM community, a debate that continues.

In actuality, it is not a case of one or the other. A KM program focused on explicit knowledge will have some people connections. A KM program focused on connecting people also will have to address explicit knowledge needed by the people.

In an extensive study in the late 1990s, professors Morton Hansen, Nitin Nohria, and Thomas Tierney found that most organizations usually had a mix. If they concentrated on codification, they had a mix of 80 percent for codification with 20 percent for connecting. Companies focusing on connecting had the opposite mix: 80 percent on connecting, 20 percent on codification.

This is another question with no right answer. Your company will have to use its own judgment as to what is best.

The Least You Need to Know

➤ A good KM strategy is a plan of action that describes what needs to be done, says what needs to be accomplished, is linked to the strategy of the organization, and gives a timeline.

➤ An executive sponsor is a critical success factor for a KM program.

➤ You need to define what KM means for your organization.

➤ You need to develop a vision for KM.

➤ One issue you need to consider when putting together a strategy is whether or not you want a strategy that spans the organization or focuses on smaller areas.

➤ Another issue you need to consider is whether to concentrate on explicit or tacit knowledge. Concentrating on explicit knowledge leads you to codify. Concentrating on tacit knowledge leads you to connect people.

Start Small

By the end of the first day of your conference you've heard the word "pilot" so often that you wonder if you're still at the airport. These knowledge management enthusiasts seem so cautious. No big gamblers here risking everything on one roll of the dice. No all-or-nothing implementations. No big projects spanning an entire organization.

They talk of picking limited projects at first. Then they carefully watch over those projects, endlessly discussing how they're going. They talk about the mistakes they've made. They report results, although the results aren't earth-shaking.

It's a contradiction. If they believe in it so much, why are they starting so small? The answer is because they are smart.

Why It's a Good Idea to Start with a Pilot

Like research and development folks working on new product development, knowledge management initiators understand the importance of developing a *prototype*. In new product development, a prototype is used to prove that a concept is worthwhile, that the crazy idea will actually work. The prototype gives people something concrete to look at and think about. It isn't just words on paper any more.

Know These

In new product development, a **prototype** is usually a physical model of the concept. It can be working or nonworking. The purpose is to get an idea of whether or not the concept is doable.

A knowledge management project is also an innovation. Think of a knowledge management pilot as a prototype for a later product launch. Also, remember that you have become an entrepreneur. To start a knowledge management initiative you must have venture capital funding. It is easier to ask for a smaller amount of capital than a larger one. Part of this is dictated by the budget cycle in your organization—depending on the time of year, you simply may not be able to get a large amount of capital investment to start a major project.

Know How

Although the steps can vary in number, a typical new development process includes

➤ Investigating the idea.

➤ Building a business case.

➤ Initial development.

➤ Testing and validation.

➤ Full production and market launch.

One of the most widely used processes is the Stage-Gate process. Robert G. Cooper is the recognized authority on this process. I suggest looking up some of his articles or one of his books. Talk to some of your R&D people about their new-product development process.

The fact is that no organization ever has enough resources. You're asking people to lay out cold hard cash and free up human resources. You may need other resources such as information technology. You also must have some time to produce results. You're asking for all of this for an innovation that's never been tried in your organization.

Know How

Chuck Seeley and Bill Dietrick have written a superlative series of articles in *Knowledge Management Review* on crafting a KM strategy. They point out that in their experience, when investment in a pilot project passes the million dollar mark, it's a good idea to have well-developed success measures. You need these measures to demonstrate a tangible impact that can sell the benefits of an enterprise-wide effort. Then you can get more funding to expand.

No matter how wonderful you are sure it could be, organizational reality means that funds have to be diverted from somewhere else. The American Productivity and Quality Center has found that the majority of initial efforts in a big company cost more than $1 million. Asking for that kind of commitment without proof that it can succeed in your organization may be too much, in my opinion. It is smarter to try something out first on a smaller scale. It's a matter of comfort, too. Not every organization likes to roll the dice when it involves significant funding. Many prefer to have some evidence. Even the Las Vegas casinos collect and analyze data to make decisions. This also taps into your personal tolerance for risk and uncertainty. If the effort fails, can you face the possibility of not being able to try again?

Another issue is getting the buy-in of senior management. The bigger the innovation you are planning to roll out and the more people who are affected, the more leadership support you need. If it's big enough, you're talking the CEO, the immediate layers below that, and all the way down to middle management. I like to have some proof before I go after that kind of management commitment. However, it all depends upon your organization, its culture and its budget process. Do what is needed to prove the concept and gain credibility. At some organizations you will need to do a pilot. At others, it might be best to launch an approach.

Usually, though, no matter how persuasive you are, it's easier to get management approval for a pilot in most organizations. It's also easier on you. There are just too many potential hurdles to launching an enterprise-wide KM approach. Even if you're confident that you have everything you need and that you can have a big win, I don't advise it. You can't afford to lose your chance to learn by starting small, learning from your mistakes, and then looking to expand across the organization.

Start with a Pilot

In classic new-product development, some prototypes are nonworking. In the KM arena you need to focus on a working model—not only working, but an initiative that shows success in either lowering costs, improving productivity, increasing sales, increasing profitability, or some combination of these. Demonstrating success not only shows that an initiative will work, it builds confidence. After a successful prototype, you know for certain that a particular KM program will work for you. You know how to make it succeed. At that point, you can move to the next steps.

Do Your Homework

Do your homework before you build your prototype. As relatively new as KM is, at first there weren't any guideposts. Now, however, there are a lot of people out there doing KM, and there are journals, books, Web sites, studies, and organizations devoted to KM. See what you can learn from such sources.

Know Nos

Don't limit your homework to written sources. A lot of KM practice still isn't written down. The practitioners in the KM community tend to be extraordinarily generous. Respect the fact that people are busy, but still don't be shy about asking people for help. At first you will receive more than you give. As soon as you can, though, reciprocate.

Define What "Done" Looks Like

Build product specifications for your project:

➤ Describe what it is that you're going to deliver. Be sure to include specific features.

➤ Explain the benefits, both to the particular group participating in the pilot as well as the entire organization.

➤ Develop a clear list of objectives.

➤ Prioritize the objectives. Separate out the must-haves and the nice-to-haves.

➤ Determine what you need for the pilot, including training, information technology support, funding, and people.

➤ Look at changes to business processes, reward and recognition mechanisms, and communications.

➤ Put together a timeline.

Involve the End Users

Be sure to involve the people who will be doing the work—the end users. They need to be your partners and participate in the planning.

And it's guaranteed they will know more about what they do than you do. They can tell you of unsuspected opportunities. They can warn you of unintended consequences of a planned action. They can point out fatal flaws in your implementation process that could sink it. They can tell you what the obstacles and barriers are—and how to get around them.

You also need their commitment to make the pilot a success. A simple fact of life is that once people have a say in how something is done, their commitment increases. You want them to feel as if they have some ownership in the project.

Users also will provide your reality check on how easy the KM process is to use. Ease of use should be a key design criterion. You should hear statements like "It's designed so that it never takes more than three clicks to get what you need." More than three clicks, and it's too much of a hassle for a user.

Users will let you know if it's easy to use, if you listen. One deafening but silent way they deliver a negative verdict is to stay away from a new system or process. Don't let it come to that. Involve them up front.

Users also are your customers. What you should deliver to your customers is something that makes their jobs easier to do. You should hear sighs of relief, not groans at additional work. To make sure you get feedback from your customers, build in feedback mechanisms. For example, you should involve users in periodic reviews. Also set up clear lines of communication so they know whom they can talk to.

Know How

Running a pilot project requires project-management skills. If that isn't one of your strengths, have someone involved in the effort who does have these skills. Good project management is a key enabler for innovation.

Know Nos

Think through all of the major players you need to involve. Remember the story of the bad fairy in Sleeping Beauty? The bad fairy also appears in organizational life. In their book *In Good Company*, Larry Prusak and Don Cohen talk about a KM effort they call exceptionally well planned. It failed because the chief financial officer wasn't invited to the party. In retaliation, the CFO killed the funding.

Picking a Winner

Like a gambler with a marked deck, go for the sure thing. Your objective is to prove the concept of KM. You won't do that with a failure. You want the definitely doable.

Another way to load the deck is find a cozy home for your pilot. The leader needs to be someone who wants the pilot and KM to do well.

You also want the group to be eager for knowledge management. They may be eager because they have a big problem, and an effective knowledge management initiative may help them solve it. If they have an urgent driver, they'll be more willing to accept your project.

What's the Buzz?

You also need to go for the gee-whiz project. You want something that is going to be visible. You want people to gossip about it in the halls and send e-mails to their friends. You want senior managers to ask each other if they've heard about it. You also want a pilot that has an impact in an area that is strategically important. You want to be able to say (and hear them say) things like, this pilot project

➤ "Cut our cycle time in half."

➤ "Gave us a brand-new capability that is going to rake in the bucks for us."

➤ "Slashed costs."

➤ "Made our jobs easier to do."

➤ "Wowed our customers."

Didn't Know

According to research by the Lotus Institute, another key factor in innovation is a passionate believer. This person makes his or her cause a crusade. Many KM efforts can be traced to one or several crusaders. Some of these people later take on the CKO role. One of these is Mike Burtha of Johnson & Johnson. I first met him in 1996 during the first American Productivity and Quality Center study on KM. He was working then in the corporate quality office but already believed that knowledge management was critical for J&J. Also believing that connecting people was the most important goal for KM, he later launched a community of practice effort in J&J.

Learn as You Go

When you're ready to scale up, you'll be smarter. A pilot gives a newly fledged KM team a chance to try out their damp wings. People on a KM team aren't any different from the rest of their organization in needing to learn. This is a chance to practice what you preach.

Take time during the pilot to stop and evaluate; identify your success factors, and examine what didn't work and find out why it didn't. Adjust as you go along, using what you've learned.

Know How

At the end of the pilot I suggest using the project-review process called a "retrospect," developed by British Petroleum. Like an after-action review, it considers the objectives, what went well, and what didn't go so well. However, there are some differences.

➤ The retrospect lasts from a couple of hours to a couple of days.

➤ An outsider facilitates it.

➤ It focuses on specific, repeatable advice.

➤ It is positioned as a celebration.

Then document the lessons you've learned as recommendations for the future. You will forget many of those lessons if you don't write them down. These recommendations should focus on concrete actions and who should do them. Some of those people will be in your group, but some won't.

In addition, look for serendipity, the unexpected opportunities that spring up. I'll bet you that you'll find benefits you never thought of. Add them with delight into your plan. Explain charmingly that this is one of the many reasons why this is even better than you had dreamed at first.

I also am sure that you will think of new ideas and ways to change the pilot as you go along. No matter how carefully you planned, as you proceed you will see new possibilities. Now is the time to be creative and try your new ideas.

Start with Several Pilots

You might want to start with several pilots. The American Productivity and Quality Center recommends starting with three. Advantages to this approach include working with different groups, trying different ways of implementing, and increasing what you can learn.

This will impact your workload, of course. It can scatter your focus. It may require that you need more resources to conduct the pilots. Only take on multiple pilots if you are sure that you still have a good chance of succeeding with the majority of them.

Plan on Going Big

Always think ahead to the time when you will do more than pilots. As you plan and implement, ask if what you are doing is scalable:

➤ Do other parts of the organization need this capability?

➤ Are you able to train the rest of the organization to do this?

➤ Does the entire organization have the information technology needed to do this?

➤ Will it require a large change in the current information technology architecture and infrastructure?

➤ Will it have a significant payoff for other parts of the organization?

➤ How much of a capital investment and other resources will it take to scale up?

Know These

The purpose of **diversity** is to establish creative abrasion, a term developed by Jerry Hirschberg. A team designed to be diverse has differences meant to rub together to produce friction. Team members challenge each other. Options are debated. The result is not placid, but it does generate options. The more options you generate, usually the better the eventual solution.

Form Your Band of Revolutionaries

You don't want clones of yourself. Often we tend to hire people just like ourselves because it's comfortable. For a KM team, though, you want the creativity that can come from *diversity*. KM is not a problem with standard solutions. Every KM solution must be customized like a tailored suit. Your new-product development team must generate multiple options and consider multiple solutions. Clones or twins don't give you that diversity.

One way to get diversity is to hire or borrow people from different functions or departments from across the organization. Depending upon what your pilot is, representing certain functions rather than others may be important. Pick the functions that are most important to you while still remembering that the goal is to scale up later.

Try for a multicultural team, particularly if your organization is multicultural. Different cultures have different ways of looking at the world. The more ways you have, the richer your team will be. Also, team members can clue you into cultural or linguistic differences that are important to the success of your pilot.

Know How

Understanding cross-cultural differences is important for your entire effort, not just your team. Hewlett-Packard Consulting hired a cross-cultural consultant who understood the cultural differences in values and attitudes for sharing knowledge. For example, the Japanese tend to be good at sharing tacit knowledge, but not as strong on explicit knowledge. In Japan, they focused on a document repository.

You also need to do the usual team basics. Make sure that you have all of the skills needed on the team. More than likely, you will need at least one person with a background in information technology, as that is a key enabler of knowledge management. The exact nature of your project will determine the rest of the skills needed.

The team basics also include working on how the team will mesh together. To work collaboratively as a team, a group must master two dynamics:

➤ Task dynamics, the actual tasks that the team must carry out to reach its goals

➤ Group dynamics, the tasks and process of how a team works together as a team

At the beginning of your project, take some time together to build camaraderie within your pilot team. You will want to schedule some fun activities to help the team members get to know each other a little better. Team games may seem silly, but the purpose is deadly serious.

At the same time you need to work on the tasks. Put together a project plan. Plan out the tasks, when they will be done, and who will do them. Define your deliverables together. Develop a communications plan.

Unless the entire team was involved in developing the vision, goals, and elevator speech, you will need to start all over. Again, you are trying to reach a consensus, not impose your views. I suggest starting with the elevator speech. It works on both group and task dynamics as the team debates what it should be. It is a powerful way to meld the team together.

The Least You Need to Know

➤ Start with a pilot or several pilots with clearly defined objectives.

➤ Choose pilots with visibility and impact that are certain to succeed.

➤ Involve the users.

➤ Concentrate on your lessons learned and recommendations for the future, and plan to scale up.

➤ Carefully put together a team that is diverse but also has the right mix of skills.

Chapter 7

Building the Infrastructure

In This Chapter

➤ Deciding where KM belongs

➤ Doing the budget

➤ Creating new roles

➤ Forming a steering committee

When people talk about knowledge management at conferences, the presentations often make you feel as though you came in half an hour after the movie started. Somewhere in the first reel important decisions were made, like deciding where authority for KM should reside in the organization, who does what, and how a budget gets approved. You wish they would start again at the beginning.

You also wonder if these people were operating in isolation on a studio back lot. Where were the studio executives? Weren't any key players in the organization involved? Surely these folks didn't start a major initiative without involving some of the senior people in their organizations.

The reason you don't hear more about these things at most conferences is the limit on time for presentations. Most speakers do the best they can, but the normal conference slot only allows for highlights. You're right, though, in thinking these are important issues. In this chapter, we will go back to the first reel.

Deciding Where KM Belongs in the Organization

Knowledge management efforts perch almost everywhere on organizational branches. A common home is the information technology organization. Other perches include

➤ Office of quality management.

➤ Research and development.

➤ Human resources.

➤ Corporate universities.

➤ Individual divisions.

➤ Individual business lines.

➤ Support functions such as services, legal, or corporate strategy.

➤ E-business efforts.

Some KM efforts even stand alone, reporting directly to the CEO or another top-level executive.

There is no single right answer for where KM belongs in your organization. However, there is a key question that might be helpful: What kind of organizational structure do you have? Is it decentralized or centralized? Many organizations are one of those two types: decentralized with numerous autonomous business units, or centralized with a strong governing core.

Decentralized Organizations

This type of organization has many business units that have a strong degree of autonomy. The units may allocate capital themselves, set policies, and determine business objectives. Organizations set up autonomous units to allow for flexibility in meeting customer needs in different market sectors. The independence of these units lets them respond quickly to changes in their particular environments.

Both Hewlett-Packard and British Petroleum are companies that are largely decentralized. While the goal of many organizations is to become global businesses, management also recognizes the need for autonomy of different units, and decentralization is the result.

The downside to being decentralized is that it becomes harder to be consistent across the organization about anything. For example, information technology may not be standardized across the whole organization, making it hard for different units to communicate and share information. Important policies and procedures may vary. Often there is a lack of corporate identity. People often see themselves as belonging to their unit, not to the larger organization.

All of these are barriers to sharing knowledge. Interestingly enough, however, being decentralized can also be a driver for knowledge management. This can happen if senior leadership recognizes this weakness and the potential for improvement that comes from implementing an effective knowledge management initiative that gets employees communicating and sharing.

Know How

An option for a decentralized organization is to put together a core KM group but keep it small. The real work is done out there in the units. The central group can provide expertise for unit projects while keeping an eye out for consistency across the organization. The key for such a group is to realize that it can suggest but cannot command and control. It has to earn the willingness of the units to collaborate with the KM group. It's a delicate dance to assist an autonomous unit.

One example of decentralization driving knowledge management is the communities program at Chrysler. In 1987, Chrysler reorganized into separate platforms for different vehicle types, such as small cars or trucks. This dramatically cut the cycle time for new vehicle design.

However, the reorganization had a downside. It moved experts who had been in a central group into the different platforms. The engineering experts became isolated from one another. They no longer could learn from each other, help each other out with problems, and share new ways of doing things.

Chrysler compensated by forming communities of practice among the engineering specialties, calling them its "engineering tech clubs." These tech clubs also created and maintained a best-practices repository called the *Engineering Books of Knowledge* to which all engineers had access, to their mutual benefit.

If your organization is decentralized, the best home for a KM effort could be in one of the decentralized units. That's how the organization is used to operating, so it will be a natural fit. Hewlett-Packard Consulting's KM effort is housed in and targets that group. However, that does mean that your KM effort only targets that unit.

Centralized Organizations

Centralized organizations have a strong governing core. This structure works well when there is a high degree of interdependence among different parts of the organization, with little local variation and a need to operate jointly. This kind of organization needs to mesh together as tightly as the gears in a machine.

The downside to a centralized organization is that it can be a sluggish bureaucracy with rigid policies. At the local level the central organization can seem like a distant despot indifferent to the needs of the local populace. Although the organization can act globally effectively, it is poor at reacting to local events.

If you have a centralized organization, it may make sense to plunk the KM effort at corporate headquarters. Again, it is a natural fit with how the organization runs. In such an organization there is a greater chance of developing and implementing corporate-wide polices and programs. A centralized organization can establish these.

Even corporate efforts inside centralized organizations may not have enough people to do all of the work needed in the rest of the organizations. Core KM teams usually are small. Like the core teams in decentralized organizations, these teams need to provide expertise and guidance but not do all of the actual work.

Home Sweet Home

The bottom line is that KM needs a cozy home, just like a KM pilot. In that cozy home you must be able to

➤ Make decisions in how to invest for KM.

➤ Get funding.

➤ Get the access you need to senior leadership.

➤ Make sure that resource allocations are in line with the organization's overall strategy and also the knowledge management strategy.

Often the organizational leader can be the deciding factor in picking a cozy home. Again, like a KM project, you want the leader of the organization to be a vocal supporter of KM, perhaps your executive sponsor.

At the least, the leader must provide a home for the KM initiative as well as help obtain funds and be tolerant of your effort.

Tolerance, of course, is a far cry from a fervent support. It's never my first choice. But it may not be as bad as it sounds. Having a perch gives you the toehold you need to prove the value of KM. After all, in most organizations so much needs to be done that almost any perch will give you a chance to do work that will have impact.

Doing the Budget

What you budget for will be determined by what your needs are. Don't think too narrowly, though. Some important considerations for you are

➤ Ongoing development of your core team.

➤ Continuous learning.

➤ Membership in outside organizations and consortia.

➤ External consultants.

➤ Celebrations.

Exact details for budget processes vary by organization. Different organizations go through the budget process at different times of the year. They require different submissions.

There is one rule, however, that applies across the board, regardless of your organizational requirements: Submit a budget with differing levels of funding. Prepare one with low, medium, and higher amounts of money (which I like to think of as dirt cheap, reasonable, and limited deluxe).

It's easy to say no to one option, but for many decision makers, it seems unreasonable to turn down a request with multiple options. It's like refusing to eat anything on a buffet. The temptation is to pause, look over what is available, and try a few things.

Giving a number of options will require more work on your part. You will need to write up a clear justification of expenses at each level, with a list of benefits you expect. You'll also need to think out the different resources you'll need for each level. Also, be prepared to mix and match as you go through the budget process. In short, you'll wind up doing several budgets, not one. But it's an exercise you must go through to get your funding.

Developing Your Core Team

You and your team members may want to attend some conferences, take some courses, or do other things to pick up additional skills. One skill, for example, that is almost universally applicable for this kind of work is facilitation. *Facilitation* concerns ways of helping a group work together more effectively. You may want to train several people in facilitation.

Didn't Know

Psychological research has shown that once people make even a small commitment to something, they have a need to be consistent. We have internal pressures that needle us to respond in ways that agree with our initial decision. On a practical level, this means you should never underestimate the power of getting even a small commitment.

Know These

Facilitation refers to skills used to improve group interactions. This includes conducting meetings, reaching consensus, resolving conflicts, improving relationships, and managing group tasks. In a team environment, the facilitator only addresses the group interactions, not the actual content. For example, in a meeting the facilitator might suggest using a particular method to reach consensus, but not a solution to whatever problem the team is discussing.

Knowledge management is a fast-evolving and expanding field. You can't stand still and let the KM world go by. Even if you have already done a lot of research, keep learning. This is also a diverse field. You may have overlooked something you need. Continue to scout for approaches, techniques, research, and processes that could be helpful to you.

Outside-the-Organization Memberships

Outside organizations are a great source of learning. Some of these organizations are stand-alone nonprofits. Two examples are the American Productivity and Quality Center (APQC) and Knowledge Management Consortium International. Colleges and universities such as Henley College in England and the University of Saint Gallen in Switzerland sponsor consortia and organizations as well.

Also look for government-sponsored or -affiliated consortia. In a growing number of countries such as Singapore and Finland, knowledge management is a critical issue on the government's agenda. Organizations such as IBM sponsor some consortia as well. All of these offer you a chance to network with those in the field and learn from them. Many current practices are too new to have been written down; the best way to learn is to talk to someone who's doing it.

Know How

You may want to form your own consortium. Intel Corporation formed a partnership with Siemens. Together they hold meetings about knowledge management topics, bringing in outside speakers in areas like communities of practice.

Fees for membership vary. Check out the pricing structure and the deliverables. Compare the deliverables against your goals. Get involved with a consortium that is consistent with your strategic approach to KM.

Celebrations

Being a revolutionary is a sometimes heart-breaking business. You will have defeats. Your team can get beaten down and discouraged at times. Counter the losses with celebrations of the wins. Budget a little money for a pizza party, T-shirts or mugs, or gift certificates for the group.

You may be surprised at the effect this will have on your team's morale and motivation. Even a small celebration says that the hard work is worth it and keeps the momentum going.

Creating New Roles and Funky Titles

Once you start building the KM infrastructure, you have your opening to create new roles and titles for those people who will be involved in executing the KM initiative. Part of the budgeting process will include deciding what roles you'll need people to fill and that you'll need to fund. You'll have to think out the things you want people to do, both as members of the KM team and elsewhere in the organization. You may discover that you need people to act in new roles.

The first place to start is with your own team. As most KM teams are small, there's a greater need to work closely with other parts of the organization. Again, the real work is done out there in the organization, not inside your KM team. Hewlett-Packard Consulting found that they needed people to provide knowledge management services to the field organization. Their knowledge services managers worked closely with the different geographical regions to help them plan and use the available KM services and tools.

In your KM team you also need to have people who design systems for knowledge and the supporting information technology. Hewlett-Packard Consulting created knowledge architect positions to develop these systems for use of knowledge processes and access to knowledge. Particularly in decentralized organizations these people are critical, for their job is to see the whole, not the parts. For knowledge sharing, you need to connect the entire organization.

Another role is the chief knowledge officer, as we discussed earlier in Chapter 3, "What's a Chief Knowledge Officer?" Someone needs to be in charge. Out where the real work is done, you also may need to look at roles to support knowledge processes, both for your pilot(s) and ongoing efforts.

Know How

Any major change or innovation takes time. You're not going to reach your vision overnight. However, human beings need interim successes. We need to see concrete evidence that things are beginning to change. Look for short-term wins that are relatively unambiguous that you can link to what you're doing.

Know How

Any KM team must have a thorough understanding of the organization's current information technology infrastructure: its capabilities, strengths, weaknesses, flexibility, and future plans. As well, a team must understand both current knowledge management technology and new trends. Predicting technology trends is worse than fortune-telling, but you need to make the attempt.

Didn't Know

The Delphi Group, a major KM consulting company, looked at knowledge leadership roles in its research on best practices in knowledge leadership. Among the companies they studied were British Petroleum, Warner Lambert, Hallmark Cards, and Dow Chemical. Some of the roles they found were

➤ Knowledge engineer, responsible for taking explicit knowledge and turning it into more useable forms such as instructions, programs, and codified applications.

➤ Knowledge analyst, responsible for collecting, organizing, and disseminating knowledge.

➤ Knowledge manager, responsible for coordinating the activities of other roles such as knowledge engineer and knowledge analyst.

Researchers at the IBM Institute for Knowledge Management discovered three distinctive roles:

➤ **Knowledge stewards.** They capture and codify tacit knowledge. They usually conduct interviews or observe and capture knowledge from internal sources. Additionally, they encourage people in the organization to actually use the documented knowledge. This may involve training people how to use the system.

➤ **Knowledge researchers.** They search, retrieve, and transfer knowledge that's already been codified. The old, familiar corporate librarian is one example of a knowledge researcher. These folks have skills in defining information requests, changing sometimes-vague requirements into doable searches.

This new breed of researcher does a lot more than answering information requests. They push information to people they know have specific interests. They also look for new topics that could be of value to an organization. Immersed in the flow of organization information, they are able to spot trends.

➤ **Knowledge brokers.** They connect people to people. They know who you need to talk to, and they connect you with that person, and then bow out of the picture. Knowledge brokers usually have strong personal networks. And since they understand both the person making the request and the person with the knowledge, they can wind up translating between the two people they are connecting.

Knowledge brokers can be hard to find. Their actual capabilities usually have nothing to do with their job titles. It seems to be more a matter of temperament and willingness to assume the role. Once you find one, however, cherish him or her. In a knowledge-sharing organization, the knowledge brokers are royalty.

Another important role is that of community coordinator for communities of practice. We will talk about that one in Chapter 8, "Communities of Practice—The Killer Application."

Forming a Steering Committee

A running theme in this book is that you need co-conspirators. The more co-conspirators you have in senior management in various functions across your organization, the better off you will be. Like the individual workers in your pilot projects, people who participate and guide an effort have more buy-in. This buy-in, which is separate from normal everyday business processes, can speed the adoption of knowledge management.

Having a steering committee with representatives from various functions also gives you better solutions. You get input from various views and types of expertise. You get a better big picture of the organization, helping you to prioritize resources. This can also help you bypass *organization silos,* creating a catalyst for change across the organization.

Know How

Have a facilitator work with your steering committee on decision making. Discuss what types of decisions you'll be making, such as strategy, funding, and recommendations. For each type of decision, agree on who has the final authority. Chart this so the results are visible. Also, plan how you will reach consensus and what type of consensus you want.

Know These

Organization silos is a term that refers to individual groups or departments in an organization. It's often used to suggest that such groups, while they work well as a team, seldom take into account what other groups are doing or how their work affects what these other groups do. This is both common and unhealthy.

While you want the steering committee to contribute ideas, this also can put you into a quandary. Up front, you must make it clear who has the authority to make what kinds of decisions.

What if the steering committee advises a course of action that is contrary to what you, as chief knowledge officer, think is best? When you are chartering a steering committee, the time to raise this specter is during the initial meetings.

You and your KM team by virtue of your expertise will fill a leadership role for the steering committee. Part of your goal for a steering committee is to increase its understanding of knowledge management. You also will assimilate and evaluate the recommendations of your steering committee. Possible sources for members of the steering committee are

➤ Human resources.

➤ Information technology.

➤ Marketing.

➤ Sales.

➤ Quality management.

➤ Organizational development.

➤ Corporate communications.

➤ Key business units.

➤ Different geographical areas.

➤ Line managers.

➤ Corporate library, if you have one.

You also want to choose people who have good reputations, good relationships, an interest in what you're doing, and the ability to lead.

Also think about forming a second steering committee of other people with experience and expertise in knowledge management. The people in knowledge management roles elsewhere in the organization are good candidates for members. People in efforts you have "claimed" as knowledge management also are potential members. This group can function as a larger pool of KM experts. Additionally, they can help you to document the lessons learned.

The Least You Need to Know

➤ There is no right answer for where KM belongs within an organization.

➤ A good strategy for developing a knowledge management budget is proposing multiple levels of investment with varying levels of return.

➤ Implementing knowledge management programs requires creation of new organizational roles, both within a core KM group and throughout an organization.

➤ Forming a steering committee of senior leaders is another critical success factor for knowledge management.

➤ Consider putting together a steering committee of knowledge management experts to form a larger pool of experience and expertise.

Chapter 8

Communities of Practice— The Killer Application

In This Chapter

➤ Characteristics of communities of practice

➤ Role of the community coordinator

➤ Launching a community of practice at SAP America

I dare you to find a serious general conference on knowledge management that doesn't include at least one session on communities of practice. Slowly over the past few years, communities of practice have come to be acknowledged as the killer application for knowledge management. And rightfully so.

But the concept may be hard for you to grasp. I'll admit that to someone who has spent years in organizational life, communities of practice look weird. They don't look anything like the teams you were on. Are they supposed to replace the standard organizational structures? If so, how? Will people belong to communities of practice, and teams, and departments?

In this chapter, we'll learn more about that elusive creature, the community of practice, and its distinguishing characteristics. We'll discuss the creature's life cycle and how to nurture it. Lastly we will discuss how to bring them into the world.

The Platypus of Organizational Structures

A community of practice (COP) is a platypus lurking among the dogs, chickens, cows, and pigs of standard organizational structures. I say that because when I began to understand what a community of practice is, I was reminded of the day in grade school when we learned about the platypus. Having been told up until then that all mammals bore living young, I thought the platypus was odd because it laid eggs. The picture in our textbook didn't help much. It reminded me of a cross between a duck, a beaver, and a seal. In real life, the platypus is a shy and wary animal. It lives in burrows on the banks of freshwater ponds in eastern Australia and Tasmania, venturing out in the early morning and night to feed.

In organizational life, communities of practice can also be shy and wary. Nevertheless, they may surround you. You just need to know where and what to look for. You may even be one yourself—many of us are, even though we're not aware of it. Also, more organizations are recognizing and supporting these rare animals, so they're getting easier to spot.

Know How

Etienne Wenger is credited with creating the term "community of practice" (although he gives the credit to his former colleague Jean Laval). Etienne believes that learning is a social activity and that people learn in groups. He practices what he preaches, working and learning with Richard McDermott and Bill Snyder. The three will publish a pragmatic, how-to guide on the subject, *Cultivating Communities of Practice* (Harvard University Press, 2002). It's the best source to learn more about this concept.

At first you may be tempted to think that communities of practice are another type of team. However, they aren't teams—but there can be teams within a community of practice. Although teams vary, they have some common characteristics:

➤ Usually formed by management, teams focus on a discrete goal or a series of discrete goals.

➤ Team members are usually draftees—they are requested by management to be a part of the team.

➤ Usually they are multifunctional, as the collaboration of team members with different skills is required to achieve the goals.

➤ They often produce orderly charts laying out the timeline needed to achieve their goals and the milestones along the way.

➤ When the team achieves its goals, it disbands.

You also might be tempted to think that communities of practice are like the work groups you've belonged to all of your organizational life. If so, you're wrong. Communities of practice aren't work groups, either. Work groups

➤ Are assigned by management to perform a particular function, such as the manufacture of a product or delivery of a service.

➤ Are composed of members with the various skills needed to carry out the work group's task.

➤ Have objectives that are ongoing with discrete deliverables.

➤ Last until reorganized or disbanded.

In contrast, a community of practice has its own characteristics—its equivalent of the duckbill, webbed feet, and egg-laying traits of the platypus:

➤ In almost all organizations, a community of practice is made up of volunteers. No one forces the members to belong or contribute.

➤ While community members learn and work together, they don't necessarily produce deliverables or operate within defined schedules and timetables.

➤ They are distinguished by their passion for what brings them together.

➤ While they may have some stated goals, they are broader and more general than the goals of work groups and teams. Their goals also may fluctuate more.

➤ Their members tend to be like each other, perhaps with the same types of jobs and skills or some other common interest or bond.

➤ They last as long as the members want them to last.

This last quality, the ability for self-sustainment, is what drew me to communities of practice. As a benchmarking manager, I was active with teams

Know Nos

Communities of practice remind me of the adage that you can lead a horse to water but you can't make it drink. I would change that for communities of practice to add that you can't even necessarily lead this horse to water. Don't assume you can dictate to a community of practice like you can a team or work group. They are volunteers for the most part, not draftees.

and work groups, promoting both learning and sharing of knowledge. I was happy with the immediate results most of the time. What frustrated me, though, was that the learning and sharing often stopped when the benchmarking stopped. I wanted to see the sharing and learning be more than a one-time shot.

The Three Dimensions of a Community of Practice

A community of practice is a group of practitioners who share a common interest in a specific area of competence and are willing to work together. A community of practice has three dimensions:

➤ **What the members care about, their area of interest.** This is the domain of knowledge for the community. It may be a skill like equipment repair, a professional discipline such as an engineering specialty, or a topic like creativity. 3M, for example, has a long-standing community around creativity. Whatever the commonality, it must be focused and defined well enough so that people identify with it. They must also have a passion for it. This passion for the area of interest is the catalyst that draws people together.

Know How

I once was involved in a community of practice effort that had mixed results. I was later told that the members felt that the group didn't "do any real work." Since then, doing "real work" has been my earmark for the practice.

Know Nos

Never underestimate the importance of social activities. Such activities aren't wasted time that could be better spent on actual work. Social activities help build the interpersonal relationships that enable a community to do real work. But at the same time, social activities should be structured so that they meet the goals of building a community. They should allow people to connect with those they already know as well as new people. You can set up luncheons for small groups, arrange for members to meet each other for coffee, and set aside time at larger meetings for people to meet each other and talk.

➤ **Who the members of the community are.** Any community is an intricate web of personal relationships. People within a community know and trust each other. They do things together. Some of these are social in nature; others are work activities.

➤ **How the community does its work.** This is the practice. As a community works together on their domain, they create tools, documents, processes, a common vocabulary, and shared ways of doing their work. Many communities solve problems that arise in the day-to-day work. Many develop and document best practices, the best way of doing things.

The Life Cycle of the Community Platypus

Think of a community of practice as a living organism. An organism, like the platypus, is born, grows, matures, and dies. Richard McDermott, Bill Snyder, and Etienne Wenger (McDermott, *Knowledge Management Review*, "Community Development as a Natural Step," November/December 2000) have defined five stages of potential development of a community of practice.

Planning

At this egg-like stage there are people in a loose network who have similar interests, capabilities, and needs. However, they may not see any value in doing any more work on the network. What they have is good enough for them, and, besides that, they have never seen anything like a community of practice. You need to find those people and talk to them. Part of the dialogue centers on the need for a community; another critical part is on beginning to define the domain of knowledge they share. Management must be engaged, for it will provide the resources required. It also can help remove organizational barriers.

Start-Up

Some communities launch with a big bang. Others ease into existence with low-key informal sharing. A problem for the members at this stage is that they must learn what they can do together: what to share, what is useful, and how to work together. It takes time to develop relationships as well. This can be discouraging, drowning an initial burst of enthusiasm.

There is a dilemma at this point: Members need value to stay in the community, but the community needs time to deliver value. Management also needs to see a return on its investment.

Growth

Good things are happening: Good work is being done, relationships are expanding and deepening, and the community itself is becoming more visible. However, as the new community adds members, the addition of those members can be disruptive. Care must be taken to handle the expansion well.

Sustainment

Sounds like the community is on easy street at this point, doesn't it? However, in this stage the community must dance the tightrope of sustaining itself and continuing to grow. Without continual growth, the community can stagnate.

It is also important to sustain the heartbeat of the community. Although every community has its highs and lows, a prolonged low could trail off into the last step: closure.

Closure

Like the notes of a bugle blowing taps, a community can fade away or the practice can disappear, leaving behind a well-connected social club.

Sometimes the best thing to do is to pronounce death, have a lovely funeral to celebrate the community's life, and help the members to move on.

Know How

Being a community coordinator takes time. Usually, the minimum amount of time needed to support a community is 15 percent of a person's work time. Percentages between 15 percent and 25 percent aren't unusual. It could even be higher when starting a community. There also is a correlation to size, with larger communities such as those in the thousands requiring more time.

The Most Important Member, the Community Coordinator

The most important critical success factor for a community of practice is having an effective community coordinator. While the rest of the community has a passion for what they do, the coordinator also must have a passion for the people in the community. He or she has two jobs:

➤ Help the community to develop the practice

➤ Help the community develop as a community

Helping the Community to Develop the Practice

While the individual members are busily engaged in the practice, the community coordinator monitors the big picture. There may be gaps the community needs to fill. There may be tools and other resources that the community needs. There may be cutting-edge issues the community needs to address. It's the community coordinator's job to help oversee the practice and help get the community members what they need.

Helping the Community Develop as a Community

On one level, the community coordinator is somewhat like a recreation director. This person should schedule events that enable the community to meet and interact. Although around 70 percent of the activity in any community occurs in the private interaction between individual members, events that bring the whole group together do have impact. Events are important for the life cycle of the community. Events such as a meeting to charter a community or a conference can spark the initial development or help a community sustain momentum. If necessary, an event can mark the closure of a community.

Taking care of event logistics isn't all that a community coordinator does. Prior to the actual event, the coordinator talks to members,

➤ Coaxing some to come.

➤ Telling others that a topic of particular personal interest will be covered.

➤ Asking some to make specific contributions during the event.

➤ Suggesting that certain people meet each other at the event.

During an event the coordinator may take notes, making it easier for the members to participate. Afterward the community coordinator follows up on suggestions and may post notes or documents from the event.

Of course, judging when to have an event is another important task for a coordinator. The community coordinator must watch what is going on in a community, particularly when community activity begins to die down. Usually, at such a time, an event is an ideal spark to rekindle interest.

Know Nos

When talking to an MBA class once, I was asked how to deliberately end a community. The question stunned me. Questions usually hone in on how to nurture, not how to stop. But the answer was easy. The most effective way is to remove the community coordinator. So remember: Don't decide that a community no longer needs a coordinator. Don't let a coordinator leave without a replacement unless the community decides that is all right.

Although events are exciting, regular forums for exchange also are important. Most communities have an active discussion area where they solve problems together and share information, often online community coordinators often serve as facilitators for such forums, making sure that questions get answered and monitoring the interactions.

Know How

I myself am a member of a community on communities of practice (groups.yahoo.com/group/com-prac). John Smith is our community coordinator. One way John keeps up with the ebb and flow of the group's activity is by tracking the number of messages per month. This chart of activity is also available on the home page. The number of members also is posted. When the community reached a size of more than 300, John felt it was time to review the purpose of the group. He posted a charter for all of us to read. This was a canny move on John's part, an experienced and capable coordinator who knows when to prod a community.

An important subgroup for any community is its new members. Bringing them on board may or may not be a role for the community coordinator. However, there needs to be a process for welcoming them to the group, giving a little of the history of the group, and teaching them the basics of the community. At the very least the community coordinator should make sure this process is being carried out and also personally welcome new members if possible.

Didn't Know

Organizations vary in how they pick community coordinators. At Schlumberger, communities of practice elect their own leaders. However, Schlumberger has learned that revered seniors make lousy leaders, as awe paralyzes the members. The best candidates have about three years of experience, a lot of smarts, and want to get to know other people. Most of all, they are too new to have big egos.

The most important role, though, for the community coordinator in building the community is networker par excellence. The community coordinator must have a widespread personal network. Ideally, his or her personal network should extend beyond the community itself. Inside the community, he or she is the primary member of the community that everyone knows and respects. The coordinator, using network skills, helps to connect community members to each other. The more members who feel a connection to each other, the stronger the community. A successful community coordinator makes building those connections a priority. And since 70 percent of the activity that occurs in a community takes place privately between individuals, the more people who know each other, the more knowledge can be shared.

Launching a Community of Practice at SAP America

There's a lot to think about when launching a community of practice. We will look at a case study from SAP America to illustrate some basic principles.

SAP America had a challenge. A competitor had come out with a product that quickly had captured a big chunk of market share. SAP's lack of market share meant that it lacked enough customers to give the company a reference (customers who would vouch for SAP's product), a key in getting more customers and thus increasing market share. One thing SAP had to do in order to win back the market was make sure its consultants (the people who worked with clients) had the best and latest information possible on SAP's offerings.

Laying the Foundation

SAP America carefully planned, launched ,and supported their community of practice effort. They began by

➤ **Creating a business case for the community of practice.** Managers pointed out that the most up-to-date information was not getting out to the field. This put the consultants at a disadvantage, adversely affecting customer service.

➤ **Identifying an initial leader for the community.** SAP got someone full-time for three months and then groomed him on the importance of knowledge management and communities of practice.

➤ **Defining the scope of the community.** The company focused on customer-implementation projects. It then identified all of the organizations and experts that supported the community members.

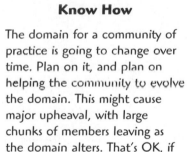

Know How

The domain for a community of practice is going to change over time. Plan on it, and plan on helping the community to evolve the domain. This might cause major upheaval, with large chunks of members leaving as the domain alters. That's OK, if it is for the overall betterment of the community. How to develop the domain is the community's decision. It has the expertise.

➤ **Designing the core activities.** SAP decided on a series of one-hour conference calls to be held biweekly. Each call had a carrot in the first 20 minutes—an expert, a hot topic, etc. Also, the community was tied into all training events, conducting a little community business during training and capitalizing on the face-to-face time.

Didn't Know

When making a business case for communities, look at three aspects:

➤ For individuals, the payoff is help in doing their jobs, a sense of belonging, a chance for learning and development, and new challenges.

➤ For a community, the payoff is increasing access to expertise, providing a means to share knowledge, and helping to build tools, documents, and processes for the practice.

➤ For an organization, communities of practice pay off by helping to drive strategy, transferring knowledge and best practices, building core capabilities, and increasing innovation.

Know How

Another important supporting role for a community is a librarian. A librarian can find, organize, post, and otherwise manage information. This frees up the community coordinator to build connections and develop the practice, while also drawing upon the specialized skills of a library to manage information. You may also find librarians maintaining databases and Web sites for communities.

➤ **Recruiting and engaging core members.** SAP picked out around 10–15 people who were passionate about sharing knowledge. They also made sure that this group represented all parts of the organization.

➤ **Aligning with current culture.** The experts were eager to share; the community provided a means for sharing. They also scheduled the conference calls so that they didn't conflict with customer projects.

➤ **Designing roles for the community of practice.** These roles included a shared leadership role among a consultant, an expert, and a respected senior member in the community.

➤ **Developing a support structure of both information technology and people.** The intranet site for the community of practice included a community calendar, a who's who, sources of information, and a discussion area. Additionally, the site has a repository of resources like white papers, how-tos, and project information.

Didn't Know

Communities of practice also can start themselves. One example is within the American Red Cross. One year, local chapters that provide transportation attended a conference on community transportation. While at the meeting they met separately to discuss their local programs. They shared and learned together as a group. They followed up with conference calls. Later, they formed an e-mail group for those who were interested. As the yearly meeting is one they all usually attend, they plan to continue meeting face-to-face then.

Liftoff for the Community

SAP America kicked off the community with their planned community event, the bi-weekly conference call. The events also were carefully staged, with scripted first calls. Despite the script, however, spontaneity was allowed and encouraged. A facilitator also assisted in the group interaction. Although SAP America limited original participation in the community event, participation soon tripled. The benefits to SAP America from this community were and continue to be

➤ Reduced costs.
➤ Improved quality.
➤ Improved innovation.
➤ Improved transfer of knowledge.
➤ Increased value to the customers.

For the individuals in the community, the similar benefits are

➤ Faster learning.
➤ Collaborative innovation.
➤ Better networking.
➤ Less time looking for information.
➤ More information available for consideration.
➤ Greater sense of connection with peers.

Didn't Know

An organizational support team for communities of practice can provide direct community support: training community coordinators, developing tools and tips, and monitoring community health. Another important task is linking communities of practice to the organization itself. Community development must be integrated with the strategy of the organization. Apart from the hustle and bustle of daily community life, a support team can attend to the global strategy.

As this example shows, although it does require planning and considerable effort to launch a community of practice, the benefits are numerous. That's why it is the killer application of KM. While no one approach is right for every organization, nothing else comes as close.

The Least You Need to Know

➤ Communities of practice are a newly recognized organizational structure, not another type of team or work group.

➤ Communities of practice have three dimensions: the domain, the community, and the practice.

➤ Communities of practice have a life cycle.

➤ The most important critical success factor for a community is the community coordinator.

Chapter 9

Strategic Choices for Connecting People to People

In This Chapter

➤ Sharing knowledge through the yellow pages

➤ Encouraging participation in the yellow pages

➤ Avoiding pitfalls

➤ Connecting knowledge and people through best practice systems

In this chapter, we'll continue to look at some of the approaches used in knowledge management. Some focus on using technology to further connect people to people, such as an electronic corporate yellow pages as well as other technological packages. Another approach—best practice systems—focuses on capturing explicit knowledge and connecting to those with the knowledge.

Look in the Yellow Pages

Up until now you might have thought that the yellow pages were part of your phone book. Or you had seen ads on TV for various providers of yellow pages, urging people to place or use ads. At knowledge management conferences, though, you heard people talk about *yellow pages* for finding other people in the organization.

There are also vendors with various packages who use technology to help locate expertise in organizations. Although those sound a bit gee whiz, they offer another way to help employees connect and share knowledge and skills. Both the corporate yellow pages (with data entered by people who have listed themselves) and the expertise finders (generated by software) hone in on finding people with distinctive expertise.

Know These

A corporate **yellow pages** is a mechanism to help people locate others in the organization with expertise they might need. They often utilize individual Web pages. They also are called *expertise directories*.

Best practices systems, meanwhile, are both a way of connecting people and a way of documenting knowledge. These approaches are driven by the need to find people who know what we need to know. Even if we aren't in a large, global, decentralized organization, we may have no way of finding out that Mary down the hall has the knowledge we need. While communities of practice can help us find our peers working in the same area of interest, they may be no help beyond the boundaries of our community of practice. Unfortunately, our jobs often go beyond those boundaries.

When British Petroleum merged with Amoco, the new organization had thousands of employees scattered across the globe who didn't know each other. BP created a corporate yellow pages system to connect employees to knowledge and each other, and called it Connect. As with their virtual-teaming program, BP experimented with a formal coaching program. However, the approach was difficult to scale up, and ultimately local staff carried out any coaching informally.

Didn't Know

Tony Carrozza, formerly of Hewlett-Packard, poses this challenge: Can you find an expert in scanning electron microscopy who belongs to a particular organization, speaks Italian, and lives in the San Francisco Bay area, all in 60 seconds? Chris Collison poses a different challenge but no less difficult: Find someone who knows about deep-water drilling, speaks fluent Russian, and is currently in southwest London. You may not ever face these challenges, but during the course of work in many different types of organizations, we do confront similar challenges.

BP found that the seniority of the employee impacted what type of information he or she entered into the yellow pages:

➤ Younger employees tended to hone in on competence and qualifications.

➤ Mid-career employees mention their job experience and network affiliations in the organization.

➤ Most senior employees describe key relationships, often external to the organization.

Best practice systems, corporate yellow pages, and other ways of finding expertise help people span boundaries and reach each other. Once found, people can share knowledge, reduce duplication of effort, and identify opportunities for collaboration. As always, connecting people to people so that they can share knowledge reaps important benefits.

Yellow Pages for Expertise

Let's look in more detail at yellow page systems and how they're used, starting with how Texaco does it.

Prior to the merger with Chevron, Texaco had a corporate yellow pages system called PeopleNet. It illustrates the types of information usually included on these systems. The main page contains the following features:

➤ **Today's featured people.** Two people selected at random appear each day. At British Petroleum, this feature is called "15 minutes of fame." Every time employees update their details, the home page shows their name and photograph. Their 15 minutes last until the next person to do an update boots them off. Both approaches offer a way to highlight individuals, which also makes the yellow pages more personal.

➤ **The ability to browse and do an advanced search for expertise.** There is a skill hierarchy that can be expanded as well.

The problem with using technology to find people is that it makes high tech something we like to do low tech (face-to-face). A database doesn't tell us if we can collaborate with different individuals, if we can trust them, or if we can rely on them. Pictures aren't a substitute for meeting someone in person, but they do make entries in databases seem more like real people. Also, databases that include other contacts may help someone identify people they know that know that person. That can help to transform the database entry into an approachable person.

Once a person has been located, that person's own page includes

➤ Basic contact information.

➤ Areas of expertise. People can rate themselves as having extensive expertise, some working knowledge, or just learning.

➤ A work history.

➤ Their *Myers-Briggs type indicator*.

➤ Key internal and external contacts.

➤ Interests and links.

Know These

The **Myers-Briggs type indicator** is a test designed to figure out how you deal with people and situations and make decisions. It deals with how people take in information (sensing versus intuition) and how they make decisions (thinking versus feeling). There are many Web sites devoted to this subject (for example, www. personalitypathways.com).

Optional items are a picture and membership in communities of practice.

Privacy laws vary from country to country. In Europe, for example, privacy laws forbid disclosing this type of information without the employee's permission. Check with your legal department when designing a yellow pages site or publication to learn what the local laws are. Also, work with your legal beagles to draft a written corporate policy governing the use of yellow pages.

Keys for Success

One key to yellow pages success is making participation voluntary. Many companies, such as Hewlett-Packard and British Petroleum, encourage but don't require participation. Employees decide on their own if they want to participate.

You may get only one chance to convince people that a corporate yellow pages is worthwhile. Unfortunately, you also need a critical mass of submissions to make the database worthwhile. Critical mass may be smaller than you think, as Hewlett-Packard discovered. But be aware that there must be enough people in the database to make it worthwhile for users to turn to.

Something that requires too much work will turn off users. Most organizations use a simple template for users to enter information about themselves. Aim for no more than 30 minutes to enter the information; in fact, you may want to aim for no more than 10 minutes. Give context-sensitive help for individual fields. Provide some selection lists and check boxes. To build momentum and encourage participation, market the yellow pages. At British Petroleum they used posters, competitions, learning fairs, and lunchtime publicity booths to grow awareness, and thus submissions. You could run promotions, giving out small tokens for entries. You may want to provide opportunities for people to learn more about technology for adding to their entries, such as how to upload pictures or use of graphics. But the bottom line for motivating people to make the effort is that knowledge workers are eager to find expertise they need. If they share what they know, others will as well.

Any yellow pages system treads on the territory of your human resources department. Team up with someone from HR to position your system as a complement to existing systems.

Know How

Another inducement for people to submit their information is the chance to be creative. For individuals, this is in effect their personal Web page. They can advertise what they know—and many knowledge workers are fiercely proud of what they know. They can talk about what interests them. They can have fun with choosing what picture to show. At some companies people have even chosen to represent themselves with famous alter egos. This also can tap into a competitive spirit: "My page is better than your page." At British Petroleum there were even duels capitalizing on the "15 minutes of fame" feature.

Danger Ahead

Any kind of data must be maintained and kept up-to-date. Yellow pages are no exception. The information that goes most quickly out-of-date is personal contact information: phone numbers, locations, and e-mail addresses. You can fix this problem by linking the yellow pages to human resources databases, so that the yellow pages can be updated automatically.

A system also can be set up to nag automatically. The system is configured to send an e-mail reminder to users who haven't updated their profiles in a certain period of time. Every 6–12 months is a good time frame for information that is less subject to change. However, nagging runs the risk of antagonizing people, either because the information hasn't changed or because they just don't like to be nagged.

Automation

Various expertise-profiling companies offer software packages for locating people. Packages vary, but can

➤ Monitor desktop behavior, like document creation.

Know Nos

As with communities of practice, yellow pages are best handled with a light hand by management. Although it may seem more efficient to develop a validation process for entries involving review by management, it could stop the knowledge worker horse from going to the water at all. Reviewing a profile during a work-review process might be a less heavy-handed method.

➤ Tap into browsing behavior on an intranet.

➤ Track e-mail, including addresses and subject matter.

➤ Track community activity such as message posting and document posting.

➤ Interface to multiple sources like human resource systems, project databases, calendars, and training databases.

One result is a profile of individuals. An advantage of this approach is that the sources of information are much more varied and comprehensive than a Web page. These profiles are also generated unprompted, freeing the user from the requirement to enter and update information. Additional benefits can be identifying patterns of knowledge, finding gaps in organizational knowledge and tracking competencies—all automatically.

By identifying people with common needs and abilities, these systems can also be useful for identifying communities of practice. This is a key feature for any organization wanting to implement communities of practice, the killer application of KM.

The stumbling block is privacy. Do you want your organization's computer system snooping through your e-mail and publishing your availability for an area of expertise? This question and related ones for this type of system can set off organizational fireworks. Therefore, managers have to know what they're getting into when they consider such systems.

The solution offered by many vendors to the privacy issue is privacy protections. Individual users decide what they wish to share. For example, if the system determines that you're the person most likely to be able to answer a question, a request is sent to you that is invisible to the requestor. You then can decide if you want to answer it. If not, you're free to ignore it.

Know How

One of the biggest barriers to transferring knowledge is that no one knows who knows what. A best practices system helps document what's known and who knows it. That's the first step in transferring knowledge.

Best Practice Systems

Remember that a best practice is something that has been shown to be effective in one place that could be effective in another. Organizations waste a lot of time and money reinventing the wheel—or, worse yet, failing at something even though someone somewhere has a method that will work. The purpose of a best practice system, then, is to make it possible to find and use what's already there.

Best practices systems also add another dimension to finding people by linking people to specific knowledge. The result is targeted: People know what knowledge they want and who can provide the full context for them.

Best Practices Help the American Red Cross

The American Red Cross has a best practices system that illustrates the principles common to many similar systems. The goals of that system are to

➤ Identify and transfer programs and business practices that are innovative and successful.

➤ Foster constructive communication within the organization.

➤ Enable the organization to recognize and acknowledge successful practices and those who submit them.

Finding the system is easy. On the home page of the American Red Cross's internal Web, CrossNet, the menu has an area titled "Best Practices." Additionally, the individual lines of service and departments have a button on their own page. The idea is to give people multiple ways to enter the system. This makes it easy to use. The best practices page has

➤ **An area for posting feedback.** This gives people a chance to comment on the usefulness of the system and also to suggest topics that need best practices.

➤ **A link to a highlights page.** This page gives a list of the most recent additions to the system and gets updated monthly.

➤ **Links to practices currently in the system.** For example, the American Red Cross chapter in Richmond, Virginia, has a best practice for working with part-time employees.

➤ **A form for submitting best practices.** Based on user feedback, this form was revised to make it even simpler.

To submit a practice, people must give information on four key issues:

➤ The objective of the practice

➤ An explanation of how it is done

➤ What showed that the practice worked

➤ Benefits and risks associated with the practice

The person submitting must also indicate the appropriate line of service or department and a name for the process.

To categorize the practices, the American Red Cross developed its own taxonomy. (A taxonomy is a

Know Nos

Don't design a best practices system in a vacuum. Design it for the users. Consultant and knowledge management author Verna Allee tells of a large technology company that spent $7 million on a best practices system for technology consultants. None of that money went toward talking to users about how they used and shared information. None of the targeted users actually used the best practices system, either.

Know How

A best practice system must have some way to organize the content in a logical manner so that users can find the practices they're looking for. Taxonomies are a common way for doing this. Arthur Andersen and the American Productivity and Quality Center One developed a well-known taxonomy for standard business practices. It's available for free on the APQC website, www.apqc.org.

Know Nos

Don't allow people to submit best practices anonymously. No one can give enough information in a best practices system. People must be available to answer questions potential users might have. One large company even designed a best practices system to have minimal information on the practice itself. The intent was to force people to talk to each other.

framework for organizing information.) Participants gave a list of topics for their areas. The goal was to come up with a list that fit every situation and line of service. There is an easy drop-down menu for users to click on when they submit the practices.

Once submitted, a best practice is subject to review to make sure it does not violate policies and procedures or that it is something that should be a part of other people's procedures. A person submitting a practice gets written notification of the review results.

In little more than a year, the system grew from a few practices to more than 100 relating to every line of service and nearly every function in an American Red Cross chapter. Feedback from the users is that they want more and more practices. They like seeing what others are doing. They often combine ideas from different practices to get a tailored solution for their situation.

The results for the American Red Cross's system include

➤ Saving time for the people who use them.

➤ Saving time for the people who submit practices. Since the practice is documented, they don't spend as much time answering lengthy questions from people who then may not use them. The calls they do get are much more specific and take less time to answer.

➤ Expanding the horizon for local chapters. One chapter printed out all of the practices on a given topic, sat down with their local board, and reviewed them. They saw possibilities they had never seen before.

➤ Giving individuals a chance to grow and succeed. People get exposure for their achievements and good ideas. One person who submitted a practice is now in demand across the U.S. Others are presenting with all expenses paid at an annual American Red Cross conference.

Some key elements to keep in mind for making a best practices system succeed are

➤ Tying it to business drivers. These best practices are aligned with lines of services and departments at the American Red Cross.

➤ The ability to contact the person who has the context for the knowledge and thus also a chance to validate the content.

➤ Monitoring the usage and the goals, as provided by the staff at American Red Cross headquarters.

➤ Recognition for those who submit best practices.

A proven best practice that can be leveraged across your entire organization is a big payoff for a best practices system. Be sure to design any best practices system to look for demonstrated practices that are transferable to many other parts of your organization.

Making People-Finders Part of a Larger System

While both yellow pages and best practice systems can provide value as a stand-alone system, I think they're best used in conjunction with other approaches. Chevron is a great example of an organization that uses multiple approaches to connect people. Their system includes the following:

➤ A best practices database

➤ A lessons-learned database

➤ Communities of practice

➤ Project documentation and reporting process

➤ Corporate yellow pages

All of these give people multiple ways to find the other people and expertise they need, an important goal for a KM program However, no single approach is enough to meet all of the users' needs. Additionally, the approaches can be linked. Linking is one of the great enablers technology provides. For example, in PeopleNet, employees can list the communities they belong to, connecting those who access their profile to their affiliated communities. Texaco has also tried combining PeopleNet and an automated package for identifying expertise. While you may want to pilot one approach initially as part of your KM program, consider an eventual architecture that combines ways for locating expertise.

The Least You Need to Know

➤ Corporate yellow pages are a way to find expertise in an organization.

➤ Expertise profiling companies also provide automated means of locating expertise that tap multiple sources.

➤ Best practices systems offer both a way to find people and specific knowledge that they have.

➤ Consider having more than one way of locating people and knowledge.

Chapter 10

More Connection Choices

In This Chapter

➤ Preventing the loss of knowledge

➤ Identifying what knowledge is being lost

➤ Consequences of knowledge loss

➤ Finding solutions to knowledge loss

➤ Choosing approaches to knowledge transfer

In the previous chapter, we looked at ways to connect people using yellow pages and best practice systems. In this chapter, we'll continue to look at choices for connecting people and knowledge. These approaches will focus on the capture and transfer of knowledge.

One approach will look at how to identify, capture, and transfer knowledge at risk for loss through attrition. Another will address ways to capture knowledge gained through experience for strategic tasks of importance for an entire organization. Then we'll look at how to capture and transfer routine—but still valuable—information. Finally, we'll review overall guidelines for selecting an approach.

Our first example illustrates a common problem and a business driver, but the Tennessee Valley Authority found that it had to create its own approach for dealing with its problems and business mandate.

Minds Going out the Door

In the United States government sector, many organizations are facing an epidemic of knowledge lost. They aren't alone. Universities, defense contractors, utility companies, and nuclear-related organizations are but a few that are affected by the same dilemma. This potential disaster is caused by a large demographic group of baby boomers—the so-called pig in the python, as Jerry Landon of the Tennessee Valley Authority (TVA) calls it—currently approaching retirement. This demographic bulge is so concentrated and large in relationship to the employees that will remain that many organizations are becoming alarmed at the upcoming loss of knowledge and expertise required to do the work that needs to be done.

The other side of the coin is organizations who have waves of new employees coming in. They key issue is how to get those employees to perform at more experienced levels. Regardless of the exact cause, the problem is the same for all organizations affected: how to identify, capture, and transfer important knowledge before all those folks box up their pictures and coffee mugs, have their farewell lunch, and boogie out of the parking lot for the last time.

One way to view this is as the loss of organizational memory, kind of like those amnesia movies. The results are devastating: repeated mistakes and reinvented wheels that can dramatically reduce productivity, taking significantly longer to get new products out and not knowing what to do when a major problem arises. It's as if organizational memory was a tape with holes punched in it.

Didn't Know

The Tennessee Valley Authority is the world's largest producer of electric power, producing more than 168 billion kilowatt hours annually. It distributes power through a network of 159 municipalities and cooperatives. Its resources include 3 nuclear plants, 11 coal-fired plants, and 29 hydroelectric dams. It has $6.7 billion in sales with 8 million customers in seven states. That's a bunch of folks depending upon TVA's knowledge.

TVA had little experience in dealing with large-scale attrition over a short period of time. It looked for, but didn't find, any published case studies or best practices. It had to start from scratch.

Documenting all of that soon-to-depart knowledge at TVA is a task of Herculean proportions, not doable by mere mortals in the time available. TVA decided it wanted no large-scale frontal assaults, no massive big-brain databases, and no huge catalogs of the knowledge and skills required for every job in the organization. Like Hewlett-Packard Consulting, it resolved instead to focus on the knowledge that is most valuable.

TVA adopted a simple guiding principle: one job at a time. TVA only devoted resources to jobs where attrition matters the most and to those jobs or tasks where attrition poses the largest threat.

In 1999, TVA created what it called the "People Team," a group made up of line managers from one section of TVA, personnel from TVA University, and a process consultant. This group conducted a pilot in order to develop methods to deal with knowledge loss through attrition. Following the pilot, the team made recommendations and suggested priorities. TVA then replicated and leveraged this process across other parts of the organization.

The process has three parts: what, so what, and now what?

Part 1: What?

Specifically, what knowledge is being lost? First, TVA looks at who is retiring and when. Estimates based on age and tenure weren't enough—TVA asked employees and supervisors directly. The resulting combination of information helped TVA identify where there was the greatest risk of knowledge loss. In addition to identifying the vital few job classifications that contributed the most to the problem, the data also revealed specific geographic locations that would encounter trouble the earliest.

Know Nos

Don't ignore the issue of departing minds, even though there's a natural inertia to do so. It isn't a problem yet; nobody owns the issue; no staff is available to work on it. There's no budget, and solutions can be expensive. TVA found that a critical success factor is moving out of the starting block early. Management must act early, move rapidly, earmark sufficient resources, and set priorities.

Didn't Know

Vilfredo Pareto (1848-1923), an Italian economist, discovered that a small percentage of people (20 percent) owned a large share of wealth (80 percent). He then went on to demonstrate that this same 20–80 principle applies in many other areas as well. It's also true in organizational process improvement; we can apply the Pareto principle to identify and prioritize problems. The goal is to categorize problems and their causes until what's sometimes called "the vital few" (20 percent) of the causes can be identified. It's generally true that these causes bring about 80 percent of most problems. So TVA concentrated on the vital few.

The next step was to analyze a single job. TVA conducted interviews with employees and supervisors to determine the knowledge content of the job. The questions began with some general, open-ended queries like, "What knowledge will TVA miss most when you leave?" and "What critical knowledge do you fear will be lost when you leave?" This group of questions was the most productive, yielding lists of complex knowledge like problem analysis and troubleshooting.

Additional groups of questions covered how to carry out tasks, what facts and information are important, and lessons learned. The lessons learned honed in on predictive failure patterns, easily repeatable mistakes, and complex diagnosis.

After completing the interviews, TVA compiled lists of potential knowledge-loss items to be analyzed and drive decisions on further action.

Part 2: So What?

What are the business consequences of losing each item of knowledge? All items aren't equally important. Some can be recreated and relearned quickly, resulting in a minor slowdown of work. Others, though, can have major consequences with a long, costly recovery period. Again, TVA focused on the vital few. It looked at four knowledge factors:

➤ **Importance.** This addresses the potential impact of the knowledge loss. Would not knowing something cause major or minor losses? Would it affect system reliability from the viewpoint of the customers? Would the loss affect one location or multiple locations? All of these were rated for each item.

➤ **Immediacy.** This gets at how quickly a solution must be developed and deployed if a problem occurs. One issue is how long it will take to transfer or reacquire the knowledge to deal with certain problems. Activities like troubleshooting can take at least two years of on-the-job training and experience to gain real proficiency. Losses also can be gradual, perhaps spread evenly over time, or they can be sudden.

➤ **Recovery.** Next, TVA considered the cost and feasibility of recovery for each item. Few knowledge items will be lost completely. In most situations, several people have knowledge and skills, and they aren't leaving all at once. Also, is it feasible to recover it? Only rarely is the answer an absolute "no."

➤ **Knowledge transfer.** Lastly, TVA addressed the difficulties involved in knowledge transfer. Tacit

Know How

In the pilot, TVA did look at extracting knowledge, codifying it, and then building databases and expert systems. They found only limited value for this approach. Participants pointed out that because TVA is a technical, engineering-oriented organization, it already produces procedures, field manuals, and other forms of codified knowledge. The critical gap was in tacit knowledge, what TVA calls the higher-order experiential knowledge.

knowledge is difficult to transfer, while explicit knowledge is fairly easy to transfer. Questions in this area try to tease out whether knowledge a person has will be easy or hard to capture and transfer to others.

Once it assessed the consequences of losses, TVA's People Team categorized and prioritized them. Some were classified as "do nothing." The consequences were minor and self-correcting over time. Some were typed as "fix it later," with minor to moderate consequences. After all, someone somewhere still has the know-how needed. Some of these problems can also be dealt with via existing processes. The last category was "immediate action," where not knowing would have major consequences. For this type of knowledge, it was time to figure out how to capture it, and do it fast—otherwise there will be major, unpleasant consequences.

Part 3: Now What?

What can be done about each item of important knowledge? The pilot team found that there was a limited number of possible solutions. One group of solutions centered on training: formal classroom, on the job, computer-based, or video-based. The second group of solutions consisted of nontraining options: establishing a designated expert or experts, codifying the knowledge, or eliminating the need. Once a list of knowledge items was assessed for business consequences and the possible remedies were identified, it was time to put together a plan and execute it. Execution involved getting commitment and resources, to include staffing and funding. Of course, routine project planning was employed to manage the process.

While this approach may seem overwhelmingly burdened by detailed work, analysis, and planning, plus considerable project management, it's balanced by a narrow focus. One job is handled at a time, and that job is selected through careful data collection and analysis.

Know How

Videotaping can be used to capture knowledge from people. The technology is easy and cheap to use. Video can be digitized, transcribed, and put on a server. It captures body language, tone, inflection, and other aspects of nonverbal communication. It also captures stories, ideas, alternative solutions, rules of thumb, and informative mistakes.

Know Nos

A lesson learned by the TVA was that everyone must play in this game: management, human resources, trainers, supervisors, process owners, and knowledge management professionals. It is a case of all for one and one for all.

Minds in Different Places: Transferring Strategic Knowledge

A CKO pal of mine once called me up to ask for suggestions. Her company was looking at starting up in a new country, an entirely new market. It didn't have anyone with extensive experience in that country. That didn't worry her—she figured they would hire locals—but she *was* worried about how to go about the start-up itself. However, she told me there was a group at her company that previously had launched a new effort in the United Kingdom. While the people involved didn't know about the new country, they did know how to go about doing the launch. Her question to me was, "How do you do this type of knowledge transfer?" It isn't something that happens every day. There would be a lot of differences: different competitors, different locations, different people, different cultures, and perhaps even different technology.

In your organization, you might be launching a new product or are in the process of acquiring another company. Perhaps you're building a new manufacturing facility. Whatever it is, you haven't done it before, either. You're certain that someone somewhere has done this before in your organization. But who? And how did they do it?

British Petroleum has a methodology and a product for this quandary that they call "knowledge assets." A knowledge asset is a package of BP's accumulated knowledge about a narrowly defined topic designed for an identified end user.

Know How

Along the way TVA found more opportunities for using what they'd learned. Some were for redesign and reengineering. It also discovered that the process could drive the development of communities, technology, and other responses. Always look for serendipity. Once you start looking around, you'll find more than you had thought originally.

Creating a knowledge asset, however, is far from trivial. It takes a huge amount of time, and it takes people in knowledge management roles to develop the asset. As in the example with TVA, it's only carried out for critical knowledge because of the investment necessary. BP has only a handful of knowledge assets for such situations as building a retail site, restructuring, refinery maintenance shutdowns, and joint ventures.

The people performing the task aren't the ones who create a knowledge asset. Knowledge specialists, who have skills in processing and documenting knowledge, do that. They travel to teams that have special experience in the task and interview the team members. They assiduously collect documents, checklists, and tools that different people have developed. However, they don't track down and write down every possible detail. The goal is to have just enough of the right stuff the end user needs, not every scrap of information they could gather.

Know How

In her typology of knowledge transfer Nancy Dixon calls this a strategic transfer. In her book *Common Knowledge* (Harvard Business School Press, 2000), she explains that strategic transfer takes place when the collective knowledge of an organization is needed to accomplish a strategic task that occurs infrequently, but is of critical importance to the whole organization. The business driver for the knowledge is the need to reduce costs and time involved in reinventing solutions to strategic issues. This is particularly important in large multinational companies where the same issue is bound to happen again and again, but in different parts of the world. One example is starting up a chip-manufacturing facility, which Intel does repeatedly in different locations.

The knowledge specialists add value by

➤ Collecting knowledge from across the organization.

➤ Offering multiple perspectives.

➤ Synthesizing what they collect.

➤ Identifying key issues.

➤ Selecting critical information.

➤ Producing a package that's available to the entire organization.

Team members don't have the time, skills, or the resources to do this.

A completed knowledge asset has the following sections:

➤ **Business context.** This explains why you would need to do what is explained in the knowledge asset.

➤ **Guidelines.** This is a distillation of the key messages, a transformation of the myriad details into the vital few nuggets of wisdom someone would need to know to deal with a particular situation. This is probably the most important part of the knowledge asset.

It can be in the form of a checklist, bulleted list, rules, or set of questions. It's illustrated by stories and quotes, and perhaps even by video clips. It also can be linked to important source documents, so that people can drill down to more detail if they need to.

113

➤ **Links to people.** The knowledge asset can skimp on details because it's expected that people who need the knowledge will connect with the people who have the knowledge. The knowledge asset includes names and photographs, and usually there are hot links to personal home pages and e-mail addresses.

In addition to individuals, it is also important to give details of the involved community of practice: the name of the community coordinator, access to a discussion forum, or perhaps a mailing list.

➤ **Performance histories.** These are the actual case histories on which the knowledge asset is based, including stories and quotes.

➤ **Artifacts and relevant records.** These include things like project plans, schedules, memos, and other things that could be reused.

Every knowledge asset is linked to a community of practice. To begin with, the community is the source of the knowledge. The community is the best source to validate the guidelines. The community also will maintain the knowledge asset. A lesson learned at BP is that despite the amount of work required to produce a knowledge asset, creating one is easier than maintaining one.

Didn't Know

You may be wondering why organizations waste time on pictures. British Petroleum for one believes that it is psychologically easier to contact people if you know what they look like.

Know How

A guiding principle for BP knowledge management efforts is to avoid dry, colorless, lifeless documents. The goal is to produce publications that will be read, not stuffed into file drawers with a sigh of relief. Stories and quotes are used to liven things up.

The Day-to-Day Stuff: Capturing and Transferring Knowledge

On a day-to-day basis you don't worry about strategic once-in-a-blue-moon tasks. Your worry is your basic, garden-variety tasks, the ones you do routinely and frequently. You aren't alone. Others across your organization also do these tasks all the time.

Despite the differences between these routine tasks and strategic tasks, your organization has the same underlying need: how to capture and transfer this knowledge to meet certain business drivers.

Within consulting firms the business driver for addressing routine tasks is clear. The best example is producing proposals. This is a time-consuming and costly part of the engagement process. The ability to reduce time to prepare proposals has a huge payoff.

Additionally, utilizing the collective knowledge of the organization produces a better proposal.

Ernst and Young's solution to this problem was what the company calls a "PowerPack." Initially PowerPacks were lowly collections of multivolume three-ring binders—not exactly what consultant road warriors wanted to throw in their suitcases for extended trips. However, Ernst and Young recognized that it needed information technology to transfer knowledge globally. So, by 1995, every consultant had a laptop loaded with standard applications. Nowadays all PowerPacks are part of E&Y's Knowledge Web.

For a specific topic, a PowerPack is a compilation of the best

- ➤ Proposals.
- ➤ Presentations.
- ➤ Competitive information.
- ➤ Models.
- ➤ Specialized tools.
- ➤ Articles.
- ➤ Work plans.
- ➤ A variety of other relevant business resources.

PowerPacks are created using a compact Lotus Notes database. Since consultants tote laptops, PowerPacks must be large enough to have the best and most needed information, but small enough to download to a laptop. Consultants then can work with them in their hotel and meeting rooms, not needing to access the organization's much larger databases.

Each PowerPack has the same look and feel, regardless of the topic. That way consultants aren't distracted by variations in format, but can hone in on the content. The familiarity also reduces the amount of time needed to work with one.

PowerPacks are produced by people within the appropriate community of practice, called "Communities of Interest Networks" (COINs). Each network is responsible for developing and maintaining its PowerPacks in addition to new content for their communities. Individual consultants access Power-Packs through their community homespace. Homespaces also have discussion databases, navigators, team profiles, external content, and a newsletter.

Know How

Less is more. For both the strategic and routine tasks, the goal is to deliver enough ... but not too much. People with experience can wade through a mountain of material, but they usually lack the patience and time to do so. A newcomer is bewildered and overwhelmed. The reason both knowledge assets and PowerPacks are pure gold is because the dross has been removed. Only the true gold remains.

115

Choosing Approaches

When choosing an approach, never forget that one size does not fit all. Some of these may be good for your organization. Some may be great, just what you need; some may be lousy, not at all what you need. You may even decide that none of the approaches described in this book are what you need. (Although, I then will nag you unmercifully to reconsider communities of practice.)

The goal of this and the two preceding chapters isn't to tell you what's best for you. It isn't to list all of the possible approaches for implementing knowledge management, either. It is to give you some examples, some ideas to spark more thought and some guiding principles. In the end, you have to choose a knowledge management approach or approaches that

➤ Help achieve your business strategy.

➤ Match your business drivers.

➤ Focus on important knowledge, the knowledge you need to manage.

➤ Connect people to people.

➤ You can steal, modify, or create.

➤ Connect people to the information and knowledge they need.

➤ Fit in with your culture.

➤ Have the appropriate technology available.

➤ You can get the resources necessary to implement and support. (This can include developing new knowledge management roles, assigning people to those roles, and training them.)

➤ Deliver value.

I wish you luck.

The Least You Need to Know

➤ There are many approaches possible for implementing knowledge management.

➤ Approaches may concentrate on connecting people to people.

➤ Approaches may focus on connecting people to information or on documenting information and knowledge.

➤ There is no one-size-fits-all approach, although communities of practices come darn close.

Part 3

Can't Live with IT; Can't Live Without IT

Long ago and far away I was a system administrator for a local area network. One dreadful day the primary server for the network began to malfunction on an intermittent, seemingly random basis. No e-mails could be sent. As the users had been encouraged to store their documents on the server (as opposed to their local hard drives), they couldn't retrieve their documents or access other resources.

The first day or two the natives remained calm, as did I. By the end of the first week they were pretty testy, as were the frantic technicians trying to identify the problem. What surprised me most, though, was that after the first week some people took a vacation. They told me simply that without the system there was no point in coming to work.

At the end of the second week a technician identified the cause—a small mechanical part that literally had a hole worn in it. I kept the part for years to remind myself how important information technology has become for knowledge workers. The purpose of this section of the book is to look at the bare necessity of IT savvy that you'll need in order to implement knowledge management.

Chapter 11

Why Your CIO Has Gray Hair

To successfully implement knowledge management you must work closely with your information technology department. That doesn't mean pestering them with unrelenting and perhaps unreasonable demands. The last thing you want to be is another person in the long line of internal supplicants. What you need to be is a partner, working together for the benefit of your organization. Best of all, you could become allies, working for common goals. But to be a good partner or ally, you must understand what makes the other person tick.

The size of IT organizations varies widely, depending in part upon how large the company is and whether or not it is global. In larger companies, IT functions are so large that they often are specialized subdivisions. In smaller organizations, an IT department can be made up of a lone ranger. This can also happen in satellites of larger companies. Lastly, IT functions can be centralized or decentralized, as discussed in Chapter 5, "Developing a Strategy."

Depending upon your organization, you may find yourself building a relationship with the chief information officer (CIO). If not, you'll be working with someone in the information technology department who will be making some similar decisions and operating under similar concerns. Either way, forming a good partnership is a critical success factor for you. In fact, I'd suggest that it be one of the first, if not the first, internal partnerships you form. To help you be a good partner, this chapter will focus on the role of the CIO in detail. We'll also look at some of the issues and concerns that affect a CIO that you, as a knowledge management implementer, could bump into.

IT Serves the Needs of the Business

You may be surprised at how much you have in common with the people in the IT department once you get past the technology and the jargon. That's another reason to partner with them. If they're successful within your organization, in addition to helping with the information technology, they also can coach you on things like how to form working relationships with senior managers, how to justify the costs of a project, and how to train users. A successful CIO knows a lot more than information technology.

Didn't Know

Organization managers such as the CEO, president, and business unit leaders vary widely in how they view IT. Without much questioning the value received, some eagerly invest huge sums, giving the CIO a free hand and an influential role in how the company's run. Others see IT as an unfortunate cost center, with the costs to be rigidly controlled by the hirelings who keep those darn computers running. Most fall somewhere in between those two extremes.

Understanding the Business

Firms don't want a technical geek who lives for the latest gee-whiz technology. They want CIOs who deliver business results and show value. Even though CIOs must be experts in information technology, their primary role is to help the organization succeed. To do that, one requirement for CIOs is to thoroughly understand the organizations for which they work—in effect, the internal customer. They should understand the following:

➤ What the organization does

➤ The organization's vision and goals

➤ The organization's business strategy

➤ The industry in which the organization operates

➤ The organization's competitors

➤ The organization's customers

➤ The organization's suppliers

➤ The organization's partners

➤ The internal users

➤ The corporate culture

➤ The history of the organization, particularly any formative experiences with information technology

➤ How the organization views the importance and value of information technology

➤ Management's level of sophistication and understanding of IT

Building Internal Relationships

The understanding of the organization helps a good CIO communicate effectively with people who work in other departments. Like a good CKO, a CIO should be a superlative communicator who builds credibility within the organization. Good CIOs don't sit in their offices playing with new technology all day long. They're out and about forming relationships by listening to other managers, asking about problems, soliciting suggestions, and discussing solutions. Ideally, a CIO also either sponsors or participates in collaborative planning processes.

After all, how many organizations today can accomplish their goals without using information technology? The CIO has a potentially strong and powerful role to play in any organization. However, depending on the organization, the CIO may have to establish credibility and build an appreciation for what he or she can contribute. Building strong relationships within the organization also helps do that.

Looking Ahead

A CIO lives in both the present and the future. As one information technology specialist told me, while you take care of today, you're also getting ready for the future.

For example, how many times have you replaced your home computer (or argued with your significant other about the need for a faster machine)? Compared to your CIO, you have it easy. Business computers usually become obsolete in about five years. One rule of thumb for a CIO is to replace one third of an organization's computers roughly every three years. A CIO must continually renew the IT infrastructure.

The CIO also has to know what's coming down the road. Think about the shift from mainframes to personal computers. Think about the change from expensive storage capacity to cheap storage capacity. Think about the change from desktop computers to mobile computing. A CIO has to be a seer for information technology, keeping on top of trends in technology, communications infrastructure, and software.

An organization's competitors can also be a cause for change, by offering a new service or benefit made possible for IT. Ever known a company whose chief competitor developed e-commerce capabilities first? Anticipating what the Joneses are going to do keeps many a CIO hopping. Competitors aren't the only cause of change in a firm. Changes, such as a merger or acquisition, bring with them their own headaches for coordinating two disparate systems.

Know How

A good CIO should partner with others for particular expertise. Some possibilities are

➤ The training department, as training users is an important part of the CIO's job.

➤ The communications department, as the CIO, too, is a change agent who needs help with internal marketing.

➤ The human resources function, as hiring and keeping information technology talent is difficult.

➤ The strategic planning function, as the CIO should be involved in strategic planning.

Showing Value

Perhaps you're in the majority of organizations that regard IT as a cost center—as a function that swallows up resources, but brings in no revenue. In that case, the need to show value is something else you have in common with the CIO. Like knowledge management, it's difficult to quantify the payoff for IT. The usual challenge quoted is quantifying how much return on investment e-mail provides. Like air, having IT is simply necessary. However, it's hard to translate that necessity into dollar amounts for support and maintenance and for specific projects.

This is also where those internal partnerships and knowledge of the organization pay off for the CIO. If the CIO has credibility as a person with a strong business orientation, a track record of delivering results, and the willingness to listen to others, then it's easier to explain that something is needed. Also, if any IT investment is tied to the firm's overall strategy, threat from competition, or change in the business environment, then it makes more sense to those forking over the money (not to mention those who may not get other funds they request).

Like a CKO, a good CIO also relies on pilots. Pilots show that a project does provide a return on investment, that it's doable, and that the project can be done better in the future. A CIO can't wait until a project is over, though. Progress reports along the way help detail the return and viability as well as building support.

Of course, attaching cold dollar amounts never hurts, either. Increases in efficiency (such as reduced costs) and effectiveness (such as increased customer satisfaction or a competitive advantage) are usually easier to come by.

Know How

The need for standards also applies to applications. While you may see the burning need for a software package, the CIO must consider how the IT folks will support, maintain, and fit your request into the overall system. If you're asking at any time other than at the beginning of the budget cycle, you're also impacting funds for support and maintenance that have already been allocated.

Setting Standards

Personal computers are just the tip of the iceberg for an organizational IT infrastructure. There's the multitude of hardware needed—file servers, disk systems, and backup drives, to name a few. There's the communications infrastructure, to include data cabling, phone lines, and data lines. There's the software that runs on the hardware.

That multiplicity of things in IT systems makes saying "have it your way" to users impractical for a CIO. Instead, a major concern for any CIO is standardizing as much as possible. For one thing, disparate systems can hamper collaboration across an organization. If everyone has a particular word processing package, for example, it's easier to exchange documents. I've known organizations that couldn't even exchange e-mail among all locations.

Know Nos

Don't set your heart on any information technology without checking with your IT people first. Their job is to stay abreast of IT developments. You could very well find out, for example, that there's a better software package than the one you're recommending—or one that's just as good, but much cheaper.

For another, if a firm buys in bulk, it's usually cheaper. Standardization also decreases maintenance costs, since it decreases the need for additional specialized support. It decreases the number of parts that have to be stocked and ordered. It decreases the training needed for to both IT personnel and the users. It's simply more cost-effective for a CIO to create and enforce standards.

You'll bump into these concerns about standardization when you, cap in hand, ask for any information technology that's near and dear to your heart. A CIO isn't being cold-hearted when he or she turns down your request because it doesn't fit into the standards. What's going through the CIO's mind is the cost of accommodating your request and whether or not it's compatible with the current or planned system.

The CIO also might know that your request would be difficult to apply across the globe, which is yet another concern.

Going Around the World

As a young soldier, I was stationed in Germany. After my first month's phone bill, which was higher than my monthly rent, I installed a meter on my phone. Having grown up in the United States, I was used to one monthly fee for local phone service. This wasn't the case in Europe.

Some other potential global differences for your CIO to consider include the following:

➤ **Telecommunication infrastructures.** The thing that comes to mind first is the difference in data communication lines. I myself had a formative experience when I visited one country where I was limited to transferring data (like receiving e-mail) to 9,600 bits per second. Even when I left my computer running to download large files, there often was so much static on the lines that my file would be kicked out. Some Web sites became too cumbersome to work with, as well.

Depending on the countries in which your organization operates, the capacity of data communication lines in some locales could be much lower than what you have back at corporate headquarters with a T1 line. Such a difference considerably lowers the common denominator for your IT infrastructure.

➤ **Electrical power.** We're talking differences in voltage, such as 110 or 220—an electrical-plug Tower of Babel every bit as diverse as differences in languages. If that weren't enough, there also are differences in how stable power supplies are. Even a mild surge can fry computer systems or knock out cooling systems.

➤ **Encryption.** *Encryption* is a way to make data secure. The federal laws of the United States place many prohibitions on the levels of encryption that can be transferred overseas.

Know These

To **encrypt** data, the data is first created with a key before being sent. The recipient then uses the same key to decrypt the received data. If someone intercepts the data who doesn't have a key, hopefully that person won't be able to read it. Encryption of data is *de rigueur* for e-commerce to protect information like consumer credit card numbers.

Didn't Know

To explain the difference in capacity for data lines, here are some terms:

➤ A bit is the smallest unit of information, usually a 1 or 0.

➤ A byte is a set of bits representing a character, usually 8 bits per byte.

➤ So, at 9,600 bits per second it would take about 18 minutes to download a megabyte of data.

➤ A transfer rate of 56,000 bits per second (as with a 56K modem) means that it takes about three minutes to transfer that same megabyte.

➤ A T1 line is a leased-line capable of carrying data at 1,544,000 bits per second. At its best, a T1 line can transfer a megabyte in less than 10 seconds. It is the fastest speed commonly used to connect networks to the Internet.

➤ **Political standing.** A thorny issue that plagues international corporations is political situations such as embargoes. If you're headquartered in the United States, even though your corporation may be operating in such countries as Iran, you'll face a myriad of problems when trying to work within that country.

➤ **Education.** Many poorer countries have much lower levels of education than more economically developed ones. This affects the education of the people who work on the system.

➤ **Language.** As we discussed earlier, even when there is one "official" language for a corporation, there usually are wide variances in mastery of it.

➤ **Cultures.** We'll talk more about this in Part 4, "The Showstopper of Culture."

All of these potential differences are important for a CIO with a global IT system, and also for you when implementing knowledge.

Other Causes of CIO Stress

At the end of a hard day being a knowledge management revolutionary (or gadfly, depending upon your point of view), I look in the mirror and say to myself, "It could be worse. I could be a CIO." So I always approach a CIO with the respect due someone who has a tough, important job and resolve to cooperate with them as much as I can.

In case you haven't already reached that conclusion, let's cover other things a CIO also must do:

➤ **Run an IT department.** Given that there's a tremendous shortage of qualified IT personnel, I know more than one CIO who doesn't allow organizational charts to be printed up with people's names. It makes it too easy for those people to be identified and stolen. And once IT people have been hired, they must be trained and otherwise managed.

➤ **Purchase hardware, software, and support services to include infrastructure support and possibly consultants.** They also have a bewildering variety of options for purchasing: direct sales, computer stores, office supply stores, and independent computer sellers. Not to mention they have to think about what to do in-house and what to outsource.

➤ **Focus on the challenges of mobility**—how to support laptops that are on the move, how to secure mobile computers, and how to support users who aren't sitting in the corporate office. Additionally, laptops that move around are more likely to be dropped, left in hot cars, and otherwise damaged.

➤ **Provide technical support.** Like purchasing, support can come from a variety of sources like vendor Web sites, other Internet sources like independent Web sites, and bulletin boards, suppliers, and internal sources. This also includes setting up a help desk for internal users.

➤ **Keep the system secure.** If you haven't encountered a computer virus up until now, I congratulate you. In addition to protecting the networks from viruses and hackers, a CIO must insure that the IT system has its own internal security.

➤ **Maintain an inventory** for what's contained in the system.

➤ **Manage projects.** This is also part of the bread and butter for a CIO.

If you're implementing a knowledge management approach, as a CKO (or other funky title), you'll need to develop a good rapport with your over-worked CIO. IT won't make knowledge management happen, but KM won't happen without it.

The Least You Need to Know

➤ To implement knowledge management, you need to partner with the CIO or your organization's equivalent.

➤ A good CIO's job is to make information technology serve the needs of the business. To do that successfully, a CIO must understand the business, build internal relationships, and plan for the future.

➤ While it's hard to show dollar amounts for the value from IT, there are other ways a CIO can demonstrate value.

➤ To operate efficiently and reduce costs, a CIO must set standards for IT.

➤ Depending on the nature and size of your organization, your CIO must design an IT system that operates globally.

Chapter 12

Nets, Nets, Nets

In This Chapter

➤ Reviewing terminology of the Internet and the World Wide Web

➤ Understanding what an intranet is and does

➤ Building and maintaining a corporate intranet

➤ Facts about extranets

Having enjoyed the benefits of a corporate intranet since the late 1980s, I can't imagine implementing knowledge management without an intranet. Without the quality of connectivity and the simplicity and commonality offered by the software interface to application that is provided by an intranet, an organization's ability to create, share, capture, and leverage knowledge is stuck in the Stone Age, just above the level of typewriters, faxes, and snail mail.

In this chapter, we'll devote considerable time to corporate intranets. Before that, though, we'll look at the predecessors of the intranet, the Internet, and the World Wide Web. Lastly, we'll look at the hybrid of the two: the extranet.

Warning: This chapter will contain a considerable amount of technical terms. Knowing the basic terminology and how the technology works will help you when working with your information technology staff. I can't emphasize enough how being literate in some of the technology talk will help you work together to develop solutions.

Net 1: The Internet and the World Wide Web

Back in the 1960s, the Advanced Research Projects Agency (ARPA), part of the U.S. Department of Defense, was charged with looking for ways that defense researchers could share computer resources and information. A crucial issue was how the bits and bytes of information could find their own way around any gaps or outages in the network (for example, if a missile knocked out part of the system). To solve this problem, it developed a new way to send information in a network. The IT term for a way to communicate in computing is a communications protocol. The particular communications protocol developed by the ARPA is called TCP/IP.

Know These

Transmission Control Protocol (TCP) routes and transfers data. It does so by breaking data into smaller units, which are stamped with the size and the sequence number.
Internet Protocol (IP) handles the addressing and routing of the data to specific computers. Together, the TCP/IP protocols are the electronic "orders" that make Internet and intranet communications work.

The *TCP, transmission control protocol,* handles how the information being sent is organized and put back together. TCP divides the information into smaller units that can be sent more easily. To keep everything straight, each unit is stamped with its own size and sequence number. This helps the computer on the receiving end to know how big it is and how to put all of the pieces back together.

IP, the *Internet protocol,* makes the containers for the small units of information. Each container is stamped with the address of the computer sending the message and the address of the computer that should receive it. Every computer connected to the Internet has its own IP address, which is a string of numbers.

Know These

The **Internet** is the global network of individual networks that are interconnected through public links. All of these networks use the TCP/IP protocol for communication. Anytime you connect two networks together, you have an internet.

This communications protocol made it possible for ARPA to build a network with four universities. However, within a few years the number of organizations connected expanded to 40. Over the next two decades, other networks were developed. In the early 1980s these networks started connecting to each other. That was the beginning of the *Internet.*

A common mistake is to use the terms Internet and the World Wide Web (WWW) interchangeably. Strictly speaking, they aren't identical. The Internet began in 1969 when the Pentagon linked with four universities. However, until 1990 the Internet was not well-known.

That year, particle physicists at the European Particle Research Center (CERN), most notably Tim Berners-Lee, proposed an approach for marking text (called hyper text mark-up language or HTML) so that it could be published online, as well as a communications means for sending and receiving the resulting documents over a network. Strictly speaking, the World Wide Web refers to the global network that uses this means of communications to access materials and HTML. These include documents, graphics, sound, video, and other computer resources.

Didn't Know

Ever wonder why you have to type in http:// to reach something on the WWW? You owe thanks to CERN. The communications protocol that they developed is the HyperText Transfer Protocol (HTTP). HTTP is the standard protocol for communications between Web servers and those requesting information from the WWW. Additionally, HTTP uses a standard request format called a Universal Resource Locator (URL). When you type in a URL, you're sending a request to a specific Web server.

In 1993, there were only 50 WWW sites, mainly for particle physicists. An enterprising young student at the University of Illinois (Marc Andreeson) developed simple browsers called Mosaic and later Netscape that anyone could use to view WWW content. The number of sites quickly zoomed to more than 10 million, and today who knows how many millions. To locate anything on the Web, you have to use a browser, one of the critical pieces of Internet and WWW technology.

A *browser* is any piece of software that helps users search and retrieve information. A *Web browser* is a type of browser that requests and receives information from Web sites. It lets you search quickly through large sets of information available on the WWW. We'll talk more about browsers when we discuss how to set up an intranet. You can't do it without a browser.

Know These

A **browser** is a piece of software that searches large amounts of information. A **Web browser** is software that interfaces with the WWW, making it easier to locate Web pages, download files, play video, etc., then download the contents on your monitor.

What an Intranet Is

The next step was to apply Internet technology internally to organizational networks. An *intranet* is

131

Know These

An **intranet** is a private Internet. Most use the TCP/IP protocols that help provide a number of services.

essentially a private Internet. Internet-type services are installed on an internal network using the TCP/IP protocol, which helps provide Web services, e-mail, and transfer of files between people who have access to the intranet.

Although the technology is the same, there are some important differences between the WWW and intranets. The most important difference is that the purpose of a corporate intranet should be to serve the business needs of the organization. It should be created for specific business reasons, provide specific services for the needs of the business, and support the growth of the organization. I'll admit that the freedom of the WWW (I sometimes think of it as the Wild Wild West) is attractive. It certainly has allowed an explosion of connectivity, information, and creativity, but no one's in charge on the WWW. Someone is more likely to be in charge of a corporate intranet, and he or she has to show a return on the investment. It also has to be easy for the internal folks to use. There are other differences as well:

➤ **Ease of setting standards.** Since an intranet is controlled internally, it's easier to specify standards, such as having a particular browser. Since the intranet is set up and supplied internally, it's relatively simple to provide standardized software. It's also simpler to update through available downloads.

➤ **Easier security.** All the users should be from the organization. Sabotage still can occur, but it is less likely than on the wide-open WWW (or WOWW as it is sometimes called).

➤ **Greater bandwidth.** When I have some serious surfing to do for work, I'll drive into the office over the weekend to use the T1 line. It's so much faster than my modem at home that I consider the time spent driving worth the savings in aggravation waiting for Web pages to load. Greater bandwidth is an advantage an intranet can offer. This enables not only the faster movement of text and graphics, but also faster movement of other content like sound and video that take enormous chunks of bandwidth.

What You Can Do on an Intranet

There's a lot you can do with an intranet, depending upon what your goals are:

➤ Providing e-mail

➤ Delivering training

➤ Publishing information, such as news

➤ Delivering information to exactly whoever and wherever it's needed in the organization, no matter how remote

➤ Managing documents by allowing users to work collaboratively on office documents such as spreadsheets, word processing documents, and presentations

➤ Automating work flows such as administrative processes

➤ Providing discussion areas for users to address issues

➤ Increasing collaboration through use of tools such as shared calendars and project-management tools

➤ Unearthing new business opportunities and revenues

➤ Providing a front end to organizational databases, such as a corporate yellow pages

It's a matter of what your priorities and your resources are.

Benefits of an Intranet

Intranets can pay off, and pay off big. One study by the Meta Group of 85 companies found that the average return on investment (ROI) was 36 percent. To give you just a few specific examples, Bay Networks, a computer networking hardware and software company later bought by Nortel, cited $10 million per year saved on an initial investment of $3 million. Mitre Corporation, an independent, not-for-profit company, calculated a ROI of $62.1 million on an initial $7 million investment over five years. Where's the savings coming from?

➤ **Reduced labor costs.** An intranet can reduce the time it takes people to carry out a task—making information that people need to do their work easily available and easy to use.

Know How

Of course, the more bells and whistles you put on an intranet, the more the initial investment will cost. It is possible, however, to build a cheap intranet. I've seen figures as low as $4,000. You won't get much for that level of investment, but you will get started. Sometimes that's all you need for a success to prove the concept.

Didn't Know

Putting material such as policies, manuals, regulatory information, and contact numbers on an intranet also makes it easier to update and more readily available to users. Analysts estimate that 18 percent of corporate printed material becomes outdated within 30 days.

133

I've even seen a tool that lets you calculate the cost of not finding information using the number of employees, number of Web pages visited per day, average time wasted, and the average employee's salary. Those numbers can add up pretty fast.

➤ **Reduced costs in other expenses.** For example, the cost to print and distribute a large manual across a global corporation can add up to a pretty penny. Putting the manual on the intranet costs a fraction of printing and distributing.

➤ **Increased productivity.** An intranet also can help employees become more productive through increased sales per employee, lower costs per sale, and faster decision making.

➤ **Compliance with laws and regulations.** This is important for many organizations. For example, Mitre must comply with federal regulations for property management, purchasing, and time card submission. Since Mitre started putting the data on their intranet, they've had no noncompliance penalties.

Of course, not just any intranet is going to provide those kinds of payoffs and benefits. A valuable intranet must be relevant to the business, with the users deciding if the content is relevant to them. The information on an intranet must be kept up-to-date. The sites on an intranet must be easily navigable, making it easy to find information. And so on. Most of these issues should be addressed during the inception of an intranet.

Building an Intranet

While the majority of larger organizations now have an intranet, not everyone does yet. If you think that your organization is too small to benefit from an intranet, think again. Granted, if you spend less you'll get less; however, even a small application can have big rewards. Keep in mind that you can start small and scale up later. Pilots are just as applicable to intranets as they are to other endeavors.

Before You Leap

The first thing is to assess your current network. Are you using the TCP/IP protocols? This is absolutely necessary. TCP/IP is the protocol that you need in order to set up an effective modern network. If this isn't the case, it may not be a showstopper, as long as the network will support TCP/IP. If you don't have it and your network doesn't support it, you'll have to

Know How

You can outsource development of an intranet. That'll get you a faster development cycle and the help of experienced web designers. However, make sure that your internal staff is ready to take over when the consultants leave. Also make sure that the initial intranet has allowed room for growth.

make a bigger investment in funds to adapt the current network. Next, you'd best look at how connected your internal networks are. You may have a mix of LANs and WANs. That's okay, as long as they're connected. The amount of connectivity in your internal networks also determines how much connectivity there will be in your intranet. If you have separate islands of LANs, you'll only be able to handle one island at a time.

Last, it's a good idea to think about how ready your organization is for an intranet. Like knowledge management projects, it isn't a case of "build it and they'll come." Depending on the mindset of your organization, you also may face some fierce resistance. You're going to be making changes, and that's never easy.

The Minimum It Takes

The most important component of an intranet is a *Web server*. A *server* in general is a powerful computer that provides services and resources to other computers in a network. A Web server is a specialized device that has three components:

➤ The Web server software, which automatically sends information such as files and data to any user who requests it. The software also includes an operating system.

➤ The hardware, which is a computer connected to the network that hosts the software.

➤ The content, which is whatever will be provided. You'll also need browsers to access the content.

How to Start a Pilot

When starting a pilot, you have a number of concerns you need to address. Some of the most important ones are as follows:

➤ **Look at the needs of the business.** Like developing a knowledge management strategy, you need to pick some important applications for your intranet. What would have a big payoff for the organization?

Know These

A **server** is a computer that shares resources with other computers on a network. A **Web server** is a specialized server that acts as the linchpin of an intranet. It includes the computer itself, the specialized software, and content.

Know How

Give your intranet a catchy name so that it has a memorable identity. My favorite name is one for a company known for making underwear: the Undernet. Others I've seen are Kite, which stands for Knowledge and Information to Everyone, at BG Group, an energy company. Another is the Global Village at US West. At the World Bank the intranet is called YourNet.

135

➤ **Identify the needs of the users.** What are things that everyone would want to use? How do people actually do their work? What would help make the intranet part of the way that everyone does business?

➤ **Determine the content and format.** You need good content to attract people initially. Also, if you carefully design a format up front, you're establishing a standard for further development.

➤ **Start working on standards.** This is a great time to decide what your standard software tools should be. Purchase, install, and give training on them right at the beginning. Also, think about what the standards will be for publishing on the intranet. Who will be allowed to do what? Also, give some thought to how content will be managed. You don't want to wind up with an intranet junkyard.

➤ **Get ready to train users and market the intranet.** Marketing will create a demand. Training helps people to actually use it and is a critical success factor.

➤ **Plan for the future.** This isn't a one-time fling. The utility of an Intranet benefits from continual improvement. You also have to plan for growth. Intranets can grow just as quickly as the WWW did. If you're unprepared, an expansion in content and use can catch you flat-footed.

Didn't Know

Every year *CIO Magazine* recognizes the top 50 intranets and extranets. Judges Tim Horgan and Lew McCreary analyzed the submissions for the 1999 awards and identified 10 major intranet trends. One of these trends was intranets becoming critical for doing business. Ninety-eight percent of the employees at Cisco use their intranet on a regular basis, for example. At Ford, the motto is "the Web is the way." Its goal is to have as many employees as possible find most of their information on the intranet. At each company where the Web was becoming a critical part of doing business, Horgan and McCreary saw strong support from senior management for the level of investment needed to bring about widespread deployment.

Maintaining the Intranet

Even if you don't scale up and expand, you'll still have to maintain what you've got. The initial cost is the tip of the iceberg. You also have to look at maintenance costs:

➤ Staffing needed for maintenance. This includes not only internal staff, but outside consultants whose expertise is needed.

➤ Upgrades to handle increased traffic and to keep up with changes in technology.

➤ Software licenses and upgrade fees.

➤ Communications infrastructure costs, such as the cost of phone calls and data lines.

➤ Costs of archiving information.

➤ Additional training on upgrades and other changes, both for users and for IT personnel.

What Is an Extranet?

An *extranet* is an intranet that uses Internet protocols and the public telecommunications system to work with selected external users. It also can be described as an extension of an intranet to users outside the organization. Those users could be customers, suppliers, partners, vendors, and perhaps even members of the organization who are connecting externally.

There are many possible roles for an extranet:

➤ Collaborating with partners on joint efforts

➤ Purchasing supplies and services

➤ Giving information about your products and services

➤ Selling products and services

➤ Supporting customers, suppliers, and sales personnel

➤ Recruiting employees

➤ Exchanging large amounts of data

The catch is that with an extranet you, in effect, unlock the door to your house. You've heard in the news about hackers gaining access to popular Web sites, sometimes with the intent to cause damage. A favorite pastime is erasing data. Another well-publicized action is hijacking a computer to carry out what the hackers wants it to do.

Think of all the sensitive information you have on your intranet. New-product development, patent information, customer records, financial results,

Know These

An **extranet** is an extension of an organization's intranet that has been opened to selected outsiders. Such outsiders may be customers, suppliers, partners, vendors, or even members of the organization itself. An extranet uses Internet protocols and a public telecommunications system. Strictly speaking, an extranet also has restricted (password-protected) access to provide security.

Know These

A **firewall** is a combination of hardware and software that protects a private network from unwanted intrusion. A firewall filters predetermined types of information from the Internet in an attempt to stop hackers from using the Internet as a means of entry.

employee records, and contracts are just a few of the things you most likely don't want to share with outsiders. But connecting your intranet to the Internet gives hackers a door they may try to open.

What stops unwanted intruders is a firewall. A *firewall* is a combination of hardware and software that examines what's coming in and filters out undesirable characters. A firewall usually is housed in the first computer reached by the Internet connection. This computer is sometimes called the bastion host, named after the defensive bastions in medieval castles. A friend of mine tells me you haven't lived until you've watched IT specialists don their armor to joust with black-hearted hackers.

Security issues shouldn't stop anyone from developing an extranet. However, the dangers, the necessity, and the options for protecting the internal network must be a primary concern in extranet development and maintenance. As the old saying goes, you aren't paranoid if they're really out to get you. Paranoia about firewalls is a survival trait.

The Least You Need to Know

➤ The Internet is the global network of linked private networks.

➤ An intranet is essentially a private Internet for an organization.

➤ Before an organization can build an intranet, there are some requisite capabilities for its internal network. However, if those requirements are met, setting up a simple intranet requires relatively little investment.

➤ If your organization plans to develop an intranet, start with a pilot.

➤ An extranet is an extension of an organization's intranet to selected outsiders. Security is a primary concern for any extranet.

Chapter 13

Between You and Me with Collaborative Tools

In This Chapter

➤ Choosing collaborative tools

➤ Tools to facilitate working together

➤ Benefits of integrated solutions

It's one thing to want to collaborate. But do you have the tools to do it? We count on having spreadsheets (pun intended) to do our financial calculations. We wouldn't dream of going back to typewriters to do word processing. We expect to have electronic databases for collecting, storing, and sorting data. Yet I've been struck many times by the lack of similar expectations for the IT tools that make it possible for people to collaborate online, usually one of the principal goals of KM. To me, it's the same issue: having the tools you need to do the job.

In this chapter, we'll look at some of the electronic tools that support collaboration. We'll start with one that I expect everyone to have—e-mail—and move up in terms of complexity and capability to support collaboration. We'll also look at two ways to describe collaborative tools.

Characteristics of Collaborative Tools

No matter what kind of collaborative tool you use, a common framework for describing it has two elements: time and place.

➤ **Time.** Is the collaboration taking place simultaneously (synchronous) or at different times (asynchronous)? Some examples of synchronous collaboration are videoconferencing, and presentation support. Examples of asynchronous collaboration are e-mail and *work flow*.

Know These

Work flow refers to tools that help automate business processes. For example, insurance claims and loan processes are both business processes involving documents that need to be reviewed and approved by several people in sequence. By automating the flow of documents through the process handling, delays can be reduced significantly and the status of an individual document can be easily tracked.

➤ **Place.** The collaboration can occur at the same place (collocated) or at different places (distance). Both of these can be combined, creating four sectors.

	Same Time	Different Time
Same Place	Decision-making, presentation support	Shared computers
Different Place	Videoconference	E-mail, workflow

Synchronous and asynchronous tools are complementary. You need both, especially for geographically distributed teams, to be effective.

Another characteristic of collaborative tools is how information-rich they are. *Information richness* is the amount and types of information that a tool provides. A tool with high information richness, such as videoconferencing that includes a whiteboard, gives more context than e-mail, which has low information richness. You're able to see facial expressions and body language. You can hear the tone and inflection in people's voices. You can see what the room looks like where other people are.

Know These

Information richness is a characteristic of a collaborative tool that indicates how much information and how many types of information it has. The more information-rich a tool is, the more context it provides.

Social presence is the last characteristic we'll discuss. It focuses on how well the collaborative tool helps people to connect with each other. For example, a face-to-face meeting has high social presence. An e-mail message has poor social presence. Synchronous communications have more social presence overall than asynchronous. Tools with high social presence are good for solving problems, building trust and relationships, and generating ideas. My rule of thumb is that when I think a face-to-face meeting is what's needed, that's when a tool with high social presence is more suitable.

However, there are times when you want a tool with low social presence. Let's say you have several people in a group who'd prefer to be meeting for a gunfight rather than a collaborative effort. Using a tool with low social presence cools the personal differences by making the people seem less real. Also, if a group is handling routine information, there's no need to get real and personal. E-mail or some other method works fine.

The bottom line is that no one collaborative tool is ideal for all situations. Think through your goals for KM, the group who would be using it, and the suitability of your available tools. Pick what's best for the situation.

The Lowly but Popular E-mail

Tell me, do you get enough e-mail at work? (Don't yell.) Do you sit up at night while you're on the road checking your e-mail? Or, at home, do you get up in the wee hours to do it? Or do you have a mobile device that beeps you while you're in transit?

E-mail is ubiquitous. In a recent consortium benchmarking study on communities of practice, the American Productivity and Quality Center found that the most frequently used tool for communities was e-mail. Professors Peter Lyman and Hal Varian of the University of California—Berkeley estimated that 610 billion e-mails are sent worldwide per year, compared to the creation of 2.1 billion static Web pages.

E-mail is nothing more than an electronic version of written mail, now sneered at as snail mail. Messages are sent via an electronic network. Attachments can be added to include files such as documents and presentations. It also gives people a chance to think about what they want to say.

Another advantage of e-mail is that it can be used to broadcast messages to a number of people. You can even set up group e-mail addresses for groups of people you frequently contact, such as team members.

Know These

Social presence indicates how well a collaborative tool helps people to connect to each other. When a tool has high social presence, such as video-conferencing, the interactions are more social and warm. In contrast, tools with low social presence can seem distant and impersonal.

Know How

There are other things to think about when you're picking a collaborative tool. How much time will it take to get and train employees to use the tool? How much training and technology is available? How comfortable are people in your organization with technology? Also, you may want to think about whether or not you want a permanent record, such as an e-mail.

A relative of e-mail is *instant messaging.* Instant messages are short text messages sent and received in a flash. Currently, one drawback is that there is little interoperability between different systems for instant messaging. For example, as of this writing AOL is incompatible with other types of instant messaging. An approved messaging standard is still needed.

Another way that e-mail can be used is via e-mail repositories. In these repositories, e-mails can be collected, tracked, retrieved, and reviewed.

Yet as much as e-mail is used, it's not perfect. The most common complaint people have is that they get too much of it. Most systems do offer ways to filter messages. For example, you can route messages on which you are only cc'd to a folder to read later. Messages sent directly to you instead go to a different folder. You can route messages sent by particular people to separate folders. You also can set up which messages you want to see immediately. To me, the beauty of filters, used well, is that they sort your mail for you, much like an electronic secretary.

Another drawback of e-mail is that it is low in information richness. Effective communication is not always a matter of what you say; often it's how you say it. In e-mail there are no facial expressions, no tone in the voice, and no winks of the eye. Without the nonverbal communications, it's all too easy to misunderstand what someone has written. It's also a poor way to discuss complex ideas and issues. Even something as simple as agreeing when to have a meeting is hard to do via e-mail, let alone prioritizing actions, brainstorming, or resolving conflicts.

An issue that's becoming of greater concern is security. For example, how do you really know who sent a message? If you've ever been *spammed* with pornographic material, you know that it's easy to disguise the true sender of a message. A digital signature can help verify the true sender of a message. Additionally, how do you know if someone or something has changed a message? This also can be handled with a software application. Depending on what you're doing, perhaps something sensitive like new-product development, it might be something to think about and handle.

Know These

Instant messaging is short text e-mail messages that are sent and received immediately. Some applications have the capability to see who else is online. Others enable the messages to be stored and resent.

Know How

People working collaboratively can have problems when it comes to using e-mail effectively. Depending on the group, you may want to mark your e-mails to show how urgent they are. You may set a time limit for reading and responding. You may agree that if someone is cc'd, he or she is not required to respond. Your group may have other issues as well.

Another potential issue with e-mail is privacy. If you send e-mail at work, expect that others can look at it, regardless of whether you want them to or not. Various software platforms, as mentioned in Chapter 9, "Strategic Choices for Connecting People to People," also tap the content of e-mail. Your e-mail can identify you as an expert, whether you want to be or not. Although such e-mail systems as the ones mentioned in Chapter 9 usually allow people to keep their anonymity, the software's capability to search them out can threaten some people, unless handled with tact and diplomacy. Otherwise they feel as if big brother is looking over their shoulder.

E-mail is well suited for:

➤ Sending information to a group.

➤ Exchanging information.

➤ Sending and revising documents.

➤ Sending data.

➤ Defining problems.

➤ Sparking a debate.

Know These

Spam is a term used for junk e-mail. The term may have come from a skit by the British comedy group, Monty Python, in which the actors repeated the word "spam" over and over again. Or it may come from the canned meat, Spam, that can be used on anything. As with junk snail mail, your e-mail address may have been put on a list, and the unwanted messages are a nuisance.

Didn't Know

Having a permanent record in e-mail can be a disadvantage. Microsoft is one of the organizations that learned this the hard way. In the antitrust suit against them, a mainstay of the prosecution's evidence was Microsoft's internal e-mail. But where there's a market, there are entrepreneurs. Software that can make e-mail temporary is now available. Features include the ability to decide how long an e-mail will be readable or if an e-mail will be readable at all (giving people the option of sending private e-mails from work). Also, e-mails stored on a laptop can be made to vanish after a certain amount of time, which is helpful if the laptop is stolen.

143

Talking Together Electronically

One drawback of e-mail is that it's hard to connect the meaning of e-mails on a particular topic scattered among other messages. Another important group of collaborative tools— message boards and chat rooms—solve this problem. Message boards (sometimes called forums, bulletin boards, or conference servers) give people the ability to post and reply to messages in a common area. Often there's a moderator for the message board—a combination of cop, social director, and discussion leader. Chat rooms are similar, but users type comments back and forth to each other in real time.

Chat rooms and messages boards offer a number of features. Some common ones are:

➤ **Threaded vs. serial discussions.** A threaded discussion is one in which all replies to a message are indented and grouped under the message. This makes it easy to see what the replies to a particular message are and to follow the thread of the discussion. In contrast, a serial discussion lists messages as they are received, in no particular order. Some applications use threaded discussions, others serial. Some people hate threaded and prefer serial; others hate serial and prefer threaded.

➤ **Handling of unread messages.** Some applications allow the user to view the messages they haven't read.

➤ **Editing of posted messages.** Sometimes users change their minds about what they've posted. Some applications allow users to edit what they've posted, perhaps in a specific time frame. Of course, other users may have already read the message. Also, some applications allow moderators to screen and delete messages.

➤ **E-mail notification.** Some software packages notify participants when messages get responses.

➤ **Banishing of participants.** If necessary, a moderator should have the ability to block someone from participating.

➤ **Archiving of messages.** How are the messages archived? How are they then retrieved? Also, how are archives searched?

➤ **Links to other functions.** For example, some applications cross-link to e-mail, chat, and instant messaging.

➤ **Editing of posted messages.** Sometimes users change their minds about what they've posted. Some applications allow users to edit what they've posted, perhaps in a specific time frame. Of course, other users may have already read the message. Also, some applications allow moderators to screen and delete messages.

➤ **Registration systems.** Depending on the software package, there may be no security features or strict confirmation of new users. You'll have to check the specific packages you're considering using.

➤ **Spell checkers.** This is a pet peeve of mine. It is beyond me why so many applications don't include spell checkers in message boards. But they don't.

Message boards are good at:

➤ Giving people a meeting place, much like a café.

➤ Solving problems.

➤ Sharing information.

➤ Meeting other people.

➤ Learning who the experts are.

➤ Learning about the topic.

Chat rooms work well for:

➤ Solving problems in real time.

➤ Providing more social presence than message boards.

➤ Holding scheduled events.

➤ Building communities.

Electronic Meeting Systems

Another step up from chat rooms and message boards are electronic meeting systems. I remember years ago going to a special team room to use an electronic meeting system. Each of us sat at a computer and typed in our input. All input then was displayed anonymously, helping to skirt any personality clashes in the group or a tendency for one person to dominate. We also used the system to vote on issues. Such systems are still in use, and they can range in complexity. Some are simple polling systems while others have the ability to collect input from the group members and display it on a central screen. Such electronic meetings systems also are now available on WANs, intranets, and the Internet. Such a system is good for

➤ Dealing with controversial issues.

➤ Helping a group with many conflicts to work together.

➤ Generating and prioritizing options.

➤ Defining problems.

➤ Reaching consensus.

➤ Creating a permanent record.

These systems are also becoming more compatible with other work tools, to include project-management software, spreadsheets, presentation software, and word processing. If needed, these systems can be integrated with other systems such as desktop

video. The combination of electronic meetings systems with other tools increases information richness and, depending on the tool integrated, the social presence as well.

Working Together

In addition to electronic meeting systems, there are a number of tools that make certain activities easier for groups, whether you have teams, work groups, or communities. We'll look at shared documents, shared databases, and electronic whiteboards.

Shared Documents

When a group is working on the same document or group of documents, there needs to be a way to

➤ Make the document centrally available.

➤ Allow people to make changes, if permitted.

➤ Synchronize the changes made.

➤ Maintain the most up-to-date version.

A variety of software packages can provide these functionalities. The benefits are obvious to anyone who has tried using e-mail to create a group document. It's just too hard to keep track of the changes, not to mention who did what and what the most current version is.

Shared Databases

Shared database systems were some of the first collaborative tools to come out. Such systems usually can handle many kinds of data, including multimedia. Such systems are good for

➤ Storing the work of individual members.

➤ Storing the work of the group, such as lessons learned, reports, and other documents.

➤ Accessing and saving information from other sources like organizational databases.

The Electronic Whiteboard

An electronic whiteboard is similar to the whiteboards and blackboards you're used to scribbling on. However, an electronic whiteboard gives a group the ability to share documents and drawings. I'd suggest using these with a communications link, such as voice, audio, or video. That way the group can discuss what's being displayed on the whiteboard. An electronic whiteboard works well for these tasks:

➤ Preparing information

➤ Displaying and analyzing data

➤ Generating and listing options

➤ Drawing concepts and other visual ways to express ideas

➤ Brainstorming

➤ Creating a permanent record

Similar in nature to shared whiteboards are applications that enable users to share PC screens, such as NetMeeting. This goes beyond the shared whiteboard, though, to enable users to tap into their software applications as they collaborate. I once had a virtual meeting with someone to look at his intranet. We talked by phone while I looked at his screen as he surfed through his Intranet. It saved me a trip and got me the information I needed.

Videoconferencing

One collaborative tool that has both high social presence and information richness is videoconferencing. It comes in two flavors: specialized video facilities and desktop.

Your organization may have specialized videoconference facilities that are set up with the hardware and data links needed. Vendors also provide such facilities if your organization doesn't want to invest in the technology. Either way, a specialized videoconference facility usually has a data link that provides high bandwidth (allows more data to flow faster through communication lines) for better quality. It also may have video equipment. However, even with high bandwidth the transmission still may not be the best for a number of reasons, particularly if you have more than two locations linked together.

Know How

The cousin of the videoconference is the audio conference, which is voice transmission only. While a videoconference with its combination of the visual and the auditory has more information richness and social presence, an audio conference still has more information richness and social presence than such technologies as e-mail. It can be very effective when participants already know each other.

Didn't Know

Can you trust someone you can see more than someone you can't? British Petroleum made an interesting discovery during its work with virtual teams that used desktop video and other collaborative technology. When people made promises using video, they were more likely to keep those promises than ones made via e-mail. Here's looking at you, kid.

Know How

Designing, implementing, and facilitating an online community requires a lot of know-how. Some vendors will provide these services. For example, a vendor provides the software and facilitates online customer communities for Hallmark and Sara Lee. Check to see what services a vendor provides in addition to the package. Other possibilities are training and consulting, in addition to hosting.

A desktop video usually also has a voice capability and a way to share documents. One advantage of desktop video is that most computers already have the hardware needed, although older computers may need a video card, microphone, speakers, and a video camera. However, the picture often is poor and small. Discerning body language also is difficult.

However, not everyone likes videoconferencing. Depending on the amount of bandwidth in your data link, you may wind up with a picture that looks out of focus. Motion may also appear jerky, as if the people you're talking to are stiff puppets. If you're connecting via the Internet and there's a data traffic jam, you could have a poor-quality transmission as well.

Another issue is the cost of the call. Because videoconferencing may require several lines, a lengthy call between continents can run up a bill considerably more than phoning your mother back home. Granted, it's still much cheaper than traveling.

Videoconferencing works well for the following:

➤ Defining problems

➤ Discussing issues

➤ Generating and prioritizing options

➤ Fostering a communal spirit

➤ Helping to build trust

➤ Situations where you don't need a detailed permanent record generated automatically

Putting It All Together: Integrated Solutions

If you find the variety of options bewildering, there's good news. There are now packages out there that tie together many of the options into an integrated solution. The packages vary a good bit. However, these are some of the features that you'll see:

➤ Instant messaging

➤ Document sharing

➤ Polling

➤ Video, voice, and text chat rooms

➤ Threaded discussions

➤ Project-management tools

➤ File storage

➤ Online brainstorming activities

➤ Desktop paging

➤ Member profiles (A member profile is information about individuals—an electronic introduction of sorts.)

➤ Expertise location

➤ Member directories

➤ Profanity filters

Some vendors also are offering the ability to choose which functionalities a customer wants. Others also will host the system usually via the Internet. This might raise the issue of security, particularly if the information involved is proprietary or sensitive. Many companies are leery of hosted systems for this reason.

Custom integrated solutions are good for:

➤ Virtual Teams

➤ Collocated Teams

➤ Communities of practice

➤ Customer communities

➤ Working with customers, suppliers, and partners

The Least You Need to Know

➤ Collaborative tools can be categorized as to whether they are synchronous or asynchronous, and also whether they are used in the same place or in different locations. Other characteristics of collaborative tools are how well they connect people to each other and how much and how many types of information they carry.

➤ Despite its limitations, e-mail is the most commonly used collaborative tool. However, message boards and chat rooms offer additional features that often make them more effective than e-mail.

➤ There are a number of options for collaborative tools—to include chat rooms, shared whiteboards, shared documents, audio conferencing and video conferencing.

➤ No one collaborative tool is right for all situations.

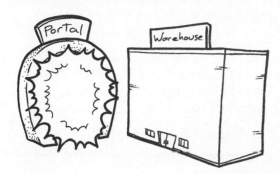

Chapter 14

Finding the Information You Need

In This Chapter

➤ Making the best use of all that information

➤ Managing content with taxonomies and search engines

➤ Understanding the role of a portal

When we talked about intranets, we discussed planning for growth. Some of you may have grinned ruefully at that point. It's already too late for that, you thought. Your intranet has already grown. There's so much content that you can't find what you need to find. Your intranet has become a data junkyard, forcing you to root around the piles of debris, hoping you'll find what you need. Your desktop is a mess, icons crammed together, but you need all of them for the various applications you use. In short, the problem isn't that you have too little. What you have is too much. And if your intranet isn't bad enough, there's always the Internet to overwhelm you with content.

In this chapter, we'll look at ways to access, organize, and use the information in your intranet and, in some cases, the Internet. Information technology evolves rapidly, so some of this chapter undoubtedly will become dated in a few years. However, some basic information such as the description of taxonomies, the need for taxonomies, the definition of a portal, and the steps for managing content should remain relevant.

Staying Out of the Junkyards: Managing Content

It's possible to have too much success. Perhaps your organization is one that successfully built an intranet that subsequently grew and grew. The result was a network full up to its electronic eyeballs in content—not only a lot of content, but many different kinds:

➤ Databases

➤ Presentations

➤ E-mail

➤ Documents

➤ Spreadsheets

➤ Archived discussions from bulletin boards

It's a jungle out there. But sadly, the amount and variety of content doesn't guarantee that users will be able to find what they need quickly.

Regardless of the way it's implemented, any system for managing content has three critical processes:

➤ **Collecting the content.** Content can come from both internal and external sources. In fact, it should come from both.

➤ **Using the content.** This includes the technology for finding, accessing, and delivering the content to users. One important technology for finding and accessing content is search engines, which we'll cover later in this chapter.

➤ **Managing the content.** One important concern is organizing the content. We'll talk later in this chapter about taxonomies, an important tool for organizing content. Here are some key concerns for managing content:

    Collecting the right content

    Finding sources for content

    Selecting the best technology to deliver the content

    Developing ways to organize the content

    Establishing processes to manage the content

Didn't Know

It's not just your intranet that's growing. In a research report released in January 2001, Forrester Research found that 79 percent of the people they studied said their sites would grow in the upcoming year. One-third expected their content to double through 2001.

Know How

Another important element of any content management system is people to manage the content—people who know the content and have expertise. For example, a key role in a community of practice is the equivalent of the community librarian. Such a person can teach community members how to manage their content and oversee the whole process.

Additionally, there must be a process in place to make sure the content stays current. Deadwood such as out-of-date material or even abandoned Web sites has to be pruned. Additionally, the needs of the users will change over time. New content will need to be added. There must be an ongoing process to monitor the content and how well it meets the needs of the users.

Something else to think about is legal liability. What if a customer misuses the information on your Web site and dies or is severely injured? You'll need to include disclaimers if you're making content available to customers. Additionally, if you bring in content from the outside, you're entering the murky world of copyright issues. Unfortunately, copyright law hasn't kept up with the times, and there are many cloudy and unresolved questions about the electronic use of copyrighted material. It's not even clear if it's okay, legally, to link to Web sites.

I wish I could tell you that there's a multitude of great technology out there for content management that would solve the problem. Forrester Research, in a report issued in January 2001, concluded that current content-management software is in an early stage. It cites three so-called classic signs:

➤ Incomplete products that don't address all of a customer's needs

➤ Lack of a clear understanding of what content management is and what it involves

➤ Diverging visions of the future of concept management

However, there is hope. We see an increasing use of an enabling technology for content management called *XML,* or *extensible markup language.* XML is a set of rules for defining structures that indicate what the function of the data is, not just the way it is supposed to appear on your screen like HTML does. If all the available content is marked using XML, it's considerably easier to find, access, categorize, integrate, and otherwise manage the information. This extensive use is just over the horizon, as XML is an emerging standard. The impact should be considerable, though. One expert I read enthused that it will be as big a leap forward as the technology that enabled the explosion of the World Wide Web, HTML.

Know These

Extensible markup language (XML) is an important technology for content management. It is a set of rules for defining data structures. It specifies what the function is of text on a Web page, unlike HTML, which only says how things will be presented. One application is that XML makes it possible for key elements in a document to be categorized by their meaning. A search engine can then find these elements and then return results more intelligently.

Managing Content with Taxonomies and Search Engines

One important key for organizing and finding information is a *taxonomy*, a hierarchical structure for a body of knowledge. This structure gives a framework for understanding how that knowledge is grouped and how the groups relate to each other. From your school days you may remember that the purpose of a taxonomy in biology is to organize the vast number of known plants and animals into related categories that could be named, remembered, and discussed. The taxonomy provides a methodology for classifying a particular plant or animal to show its place in the overall scheme.

To show you an example of how a taxonomy in the animal hierarchical structure works, we'll go back to that odd animal, the duck-billed platypus. We'll start at the top of the taxonomy and go to the bottom. As we work through hierarchy down to the platypus, you'll see how it relates to other animals.

➤ **Kingdom.** The platypus belongs to the animal kingdom. Other kingdoms are Monera, fungi, plant, and Protista.

➤ **Phylum.** The platypus is part of chordata, animals with a notochord. A notochord is a rod that extends most of the length of the body when it is fully developed.

➤ **Subphylum.** The platypus is one of the vertebrata, animals with a backbone.

➤ **Class.** Despite its oddities, a platypus is a mammal, a group of animals that have hair and four-chambered hearts, are warm-blooded, and bear living young.

➤ **Order.** The platypus belongs to the monotremes, mammals that lay eggs.

➤ **Family.** Ornithorhynchidae is the family of the platypus, a lonely family with one member.

➤ **Species.** The Latin, taxonomical species name for the duck-billed platypus is ornithorhynchus anatinus.

Know These

A **taxonomy** is a hierarchical structure for a body of knowledge. This structure provides a method for grouping knowledge and how different items relate to each other. It also gives a way to classify a particular thing. In content management, a taxonomy is a classification scheme for the content in a system. It organizes and helps users navigate through the content.

If you're managing content on your intranet or a specific Web site, a taxonomy gives users a way to view what information is available, how it is organized into groups, and how those groups relate to each other. A good taxonomy will take you close to where you want to be in your sea of knowledge. Additionally, it gives people adding content a way to classify their material. Those responsible for managing the overall content also can use the taxonomy to inventory and check the content. You can see how useful this can be in a knowledge management system.

There are two ways to generate a taxonomy: automatically and manually (by people). For example, Unilever Research used facilitated teams of 6 to 10 people to develop taxonomies. During mapping sessions lasting two to three hours, participants mapped out the hierarchical structure. Unilever found that mapping a taxonomy is an interactive and iterative process. As people work, some categories may change, or even disappear. The structure may also change. All of this requires intense dialogue.

While the results and benefits can be great, developing a taxonomy using people is time-consuming and people-intensive. You'll need experts, facilitators, and possibly some outside consultants with expertise in creativity and taxonomies. However, the most important drawback of a taxonomy generated by people is that it's a snapshot taken at a particular time. Unfortunately, that snapshot may not remain current. Things change, and taxonomies should change with them.

In contrast, a taxonomy generated automatically by a software program can be updated continuously, as part of the process of performing its main task. Some software will even present the resulting taxonomy visually, as a hyperbolic tree that allows users to navigate through the information.

There are also search engines that combine searches with taxonomies. Web sites like Yahoo! are good examples. Some use existing internal taxonomies or keyword lists. Some build a customized taxonomy by analyzing internal work processes and information.

Know Nos

Don't expect a taxonomy to be a perfect work of art. Take the platypus. It really doesn't fit into the mammal class since it lays eggs, but it comes closer to mammals then any group. Any taxonomy you develop will be an approximation. Do the best you reasonably can.

Know How

Mapping out a taxonomy might spur the development of a thesaurus, which marks the relationships between concepts and common terms used at a company. A thesaurus needs to be dynamic, adding new terms and adapting to connections found in practice.

A Taxonomy in Action

If you would like to see a taxonomy for common business processes, one has been developed by the American Productivity and Quality Center in collaboration with industry members and Arthur Andersen. It can be downloaded for free on the APQC Web site (www.apqc.org). Search for the process classification framework. The top levels of the APQC framework are as follows:

➤ Understand markets and customers

➤ Develop vision and strategy

➤ Design products and services

➤ Market and sell

➤ Produce and deliver for manufacturing

➤ Produce and deliver for service-oriented organizations

➤ Invoice and service customers

➤ Develop and manage human resources

➤ Manage information resources

➤ Manage financial and physical resources

➤ Execute environmental-management program

➤ Manage external relationships

➤ Manage improvement and change

Like other taxonomies, this one gives a framework for organizing and finding information, in this case about standard business processes.

Know These

A **search engine** is a piece of software that carries out searches for information. Searches usually focus on finding content from multiple sources, such as all of the content on an intranet or the resources of the Internet. Search engines are another important tool for managing content.

Search Engines

You may be wondering, why bother with a taxonomy? Wouldn't it be easier to just use a search engine, a piece of software that finds information? It's not that simple, though. In its most basic form, a *search engine* looks for documents containing the desired word, often many of which are unrelated to your topic. This produces the 10,000-hits syndrome (and not the kind you find on the Top 40), since most people search by starting with a broad topic, and then narrow it down.

Granted, search engines have gotten more sophisticated over the years. In addition to using taxonomies, search engines now use queries in natural language (the way we speak, not computerese), linguistic analysis, contextual information, and user profiles.

No matter how well a specific search engine works, though, it only focuses on finding information. It doesn't help users who are putting information in. It doesn't help users who want to see related information to their search. It doesn't help the people who manage the content.

I'm not saying that you shouldn't have a search engine. On the contrary, you must have at least one. It's another tool you need to manage content. It's also another critical decision for your IT staff to make when they put together the IT infrastructure. However, keep in mind that the purpose of a search engine is to find information. You also need to understand how the search engines(s) you have work and their limitations. Search engines vary a great deal. They've also grown more sophisticated over time.

Also, the best approach is to combine search engines with taxonomies. Some users are skilled at guessing keywords and doing searches; others find that drilling down into a good taxonomy works best. Provide both types of tools for both types of users.

One-Stop Shopping with a Portal

A *portal* is a Web site or Web page that gathers various information resources, both Web-based and traditional data including links to ERP database systems, into a single location. The purpose is to make users more efficient, since ideally the information resources on the Web site or Web page are the ones most needed. A portal can be on an intranet or the Internet. On the Internet, for example, you may have set up a personalized portal on MyAOL, MyYahoo, or MyExcite. A portal can be used in different ways.

One potential application of portal technology is for an enterprise-wide use, called an enterprise information portal (EIP). Such a portal serves as an entry for the information resources of the entire organization. However, you probably haven't seen such a portal at your organization. A recent survey of 1,000 IT executives by portal vendor Hummingbird found that, while most companies plan to have portals, only 8 percent had completed deployment. However, of organizations with revenues of more than $15 billion, 23 percent had deployed portals already.

Know These

A **portal** is a term for a Web site or Web page that's meant to be the main point of entry to an intranet or the Internet. The purpose is to put a variety of information resources into one location to make a unified user interface. Another name for a portal is a Web top, as it is the Web equivalent of a user's desktop.

There's a good reason for this. From an IT perspective, an enterprise-wide portal is much like the proverbial problem of belling the cat. It's a wonderful tool that can have many benefits. However, it's ticklishly difficult to actually do.

But the slowness in deployment isn't caused by a lack of vendors. On the contrary, it seems as if almost every software vendor is offering something claiming to be a portal product. However, the technology itself is still rapidly evolving. The first-generation products were far from perfect, focusing mostly on aggregating data. Worst of all, they usually didn't scale up well.

The next generation is improving in this area. Also, the software is starting to include collaborative tools such as instant messaging, audio and videoconferencing, shared calendaring, and document sharing.

Given the rapid change in the technology and the many new players coming into the market, it's important to choose a vendor carefully. Things to consider include:

➤ **The vendors' viability.** The new kids on the block haven't proven themselves yet. Given the effort and cost involved in setting up an enterprise information portal (EIP), it's not a good idea to bank on an unproven vendor. Additionally, you need to think about how good of a partner the vendor will be. Having experience with other large customers is a big plus.

➤ **Scalability.** Oddly enough, the tried-and-true approach of beginning with a pilot can mask a fatal defect—an inability to scale up. What works well in one department may develop problems when it's rolled out across an enterprise. It's still a good idea to start with a pilot, but scalability must be a primary concern up front. Another thing to think about when scaling up is how fast it will work. Sluggish portals frustrate users.

➤ **Security.** Not every user on your intranet has the right to see all of the information out there or possibly available. For example, if you link to the human resources system you'll need to limit access for the everyday user, provide more access to management, and give perhaps even more access to people within human resources.

➤ **Ability to access all of the needed information sources.** Again, this may be easier said than done depending upon your IT infrastructure and the connections tools provided by the portal vendor.

➤ **Personalization features.** No matter how well you design a portal, it won't be the best solution for everyone. You need to allow users to personalize the portal so that they have what they need.

Whether you're setting up an enterprise-wide portal or one with a smaller scope, portals usually provide three kinds of content:

➤ **Applications.** At the corporate level, customer support and sales and marketing applications are used most often.

➤ **Information, both internal and external.** Frito-Lay is a good example of using a portal for information resources. Its salespeople needed information on how to market Frito-Lay products. The information was available, but in separate databases, spreadsheets, word processing documents, presentations, and PDF files. Also, the sales force routinely tapped external Web sites for information.

Additionally, if you're setting up a portal, you may want to look at it from these three lenses suggested by Geoff Smith, who is the European head of knowledge and content management at Cap Gemini Ernst & Young:

➤ **Personal.** These role-based portals provide the technical and business tools that are needed by a person doing a type of job. Geoscientists in an oil company, R&D chemists, and HR administrators are good examples.

➤ **Professional.** This looks at career development, including training. If available, you could provide a link to the corporate university or an e-learning capability.

➤ **Process.** This focuses on how employees do their jobs and the key tools and processes for doing it. If your organization has a community of practice structure or teams, they would be included here.

Don't develop a portal without talking extensively to the future users. You might want to do surveys, form focus groups, and interview employees to learn about how they do their work and how a portal would make their job easier. This could take some time, perhaps even months.

Know These

Strictly speaking, an **application** is any computer program designed to accomplish a specific task or related set of tasks. For example, PowerPoint is an application for making presentation slides.

The Least You Need to Know

➤ Content management addresses the issues involved in categorizing, organizing, finding, and accessing information by users. It also includes keeping the content up-to-date and relevant.

➤ A taxonomy is a hierarchical structure for a body of knowledge. This gives a framework for understanding how the knowledge can be grouped and how the groups relate to each other.

➤ A search engine is software that searches for information.

➤ Taxonomies and search engines both help in managing content.

➤ A portal puts a variety of information resources into one location to make a unified user interface.

Part 4

The Showstopper of Culture

When talking about her organization, a colleague of mine talks about a study that involved gorillas and a bunch of bananas hung high out of reach in their cage. A stepladder was placed underneath the bananas. Whenever a gorilla tried to climb the ladder to get the bananas, researchers would knock it off using a fire hose. Eventually, when a gorilla would try again to climb the ladder, the other gorillas would pounce on it and beat it up. Bad things happened when you tried to climb the ladder; they weren't about to let other gorillas do that.

The researchers then started removing gorillas from the cage and replacing them with gorillas that knew nothing about the perilous ladder. It wasn't until the last gorilla that had learned the dangers of the ladder was removed that a gorilla could climb the ladder without being beaten by its peers.

When an organization goes through a significant failure, the "gorillas" within learn not to climb that ladder again. When the opposite happens, the gorillas will try to climb that ladder at all costs. Both failure and success are learning experiences that help shape an organization's view of the world, its corporate culture.

Part 4 looks at what corporate culture is all about and its importance in understanding why employees and managers do what they do. You'll learn about a set of techniques called change management that can help you work with people who, through their experience, are likely to be skeptical of knowledge management. But, with the right approach, these same people can come to see the value of embracing the capture, classification, and most importantly, the sharing of knowledge, to the benefit of all.

Chapter 15

Culture Is You, Me, and Everybody Else

> ## In This Chapter
>
> ➤ Identifying the three layers of organizational culture
>
> ➤ Why organizational culture is key
>
> ➤ Uncovering the culture
>
> ➤ Understanding an organization's stories

One day when I was working with a team, I said loftily that organizational culture was the most important factor we had to consider. A team member sneered, "And just what the heck is organizational culture?" In horror, I realized the answer: "You are." Luckily, though, that particular culture included not only the obnoxious team member, but me, everyone on the team, and everyone else who worked in that organization.

Today I have a better answer for that person who had significant room for personal growth. A short answer is that culture is *the way we do things around here.* As you enter the field of knowledge management, you need to understand and work with organizational culture, and for you the answer is more detailed. An organizational culture is a set of values, beliefs, and assumptions that are deeply held by the people in an organization. These factors influence the decisions people make and how they behave in different situations.

In this chapter, we'll look at the nature of culture, how an organization acquires culture, and the inherent stability of culture once it is acquired. We'll also delve into how to understand a culture and its role in knowledge management. Then we'll also look at its companion, change management, the methodology and tools for working to change an organization's work and thus its culture.

Introducing a change of any kind is like pouring sand into a well-functioning engine. It doesn't matter if the change is as trivial as putting in an automatic requirement to make people change their log-in password every three months. It's a change. It introduces friction by changing the way people do things where they work.

The more friction, the more resistance. Depending upon your organizational culture and the nature of the knowledge management approach you use, you could be tipping a sandbag or two into the organizational engine. The purpose of this chapter and the others in this section, is to help you gauge how much sand you might be pouring into the organizational engine and how you can best handle it. Otherwise, your effort might grind to a halt.

The Three Levels of Organizational Culture

I don't know about you, but when I walk into an organization I'm like a three-year-old let loose in a new house. I look into everything. I pick stuff up. I poke my nose into where it isn't wanted. What I'm trying to do is to get a quick feel for what the organization is like. I look around for clues to the culture:

Know These

Artifacts are the visible aspects of an organizational culture. Some examples are office furniture, pictures, how meetings are run, and how people are dressed.

➤ What's on the bulletin boards

➤ What pictures or art are on the walls

➤ What the furniture looks like

➤ How the offices are set up

➤ How people decorate their office space

➤ How people are dressed

Beyond that, I also pay attention to how people act:

➤ How people greet each other

➤ How meetings are conducted

➤ How well people seem to work with each other

➤ The pace of how people interact with each other

All of these are part of the first of three layers of culture as defined by Ed Schein in his 1997 book, *Organizational Culture and Leadership*. This layer is called *artifacts,* and they are easy enough to spot; all you have to do is keep your eyes open. However, artifacts also have the disadvantage of being deceptive. It's all too easy to jump to conclusions based on the artifacts.

I compare looking at artifacts to looking at a mirror. You can't see what's behind a mirror; you only see what the surface reflects back to you. Many times you see yourself, as you interpret the artifacts accordingly to your own cultural assumptions.

The second layer is the espoused values, what the organization says that it believes. Some of these are:

➤ The corporate vision statement

➤ The overall mission

➤ The strategies

➤ Justifications for the strategies

➤ Codes of ethics

➤ Advertising brochures

➤ Material from the corporate Web site

➤ Written policies

I call these the supposed-to-be's. These espoused values are the official view of what the organization is supposed to believe. It's what people say, invariably highfalutin statements. When I start thinking of motherhood, the flag, and apple pie (with a dash of cynicism), I know I'm dealing with the espoused values.

And you need to be cynical, or at least questioning. Often the espoused values don't have anything to do with how the organization operates. There are the values hanging up on the wall, and then there is the way things are actually done around here. Words mean less than actions.

This divergence is often a function of age. As an organization ages, it can veer from its original beliefs. Sometimes you may actually see behavior that is 180 degrees off the espoused values. The potential for a gap increases the older an organization gets. The older an organization is, the more likely there is a gap between the espoused values and what really drives the behavior. Something else is driving the behavior, something unseen. This something is the third layer, a set of tacit assumptions that develop over time. And those aren't something you see when you walk around or talk to people. Those aren't necessarily the espoused values you hear.

Culture Is Learned

Culture is tacit knowledge, the seldom-discussed assumptions that are behind the actions we take. We know more than we can tell. If pressed about our reasons for doing something, we may say with annoyance, "That's the way we do things around here." If an outsider or the new kid on the block presses further, we fall back on that favorite of the exasperated parent: "Because." It is indisputably right to us, so right that we neither voice our assumptions nor question them.

More than 15 years after leaving the United States Army, I still have an intense emotional drive to arrive at least 10 minutes early for any meeting. (This still amazes my mother.) During my 10 years, the Army firmly impressed on my brain the dictum, "Be on time."

Punctuality, along with the cleanliness of a starched uniform and shined boots, was next to godliness. As one sergeant major said to me, "Punctuality and attention to detail are the two things you have to have to be successful in this Army." In all fairness, being on time is more than a quaint quirk for the military. If a coordinated military operation is slated to start at a certain time, one unit being late could ruin the operation.

For the military and some other organizational cultures, time is something concrete to be broken up into chunks. Certain tasks must be accomplished in each of those chunks. Like knocking over a pile of dominoes, being five minutes late could disrupt one thing in a carefully planned sequence, then another. Over the centuries, the military has learned repeatedly that being on time contributes to success. It has become a deeply held cultural assumption.

I'm not saying that it is a bad idea to learn the shared assumptions of a culture. On a mundane level, learning enables us to go about our lives with a minimum of effort. Just as the conventional rules of polite society have taught us the proper things to say when we meet people, our organizational cultures have taught us the proper norms for behavior. In an organization, this means that friction is lessened because people know the right way to behave. There isn't any need to discuss it or fight about it. It makes life easier.

At best, learning enables us to survive and prosper. Cultural lessons learned can enable us to repeat those actions that helped us to succeed in the past—and avoid past mistakes.

Know Nos

No matter how insanely idiotic you think some aspect of a culture is, keep that opinion to yourself. Whether you're an insider or an outsider, your job is to understand the culture with its strengths and weaknesses and to work within it. Open contempt will alienate the people you need to learn from.

Know How

During the Berlin airlift, the United States Air Force relied on timing to provide the desperately needed supplies. Aircraft took off and landed with almost mechanical precision every few minutes. Only by split-second timing could the vast amount of supplies necessary be brought in by plane.

Culture Is Stable

Sometimes I wince when I think about a PowerPoint presentation a colleague and I used to give. There was a slide on culture: "Does the culture emphasize the unnatural acts of sharing, using, collaborating, and improving?" That one was okay. That's a good question to ask about a culture when you're implementing knowledge management. It was the following slide that makes me wince: "If not, shifting to emphasizing these unnatural acts will necessitate changing the culture, with all of the difficulties that entails."

Talk about delusions of grandeur. At the time my naive (I like that word better than "stupid") goal was to take the entire culture head-on, with the goal of changing all of it. I don't think so. Changing even one deeply held assumption of an organizational culture takes serious work. Organizational cultures run deep.

These learned and shared assumptions are as pervading as they are deep. Think about how many people there are in your organization. Let's take just a few, perhaps the people in your section or department. Realistically, what do you think your chances are of changing their minds on just one thing they may have believed for years, something they don't even realize they believe? For example, it would have been an exercise in futility to tell my fellow soldiers that a few minutes here or there didn't make any difference. I could have argued until doomsday, but I wouldn't have changed their attitudes or assumptions.

Know How

New hires, ignorant of shared values, can threaten stability. One way to counter this is careful hiring for the right values. It is easier to hire the right people than to hire ones who have to be reeducated. Southwest Airlines is one company that is famous for its corporate culture. It hires for the right attitude, a sense of humor, and an ability to not take oneself too seriously. The result is that it gets the people whose values fit those of the company. They turn away job applicants in droves.

You might think that if you were the CEO you would be able to do it. Think again. There are always stories in the news of CEOs who have crashed and burned. They've joined companies and then were unable to make the changes they wanted. What you read are things like, "He didn't understand how we think. He didn't talk like us. She wasn't one of us." Even a CEO must understand and work within the organizational culture.

Unfortunately, many of these stories are also of internal CEOs who desperately needed to turn an organization around. Over time, assumptions based on past successes can become maladaptive. What worked before can ruin an organization rooted in the past. For organizations on the downward slide, massive transformative change is needed. But it is easier said than done.

Culture is inherently stable, even if it's a culture that's not healthy or when the assumptions behind it get in the way of improved performance. These assumptions and the related values and beliefs are tacit and thus not spoken much. How can you talk about what people don't know they know? The cohesive power of commonly held beliefs creates a stability that can defeat change efforts, CEOs, and even a reality that dictates change for survival.

MBA classes are full of stories of companies that continued making buggy whips after the first cars appeared. It seems like criminally stupid pig-headedness to outsiders, but the force of shared belief is formidable.

Didn't Know

An organization can learn in advance. One method is scenario planning, a way of thinking about what could happen in the future and how to handle the situation. You can build models. Simulations can be run. Experiments can be conducted. All of these nonreal-life methods also give you a chance to uncover underlying cultural assumptions and beliefs, but in a safe environment.

The Importance of Understanding Culture

The danger is that the culture can blindside knowledge management efforts. I've seen too many efforts derailed by organizational cultures. Your choice is to either understand the power of the organizational culture, or react to it after it runs over you. I prefer to understand what I am dealing with as much as I can.

In a former life, I spent a lot of time working with benchmarking teams. Our charter would be to benchmark a particular process with other organizations, find out how they did it, and then implement it at our place. Sounds simple, but I always worried intensely about the wild card, culture. To explain the wild card of culture I often drew three circles on a sheet of butcher-block paper or a whiteboard to illustrate its power:

➤ The first teeny circle in the very center had in it the process and its measures. The print was so small as to be unreadable.

➤ The second circle, which included the first one, contained organizational infrastructure, like the structure of the organization, the information technology, the communications structure, training, and so on. This circle was a little bigger; just big enough for small but readable print.

➤ The last circle, which contained the other two, I would draw so big that only parts of it were on the page or whiteboard. "This is culture," I would intone solemnly as I wrote the word in towering letters. I knew from unhappy experiences that culture was also the trump card. No matter how good the benchmarked process was, no matter how much it would have benefited our organization, nothing mattered if it clashed strongly with our organizational culture.

The other side of the coin was that the culture of the company whose process we had benchmarked helped make it work there. For example, cultures vary on how they value teamwork. If a benchmarked process depends heavily on teamwork, any organization that wants to adopt the process must recognize the importance of teamwork to make it work. Then they must assess their own belief teamwork. If an adopting organization has a culture that downplays teamwork, it may be impossible to implement the new process successfully.

In benchmarking, organizational culture was a potential showstopper. We had to understand what cultural aspects enabled a process to succeed on its home turf. We had to understand what aspects of our organizational culture might sabotage adopting a process.

That is no less true for knowledge management. To implement knowledge management you must understand the organizational culture. Otherwise, you may watch helplessly and hopelessly as culture derails your effort.

Know How

Can there be more than one culture in an organization? Sure. Any organization will have multiple personalities to a certain extent. Different divisions, locations, and functions are some of the groups that could have subcultures. Subcultures can be healthy, but can become destructive when there is conflict between different groups or if they become too ingrown. A subgroup that subverts the overall values can damage the organization.

Seeing the Invisible

There are no shortcuts to understanding culture. However, the best place to start is the history of an organization. How did the organization react to different situations in the past? How successful was it?

You may find that what people tell you has no basis in fact. Relax. In this instance, perception is all that matters. What people believe to have happened in the past is what you need to know. In fact, the difference between what they describe as happening and what actually happened can clue you into critical beliefs.

Didn't Know

Examine carefully the values and beliefs of the founder of an organization. Unless an organization fails, the rest of the organization comes to hold those beliefs. And once implanted, they are remarkably durable. In 1862, Henri Dunant, father of the Red Cross, wrote of the need for trained volunteers to care for the wounded in wartime. He believed that paid providers weren't as devoted or reliable as volunteers. Reliance on trained volunteers continues to be a cornerstone of the Red Cross. The American Red Cross is the largest volunteer organization in the United States. Other beliefs of Dunant also are apparent today: neutrality, the need for international cooperation, and the importance of tracing people who have disappeared.

Know How

If you're an insider, you have a problem: objectivity. You must put aside your own values, beliefs, and assumptions. Question and observe, don't judge. To better understand yourself, look at the groups, communities, and occupations that you belong to now or have belonged to in the past. Try to identify how they have influenced you.

I would add the evil twin of success, failure. Failures can irredeemably brand an organizational culture. None of us wants to repeat something that has burned us badly. Avoiding failure is a survival instinct.

Again, this can be good or bad. It depends upon whether the learned belief is still valid in today's reality. However, when we're trying to understand a culture, learning about the failures that shaped it help you to better make sense of it.

I call this the dead hand of history. Never underestimate its power. The world outside the organization may have changed drastically. Decades or even centuries may have passed. An organization may have undergone numerous changes. But the people within an organizational culture embody the memory by maintaining the values and beliefs of that culture. The lessons of the past continue to affect people in the here and now.

Didn't Know

In his book *The Corporate Culture Survival Guide*, Ed Schein says that organizations have different stages in their life cycle: start-up, midlife, maturity, and merger/acquisition. At each stage the culture is entirely different. Schein advises readers to first find out what stage an organization is in, because that will determine what you plan and execute.

➤ **Start-ups.** The founder's values shape the culture.

➤ **Midlifes.** Promoted general managers, not the founder or founding families, create the culture.

➤ **Old dinosaurs.** If a company doesn't change over time, it becomes maladapted. Often mature companies must undergo massive cultural transformations to survive.

➤ **Merger/acquisition.** Even if the stated aim is to combine the "best of both worlds," the possible outcomes are separation, domination, or blending.

The Least You Need to Know

➤ Organizational culture is composed of the tacit assumptions that are deeply held by the organizational members.

➤ Culture is stable, and not easily changed.

➤ To succeed in any new effort, you must understand the power of the organizational culture and work within it.

➤ Culture is complex; the assumptions are hard to uncover.

➤ One way to uncover the assumptions is to examine the organization's history from the view of the members.

➤ The stories told within an organizational culture also convey a sense of what the underlying assumptions are.

Chapter 16

Working with Organizational Culture

In This Chapter

➤ Changing the way people work

➤ Evaluating social capital

➤ Importance of leaders and middle management

➤ Looking at the rewards and recognition system

➤ Creating new heroes

Each organizational culture is different from every other one. They are as varied, as complex, and as individualistic as human beings are. That's not too surprising, considering the cultural values, beliefs, and assumptions held by the human beings who make up the organization.

In this chapter, we'll get down to the brass tacks on how to identify the cultural assumptions that could derail your knowledge management approach, ways to identify some conditions that create a favorable climate, and how to create new values and strengthen ones that are already supporting knowledge management.

Change the Way People Work

When I've been involved in blue-sky discussions of what would be the ideal culture for knowledge sharing, I've heard things like …

➤ We share freely and openly.

➤ We trust each other.

➤ The barriers between functional silos disappear.

➤ We view our mistakes as an opportunity for learning, not a chance to assign blame.

➤ We value teamwork and collaboration.

However, I've never been in a culture that had an open road to knowledge management with no cultural barricades. No organizational culture is a knowledge management nirvana.

First of all, try to define "nirvana." If you had a perfect culture for sharing knowledge, what would it look like? Come up with a list of things that would describe it, and then get even more specific. What exactly are the behaviors you'd see? How would things work differently than what they do today?

Once you have that, you have the level of detail you need for your vision. What you still don't have is a way to implement your approach. For that, you need to take it down to another level of detail:

➤ How would things work differently than they do today for the business goal or problem you're working on?

➤ How would the people involved in the day-to-day work behave differently?

➤ How would the daily work practice change?

➤ What strengths already present in the culture would help?

➤ What does that mean to you?

Know How

Think of the cultural barriers you'll face as being your opponent in judo. Judo leverages the strength of an opponent in order to overcome him or her. That's exactly what you've got to do with the culture. Apply the strengths of the culture to change the way people work. It's easier to motivate people to work for something they believe in.

Taking on the entire organizational culture is impossible. You have to do it in the context of your business issue and the day-to-day work of employees. By changing the way people behave, by showing them that new ways of working make them more successful, and by creating a new and shared history, you affect the underlying assumptions that drive behavior in the first place. That's not to say that you can do this quickly or easily! It'll take time and also involve other pieces of the cultural puzzle.

Discovering the Shadow Organization

We've talked about the importance of connecting people with our knowledge management approaches such as communities of practice and yellow pages. But we're not starting off with a blank sheet. The people in our organizations are already connected to each other. How strongly they're connected and how they relate to one another are additional clues to the organizational culture.

All of us know the organizational wiring diagram—the neat rows of boxes listing job titles and responsibilities that indicate a company's formal structure. We all know which one is our box. Our place in the hierarchy is delineated by the position of our box in relationships to other boxes.

However, the wiring diagram gives an incomplete picture of the organization. There's also what can be called a shadow organization, one that's not delineated on the wiring diagram. The shadow organization is made up of the networks and communities within an organization. And it is within these networks and communities that much of the organization's work gets done.

A *network* consists of people who know each other. While not everyone in a network knows everyone else, there is an overall pattern of connections. There is also mutual aid and reciprocity. In a network, people do things for each other. For us personally, our network is the people we call when

➤ We need to know something.

➤ We have information to share.

➤ We need to get around bureaucracy.

➤ We need help.

➤ We want to help.

They are people with whom we have built a relationship over time. We can expect them to respond. There also are people connected to the people we know, extending our reach. We call someone and they refer us to someone else. We tend to extend trust to the third person, depending

Know These

A **network** is a loosely and voluntarily connected group of people who know each other and do things for each other. However, it isn't a team, which has a fixed task and is usually appointed by management. It also isn't cohesive enough or focused enough on a practice to be a community of practice.

Know How

One way to uncover the networks and communities is by using social network analysis. It is a methodology for mapping out the participants in a network or community and the interrelationships. A social network analysis also is diagnostic. It reveals gaps, the density of the connections, and the role players in networks and communities.

175

upon how close the connection is. Often the person referring us will provide some background that gives us a better feel for whether we can trust this other person.

A close relative of the network is the community of practice, discussed in Chapter 8, "Communities of Practice—The Killer Application." Both networks and communities of practice make up the shadow organization.

The presence (or absence) of strong social networks and communities of practice gives us a sense of the social capital in an organizational culture. *Social capital* is the sum of connections between people. These connections help build trust, understanding, and a willingness to collaborate. All of these are conditions for knowledge sharing. They also make the workplace a comfortable place to be.

Know These

Social capital is the connections between people and the associated norms of trust and behavior that create social cohesion. In an organization, social capital is a vital enabler for collaboration and knowledge sharing, as it provides a basis for cooperation and coordination.

I hope you've never been in an organization with low social capital. In such organizations, it's much safer to be paranoid than trusting. Divisions and feuds characterize the organization. Never knowing who can be trusted, people continually watch their backs. Not much knowledge gets shared, and you can forget collaboration.

Evaluating the social capital in your organization can give you a sense of how well your organizational culture enables knowledge sharing. It reflects whether or not there are strong relationships between people, relationships of mutual aid and benefit. These relationships undoubtedly include the sharing of knowledge—in fact, they'll make up the lion's share of learning in the organization. It also reflects that people are able to *trust* each other, and that trust is returned.

Trust gives us an assurance that we can expect certain behavior from others. We let down our guard. We're more willing to share, certain that it is safe to give information to someone. That extends to more elaborate collaboration as well.

Know These

Trust is an expectation of how someone else will behave. It may be grounded in experience or it may be granted immediately.

However, we need more than a relationship and the associated trust to share knowledge effectively. Rob Cross, Andrew Parker, and Larry Prusak of the IBM Institute for Knowledge Management have identified four other factors for effective sharing in relationships:

➤ **Knowing what the other person knows.** This may be specific knowledge, like technical expertise. It also may be an ability to think through tough issues. Sometimes knowing the right question to ask is more important than having the right answer.

➤ **Knowing they'll respond to your request.** We may have to learn more about how a particular person responds and adapt ourselves to that. For example, I have a friend who almost never responds to e-mail. If I need something urgently, I call his secretary.

➤ **Knowing they're good teachers.** They don't overwhelm us with extraneous (to us) information. They listen carefully, and give us what we need.

➤ **Knowing we are safe to show a weakness.** Asking for help admits that there is something we don't know. Unless we feel safe with someone, we aren't going to reveal our weaknesses. That degree of safety also frees us up to be creative and try out ideas.

The factors in this list help show the complexity of trust. It exists on many levels with important differences between the levels.

Helping Leaders to Walk the Talk

Walk the talk: We all know that phrase and what it means in terms of leaders doing what they say they will do. This is a vital factor in any culture, as leaders provide the cues that give others a sense of acceptable behaviors and goals. They have an important role to play, therefore, in developing a culture that supports knowledge management and sharing.

Didn't Know

Although he once tossed my briefing slides at me, I remember with fondness and respect now-retired Marine General Sheehan. He strongly supported knowledge management and had sponsored the formation of a knowledge management section for his command. General Sheehan appreciated the power of simple gestures. At his daily morning staff meeting, General Sheehan would refer to the organizational knowledge management Web site, mentioning items and asking people if they had read them. The knowledge management staff laughed when they told me about this, saying that the word sure got around fast. For my money, that beats the heck out of a signed memo or a speech.

Leaders Are Always on Display

Even if leaders are supporters, they may need special coaching. The bottom line is that leaders are always on display. They must talk the talk and walk the walk because someone is always watching. Even a small act by someone in a leadership position can have enormous impact, because the watchers spread it through the organizational grapevine.

This Means You, Too, Change Agent

Don't look now, but you're one of those leaders, too. By setting yourself up as a force in guiding the change, you've become someone that other people watch. Perhaps more than anyone else except the CEO, people will observe you to see if you're walking your own talk. Heaven help you if they spot you hoarding knowledge, claiming the credit for someone else's work, or refusing to collaborate. You've got to take your own medicine.

Unfortunately, we overlook our own warts. I suggest that to monitor your own performance you ask your colleagues to give you feedback on your behavior. Your sponsor is also a good person to ask.

Didn't Know

I once worked for someone who was a change agent at the corporate level. The effort he led touted the importance of teamwork. I took this to heart, and ran about supporting skadzooks of teams. One day my supervisor called me in and told me I was out of the office too much. He told me to tell the teams they would have to get by without my technical support. Well aware of the message it'd send, I protested. No luck. I don't think he ever understood how much he damaged his credibility.

The Importance of Middle Management

For most people in your organization, who most affects their day-to-day work—the CEO, the head of their business unit, or their immediate supervisor? In my experience, it's the immediate supervisor. Organizational research also has shown that a person's immediate supervisor is one of the most important factors for job satisfaction. Supervisors and others in middle management also can make or break your knowledge management effort.

Unfortunately, middle managers may be evaluated solely on how well their individual section performs. Since grade school, people have been conditioned to "do well on the test," and are rewarded for such. However, sometimes when immediate supervisors have some leeway, I've seen them refuse to give someone time to share knowledge. They don't have the mind-set.

People who want to share are afraid to do so. Refusing could mean a bad evaluation, no promotions, no rewards, and other unpleasantness an immediate supervisor can impose.

The answer is to coach middle management, court their support, and involve them in your effort. Don't underestimate their influence merely because they're two or three rows down the organizational chart. On a day-to-day basis, with the employees they supervise, they have more influence than the CEO.

With middle management on board you can have the best strategy for management support—what I call the "every which way" strategy: support from the top, support from the middle, support from the grass roots, and support from the side with the KM team, champions, and sponsors.

Aligning Rewards and Recognition

Another important aspect of any culture is the rewards and recognition structure. That structure tells people what they will be rewarded for doing. Consequently, it overrides any rhetoric (including yours, potentially) promoting the values and beliefs supporting knowledge sharing.

You need to figure out if you have a clash between the current system and what you need. Analyze the current system to see what it rewards. Then identify the skills, behaviors, and attitudes you're promoting, and compare those promoted by the reward and recognition system.

I realize that you've just introduced a change in the organizational system, and there hasn't been time to catch up yet. However, any clash between

Know Nos

A problem with middle managers in knowledge management efforts is lack of a big-picture view. Some care about their own group, but not the rest of the organization. When someone works on something for his or her community of practice or inputs something into a best practices database, the response is, "If it's not for us, you're wasting your time."

Didn't Know

Steven Kerr wrote a classic article on rewards systems titled "On the Folly of Rewarding A, While Hoping for B" (*The Academy of Management Executive*, February 1995). The title says it all. It's well worth a read.

Know How

Create new rewards and forms of recognition while people are learning and standards are being established. You may want to reward reaching a milestone. You may want to reward individual contributions. In effect, you're going around the official system, but that gives you the luxury of waiting until later to overhaul that if need be.

Know Nos

Don't completely put off dealing with rewards and recognition. Granted, you can't change the system overnight, but you do need to start sending signals about what will be rewarded in the future. You also need to plan on making some alterations, if needed, in the long run. Failure to change a reward and recognition system is one of the biggest causes of failure for any cultural change.

what people are told to do and what is actually rewarded is a serious problem. While you're telling employees to behave in a new way, the old way is the one that's still being rewarded, and that's what most people will follow. You also need to analyze your reward and recognition system in some detail as to the actual rewards and means of recognition. Any system may have both formal and informal rewards. Awards like an "atta boy" plaque are more low-key and informal, requiring a minimum of paperwork and justification, but they still have meaning to people—sometimes a lot of meaning. They may fall outside the official human resources system, and thus be easier for you to initiate.

However, bonuses, promotions, compensation, and some awards are tightly linked to policies, procedures, and criteria that might as well be set in stone. Over time, people come to rely on them. They work to meet those standards. Changing them suddenly pulls the rug out from under their feet.

Trying to change substantial rewards and recognition like bonuses, compensation, and promotions could stir up a storm of organizational protest that could damage you. You could lose people who otherwise would have been supporters. My advice is to leave the established rewards alone at first; I don't think it's feasible to tackle it at the beginning. However, you do need to understand these issues early in your KM effort.

I also don't think it's fair to change the more formal rewards and recognition immediately. While the change is taking place, people need time to learn and adapt without penalties. You must give them a safe place to do that. Losing a bonus or a promotion is a doozy of a penalty.

Creating New Heroes

You need to create new heroes. One way is through the same reward and recognition system. By making early adopters into heroes, you can honor their willingness to take a leap of faith by making the recognition public:

➤ Have a ceremony with lots of hoopla and fan-fare. Take pictures.

➤ Write it up and publish it in the company newsletter with pictures.

➤ Tell stories about how the heroes succeeded.

➤ Ask people to congratulate the heroes on their willingness to be pioneers and lead the way.

If this arouses a bit of envy in the collective organizational breast, all the better.

If you've ever taken care of several kids, you know what happens when one kid is allowed to get away with murder. This is no less true in organizations. Unfortunately, you also must discipline people who refuse to adopt the new rules and behaviors. I've seen people openly defy the rules, daring the system to do anything about it. As much as I prefer the carrot to the stick, the stick must be applied to those who refuse to change. It tells that person and all of the rest that refusing to change won't be tolerated.

Didn't Know

In knowledge sharing you need to honor both ends of the equation: the person who shares and the recipient. Some organizations have specifically rewarded the recipient. Texas Instruments used to have a NIHBIDIA—Not Invented Here But I Did It Anyway award. British Petroleum's version was The Thief of the Year award. Both of these were meant to overcome a reluctance to use someone else's work.

The Least You Need to Know

➤ To identify the barriers and enabling strengths in your culture, focus on the context of the business issue and strategy your approach is supporting and the day-to-day work.

➤ Every organization is made up of both the official hierarchy as shown in the organizational charts and the unseen associations between people in the networks and communities.

➤ Middle managers have much influence. Coach, court, and involve them.

➤ Aligning the current reward and recognition system to support the values and beliefs needed for knowledge sharing may be too much to tackle at first. However, you can create additional rewards and recognition.

➤ Create new heroes and tell stories about them.

Chapter 17

Managing the Change

In This Chapter

➤ Understanding the change process

➤ Coping with resistance to change

➤ Planning the transition

➤ Meeting with resistance to change

➤ Designing training for change

In this chapter, we will move from understanding culture to changing it. Many years ago, I headed up a difficult project intended to produce a great change in my organization. From a technical viewpoint, the end result would have been an incredible advancement. I also truly believed, based on my knowledge of our business and people, that the people affected would immediately see the many benefits for them. After several years, the project was canceled. The cover story was that the funds were more urgently needed elsewhere. The true story was that we'd bungled the change management process.

Our approach had been to give a limited number of briefings well after the work had begun. We didn't enlist anyone's support up front. We never asked the people in the organization if they thought it would be an improvement. We believed that all we had to do was to explain it rationally a few times, and people would fall over themselves to support us. Instead, they shrieked bloody murder. End of funding and end of

Know These

A **change agent** is someone who is responsible for planning and implementing a change. Knowledge of the basics of organizational culture, knowledge of the specific culture, and knowledge about the discipline of change management are critical. Actual experience is even better.

Know How

One way to help visualize the future state is by holding a fake press conference. Pretend that it is your end date, and you're briefing the press (with delight, that is). Explain what your goals and vision were when you started. Report what you did to accomplish them. Talk about how wonderful things are now. Stage it to make it as real as you can.

project. The painful lesson learned for me was that managing change is as important as doing the right thing in the right way.

No matter what kind of knowledge management effort you introduce, you'll be asking people to change the way they work. For better or worse, if you're in the knowledge management business you're also in the change management business. (I hope you're keeping a list of all of your new occupations. This one is change agent.) In this chapter, we'll discuss some basics of change management. However, we'll leave communications, one of the most important areas, for the next chapter.

The Change Process

If you're going to be a *change agent* and manage change, you need a way to frame it as a process and break it down into doable parts. In classical change management we divide the process of change into three stages: the future state, the current state, and the transition state.

The Future State

You've already developed your vision, defined your goals, and linked what you plan to do to the organizational strategy. But now you should revisit these decisions and dreams. Developing these areas is an iterative process. However, one thing you probably haven't done yet is decide when you plan to get there. Pick an approximate date you expect to finish, even if it seems like a stab in the dark.

You'll probably need to adjust the date later, but it's best to start with a clear end date for the change you want to implement. Having a deadline creates a sense of urgency, which is incredible motivation for action. On a more pragmatic level, it also tells you how much time you have.

You also may need to establish some midpoints during the process. Big change is a long-term business. If you want to make big changes, plan on being in the change management business for years—but that's too long to go without getting anywhere. Give yourself some signposts along the way to let you know you're still on course.

If you have planned the process in phases, your phases should give you some idea of what your midpoints during the overall process are. If nothing else, the end of each phase is a distinct milestone.

There is also the equivalent of the television network sweeps: submission of your annual budget. This time can provide a distinct (and anxious) midpoint. Somehow the process of justifying your continued existence spurs you to show some accomplishments and make some assessments. A friend once told me nervously that this was the year their program had to show solid gains. It also was the first year they had been required to justify their budget to a new chief.

Putting the *future state* first isn't a mistake. First of all, it points you in the right direction. That can stop you from bogging down in the details of the here and now. It is tempting to fight the current fires. They're serious and they demand your attention. Also, it is more encouraging. Defining a bright future gives you something to look forward to. In contrast, focusing on how things are now may be enough to make you quit, overwhelmed by the magnitude of the problems. Most important of all, it makes you narrow your focus to your goals and vision.

> **Know These**
>
> In change management, a **future state** is the finish line. It is what "done" looks like.
>
> The **current state** is the way things are right now. It's the "what is."
>
> The **transition state** is the stage in between the current state and the future state. It is the journey that ends with reaching your goals and vision.

The Current State

The *current state* is the here and now, how things actually are.

➤ How do we describe the current state?

➤ What are the internal and external pressures?

➤ Why is there a need for change?

➤ Do we want to change?

➤ What needs to be changed to accomplish our vision and goals?

➤ What are our priorities for change?

➤ How ready are we for change?

From an emotional viewpoint, the current state seems cozy and safe. We can keep ticking along as we have been. (Can't we?) Business as usual, we say. This reminds me of the scene in the Disney cartoon *The Sorcerer's Apprentice,* when the marching brooms keep bringing in buckets of water even as the water rises higher and higher. Things may be desperate, but we tend to keep on doing things as we have been.

Didn't Know

There is some good news about the transition state. This is the time for creativity. You've realized that the current state is broken and needs fixing, you've rocked the boat, and you've made this a time that changes are supposed to happen.

Encourage innovation as much as you can. Give people a chance to add their own creative ideas. Establish that this is the time to experiment. Ask for additional solutions. Accept challenges from people as an opportunity to question assumptions. Above all, resist the urge to move to closure too quickly. You may never have this kind of freedom and elbowroom again. Slow down, even though being in transition is uncomfortable.

Know Nos

Don't dismiss people's emotions during the transition state. You must be attuned to how people feel; no matter how groundless you think those feelings are, they're still valid to the people who feel them. The stress induced by the change reduces people's ability to adapt. The bigger the change, the more stress. The more stressed they are, the less they will be able to learn and adapt.

The Transition State

The *transition state* is that uneasy stage where things are changing, but we haven't gotten to where we plan to wind up yet. We are on the move. It is darned uncomfortable. What you have done is taken a (more or less) stable system and deliberately destabilized it.

Resistance to Change

I, for one, freeze up when someone says brightly to me that something is going to be different. I can feel my blood pressure going up. It doesn't matter how good the end result should be—all change is stressful, even when it's for a good reason.

I'm not alone in reacting negatively to the word "different." Resistance to change is human nature. You have to expect some resistance, although you'll do your best to minimize it.

Consider yourself lucky if the resistance is in the open. If someone stops you in the hall and argues with you, you've got the chance to discuss it. If you're attacked in meetings, that puts the issues people care about on the table. Public resistance gives you the opportunity to both air grievances and talk about them. Keep in mind, however, that you won't be able to resolve all of the issues. Encourage people to resist openly but constructively. You then can learn and improve what you're doing based on the feedback.

What scares me is underground resistance—the sneaky, behind-your-back stuff. People breeze by you in the hall, sniffing disdainfully. They don't show up to meetings. Work that was supposed to get done doesn't. What you have is a time bomb waiting to go off, but you have no idea of its size. It could be a big bomb. It could be a little bomb, like endless griping. And you don't know when it will go off.

Didn't Know

A possible covert reaction to change is sabotage. When I was a young soldier I was told that my Army unit was getting new technology that would drastically change the way we worked. I was relieved that a sister unit would get it first, figuring they'd work out the bugs. But we soon heard that it had been a complete disaster and a grim-faced bunch of people showed up at our unit to implement the new technology. They admitted they had flubbed the change management and discussed candidly how people in the other unit had deliberately sabotaged the new technology. They asked the middle managers to make it work—and they did. We all did.

However, if you handle it right, most people will get past their resistance and accept change. Just don't expect everyone to change at the same time. People adjust to change according to their own schedule, not yours. At any given time, you'll have people in different stages of adjustment; some delightful people will adapt quickly, racing out of the gate, while others will amble out. Some diehards will opt out permanently, refusing to move at all.

A Road Map for the Journey

You as the leader will need a road map. Lay out a detailed activity plan showing the following:

➤ What exactly will happen

➤ What the sequence of activities is

➤ When the activities will happen

➤ How the activities are linked to your goals

➤ How you will get feedback

➤ What the milestones are

➤ How you will measure progress

Any organization is a system. If you tinker with one part of a system, things can happen to other parts that you didn't intend. One unintended consequence to expect during a transition is that problems you thought had been solved a long time ago reappear. Or something you thought was on the mend suddenly regresses. Weak points also will break under the strain of the change. Be prepared to cope with leaks sprouting all over the organizational dyke.

How Big Is the Change?

Another important task when planning the transition is to get a handle on the size of the change. Are you asking people to staple their documents along the right top corner as opposed to the top left corner? Or are you asking for a more significant and broader change? The bigger the change, the more potential resistance there is and the more effort required to manage the change. Some questions to consider include the following:

➤ How much of a change are you trying to make in the way people do their work?

➤ How much of their work will it affect?

➤ Will it require new processes?

➤ How different is it from the way they are working now?

➤ Will it require new information technology?

➤ Will it require new equipment?

➤ Will it require new behaviors?

➤ Will it require new skills?

➤ Will it require them to work with new people?

➤ How will people feel about it?

You also have to identify how much of the organization you will be working with. If you're starting with a pilot in one section or unit, your scope is relatively limited. The rule of thumb is that the more people, sections, geographies, and functions you have, the more work you have to do, not to mention how many more resources you will need. It's a matter of scale.

Who's for You? Who's Against You?

Spell out who exactly is going to be affected. Some of these will be groups. Some will be individuals. All of them are your stakeholders. This is your target population (or, if you prefer, your customers). The stakeholder analysis will be the foundation for other work you'll be doing, like designing communications and training for particular groups and individuals. In an article on change management titled "Change Management: A Base For Knowledge Sharing," *Knowledge Management Review,* vol. 3, issue 4, September/October 2000, Chuck Seeley, manager, Technology Manufacturing Group Knowledge Management, Intel Corporation, identified the following stakeholders:

➤ The people in the center of the target for the change. These people at ground zero will have to change what they do or how they behave.

➤ The people planning and carrying out the change. This includes support staff, both inside and outside any knowledge management group. These are all change agents.

➤ The people sponsoring the change. This could be anyone with sufficient clout, but sponsors usually are found in management.

➤ Management, to include layers above and below everyone else who is involved.

➤ People who are external, like customers, suppliers, and alliance partners.

Know How

You're not the authority on how big the change is. The people being affected are. Their perceptions are the reality with which you must deal. If handled well, a big change can be perceived as nothing much, just a ripple in the organizational waters. A small change, if bungled, can set off a tidal wave of resistance.

Didn't Know

Being a sponsor requires a significant commitment. In addition to providing clout, a sponsor should play both a public and a private role to consistently support the change. The sponsor also should monitor progress and any bumps in the road. Also, the sponsor ensures that there is follow-up. Make sure your sponsor has enough time to do all of this— and has a deep commitment to the process.

Know How

Look for both formal and informal leaders. Formal leaders are easy, but spotting the informal leaders can be tricky. Some may be technical people who are respected for their expertise. Other may be leaders because of their seniority or because they're well connected. No matter where and who they are, their perceived leadership makes them people that others look to for a cue.

Didn't Know

One way to deal with prominent resisters is to marginalize them. Give them something trivial but seemingly important to do on the sidelines. Or you can take the opposite tack and give them leadership of a significant piece of the effort, forcing them to deal with their resistance in a positive way. At that point, their success is tied to the success of the change effort.

We put these groups into the following categories:

➤ Supporters

➤ Opponents

➤ Neutrals

As you do that, think about the consequences of a person being a supporter, an opponent, or a neutral. Depending upon the person or group, any of these could be tolerable. You can't convince everybody. Trying to turn around strong resisters sometimes reminds me of the adage that it's no use arguing with a greased pig. The pig likes it, and you get dirty. If you can, it's best to concentrate your limited time where it is most useful.

However, sometimes you don't have a good choice. The group that worries me the most is the one whose support is critical but who are opponents. If you can't change their thinking to either neutral or supporting, you may be dead in the water. I don't have any easy fixes for that situation, but you're better off figuring out if you're in that fix.

Neutral also can be disastrous, depending upon who's neutral. There are some people who, if they're viewed as neutral, can prove fatal for the change. For example, if a key and respected leader in your organization does not get behind your efforts, it will send an unmistakable message that it's okay to not take the changes seriously.

It also sends the message that the leadership of the organization isn't really behind the change. Your pitch to sell the need for the change has been challenged publicly. And that leader has more credibility than you with his or her followers.

Learning the New Ropes

Part of the reason that people resist change is learning anxiety. If you're being asked to do something you don't know how to do and don't understand why you need to do it, that's a huge no-win situation for you. You zone out. Or you try to dodge the issue. Or you demand to know what's in it for you.

As a change agent, the way to deal with this is to provide training. Look at your stakeholder analysis and determine what groups or individuals need training. Do this relatively soon in the change process. The longer you wait, the more resistance can build up as people worry and gripe.

Then start designing the training. Determine what these people need to know to understand the value of this change. In doing this, you need to cover three areas:

➤ Skills (the actual how-to's of what they now need to know)

➤ New behaviors (what will be done)

➤ Necessary attitudes (why they should do it)

I'd start the training here, with why this new way of doing things is required. Obviously, there is room for improvement. Talk about waste, loss of market share, and obsolete technology, as well as the problems these cause. Turn on their motivation to change because they see it's in their best interest. Then move onto how things are going to be better. The bottom line is that what you're doing should make their work easier. Talk specifically about the payoff for them individually and for the organization.

Finally, explain how this is part of the big picture. This is the time to talk about your vision and goals, how they tie into the business strategy and the organization's future.

In helping people gain new skills and behaviors, you need to make sure they have practice time, complete with coaching. For one thing, people learn best by practicing what they're trying to learn. If people need to master a new process, let them try the process, not just read about it and take a test. You also need to coach and give them immediate feedback so they can correct any mistakes.

Another important reason to give training is that a classroom environment is a safe environment. People are supposed to not know what they're doing. It's okay for them to make mistakes and to experiment.

Know Nos

When you spell out the pain and the benefits, be as specific as you can. This isn't the time for ambiguous platitudes. The more concrete you are, the more they can relate what you're proposing to their interests. Not only does this help establish your credibility, it gives more motivation.

Know How

While you're designing the training, involve the people who will be the students. They're the best judges of how they want to learn. This goes back to one of the overriding principles of change management: Involve the users.

If you can, train an intact group, like a work group, all at the same time. Since you want to change the way people work, stick as close to the actual work as you can. People work in groups, so it's less effective to train scattered individuals. You can't focus on the group interaction if you have John on Tuesday, Julio on Wednesday, and Fredda on Friday. You also need to put together an overall training plan. This plan should include the following:

➤ The topics that the training will cover

➤ The delivery method for the training

➤ Who is delivering the training

➤ The facilities and equipment needed

➤ The date, time, and place

➤ The method of assessing whether students learned what they were supposed to learn

➤ A means of gaining feedback from the students

As always, involve the actual people as much as you can.

The Least You Need to Know

➤ Change can be described as a process with three parts: the future state, the current state, and the transition state. You need to manage each of these parts.

➤ Develop an activity plan for the transition state.

➤ Assess how big the potential change is and how many people will be affected by it.

➤ Analyze who your stakeholders are and how they feel about the change.

➤ Early in the change process, give people training on the new skills, behaviors, and attitudes they need.

Spreading the Word Far and Wide

The last thing I'd ever thought I would be is a salesperson. But then I got into the knowledge management business. All of a sudden I needed to sell knowledge management—and sell it to numbers of people.

Selling may not be your cup of tea, either. But there are systematic ways to sell KM on a large scale. You already have some pieces you need: a definition of knowledge management, an elevator speech, and a vision. It's a good start, but you have some more work to do. In this chapter, we'll look at how to fill out your message, slowly persuade people, and develop an overall plan to communicate with people about KM.

Refining Your Message

Although you have worked on some of the pieces, you haven't laid out your specific goals for communication. Although you will want to decide what's best suited for your organization, some suggestions for what you need to communicate include the following:

➤ What knowledge management means to your organization—a tailor-made definition.

➤ Your strategies and how they will be implemented. These strategies must be perceived as a strategic thrust for your organization. Avoid at all costs the appearance of being small potatoes. What you're doing is critical for the success of your organization.

➤ How your strategies explicitly link to the overall organizational strategy and business drivers.

➤ What's wrong with the present that needs to be fixed. I call this the Chicken Little angle. Tell them the sky is falling, or about to fall pretty darn soon. Give concrete examples of underperformance and failure with key customers, and opportunities that have been lost in the recent past. Focus on how you stack up against your competitors. Talk about how the problems are affecting you now. Prophesy how bleak the future will be.

After all, if things were fine, you wouldn't need to do anything different. Complacency is your enemy. Unfortunately, it is a powerful enemy. People who think the present is okay have no reason to change. Tackle complacency head-on by creating a sense of urgency.

➤ What everyone's role is in this new way of doing business.

➤ What's going to be different (and way better). Paint the rosy future, the one that is achievable this way.

Know How

Think like a salesman. Your job is to pitch knowledge management to your audience. Talk about why it matters to *them*. Tell them what *they* need to do. Speak about the benefits to *them*. Think of them as your customers. Your job is to speak to their concerns.

All of these elements make up your basic sales pitch. However, you still need a way to pitch it.

Telling a Story of the Future

For a long time, I had mixed success explaining what a community of practice is. I carefully drew the distinctions between a team, a work group, and a community of practice. I used a definition consisting of words no greater than two syllables. I made up a nifty graphic showing people dancing together (well, I liked it). I talked about how to spot a community of practice and its characteristics.

No matter how I worded it, no matter how simple I tried to make it, in every group some people would get a glazed look. They would interrupt me with the question, "So communities are another type of team, right?" I had done everything I could think of and wasn't able to explain the concept to people. In desperation, I decided to take another shot at rewriting my PowerPoint presentation. Out of new ideas, I stopped typing and started reading Steve Denning's new book, *The Springboard: How*

Storytelling Ignites Action in Knowledge Era Organizations. He had sent me a copy to get a quote from me. Around Chapter 5, I put the book down, changed the opening to my presentation so that it began with a story, and sent it off to a colleague at a high-tech company. She replied with an e-mail praising the opening, which she said drew her in. Aha! I had finally done it. I wasn't the only one hit with this blinding flash of the obvious. Over the past few years, there has been more and more publicity around storytelling. Articles have been written, books have been published, and speakers are making the rounds.

Didn't Know

This is an example of a springboard story from the World Bank, where communities of practice are a strategy:

In July 1997, the World Bank had a task team in Yemen working with a client on an education project. Then the unexpected happened. The client asked for some urgent advice on how to build an information center for its education center. The members of the task team didn't have this expertise in their heads or their briefcases. But a World Bank community of practice found that the most useful work for this situation had been done in Kenya and faxed that to the team. Within 48 hours the team discussed a solution with the client.

There are many ways to tell a story and many ways to use them. The particular type of story that I used is the *springboard story.* This type has certain characteristics:

➤ It is short and simple. You don't want to get bogged down in the details. Your goal is to spark understanding.

➤ It is told from the viewpoint of one individual in a predicament that is common in your business. Your audience can sympathize with that person.

➤ The predicament is familiar to your audience.

Know These

A **springboard story** enables a leap in understanding by the audience so as to grasp how an organization or community or complex system may change.

➤ It is the exact conundrum knowledge management is meant to solve. This clears the way for you to provide the answer.

➤ The story has an element of the unexpected. This captures the attention of your listeners. They want to know what the ending is.

➤ It has a happy ending.

➤ It is told orally. Human beings convey the majority of their meaning through nonverbals. I can't imagine telling the story of Goldilocks and the Three Bears without deepening my voice for Poppa Bear, speaking gently for Mama Bear, and squeaking for Baby Bear.

Storytelling is a new job requirement for you. Try it. Toss out your PowerPoint presentations, the ones with convoluted diagrams complete with arrows crossing and crisscrossing. Ditch some of your charts. Put together some stories and practice first with an audience. You aren't trying out on Amateur Night. Telling a story will become part of your professional repertoire for communication.

Know How

Some tips for storytelling are as follows:

➤ Your voice is your instrument. Vary your loudness, intonation, and rhythm. Express emotion. Pretend you are reading a story to a child.

➤ Understand your organization and pitch the story to people in it.

➤ Connect to people with your eyes.

➤ Believe in what you are saying.

➤ Convey your belief to your audience. You must believe before they can.

Awareness to Commitment to Passion

You have to be realistic. You can't expect someone to leap from never having heard of something to being a believer in one step. That's what we would like—for someone to hear us speak once, read one thing, or talk to one person and become a passionate believer. It doesn't work that way most of the time, though.

The field of education gives a good framework for looking at how people move from awareness to commitment to passion.

Awareness

The first level is awareness. Years of exposure to advertising have helped us to screen out what we don't want to hear. (Not to mention that marvelous invention, the mute button.) This level has three parts:

➤ **Getting on the radar screen.** People must become conscious that knowledge management exists. This doesn't mean that they will pay attention, but they'll know it's there.

➤ **Watching what's on the radar screen.** Instead of breezing by an article in the company newsletter, someone will at least skim over it. They may not pay rapt attention, but they are willing to give it a once over. They don't punch the equivalent of the mute button.

➤ **Discovering characteristics about what is on the radar screen.** This doesn't mean someone has bought into the concept. This doesn't mean they can describe it to someone else. But they are aware that the concept has different aspects. Not only do they avoid the mute button, but also they pay a little attention.

Commitment

The next level is commitment, where we start to see people doing certain things:

➤ **Complying with directions.** People do what they are supposed to, like using corporate yellow pages to find expertise they need. This doesn't mean, however, that they really believe in it yet. People in this stage worry me. This is skin-deep, shallow, and unstable commitment. Too many things can happen to move people out of this and back to noncompliance.

➤ **Responding voluntarily.** Even if no one is looking, people will do it. It is their choice. They've begun to believe.

➤ **Enjoying responding.** They like it! You hear good adjectives—"great," "bang up," "bonzer," and "jim-dandy" (adjectives dependent on the age and geographic location, of course). You know then that your knowledge management approach has proven to deliver value. People know that it is a good thing to do, and they like doing it.

Passion

I am hard to please when I am fomenting a revolution. It's a tough job, and I want all the allies and co-conspirators I can find. I won't get everyone, but I would like as many people as possible to reach this level—passion, a deeply held belief. People who are passionate will be doing these things:

➤ **Walking the talk.** People's actions show others that they feel this way.

➤ **Championing the cause.** For people at this level, it isn't enough to walk the talk. They want to do something about it. They want to convince others that this is right so they will join the cause as well.

Help from Communications Experts

Unless you have extensive experience in communications and marketing, you need some help. Look for the experts in your organization. People in corporate communications have both the background and experience you need. Like your new pals in information technology, these are people you need to enlist.

Additionally, they know the ropes within your own organization. They can tell you about the various vehicles available.

Communications experts also can hook you up with the graphics, audiovisual, or other type of support you may need. At the same time, don't depend on them for the message. It's up to you to provide the content and tie it to the business. You're still the expert on knowledge management, your strategy, and your goals.

If you have a corporate intranet, you need a Web site. Some basic Web site design principles are:

➤ Describe your intended audience in detail and build the site for them.

➤ Choose a visual look and feel that fits your audience.

➤ Make it easy to navigate.

➤ Make it "sticky" with interesting content.

➤ Update it regularly.

➤ Keep people engaged. One way is to offer a sign-up for e-mail notification every time the Web site is updated.

Meetings offer a vehicle, from the internal professional organizations to periodic business meetings.

Know How

If your organization doesn't have a corporate communications department (or at least a person assigned to this task), talk to the people in marketing and public relations. They have expertise in crafting a message and pitching it to a particular audience. Salespeople also have many tricks of the trade.

Beat the bushes looking for meetings—people often need speakers for meetings and are glad to have a volunteer. Speak to everyone and anyone who will give you a pulpit. At the same time, tailor your message for the interests and needs of each group.

Know Nos

Don't neglect external communications, such as interviews, press releases, and advertisements. Your employees pay attention to these, more than you may realize. Speaking at external conferences is another means. It builds your credibility, gives you more practice in delivering your message, and gets the message out that your organization is doing some neat stuff. More than once I have finished giving a presentation, only to be approached by a customer who wants to talk about what we are doing. Another group you need to reach is your stakeholders, suppliers, customers, and partners. They, too, pay attention to external communications. You need to show them how knowledge management adds value for them.

Other Tools in Your Communication Kit

You may want to consider other set pieces for your communications kit. One potential piece is a *code of conduct* or a code of ethics. Many organizations have such codes, which usually talk about the values and beliefs of the organization and lay out ground rules for people to follow.

A Xerox Tool

Xerox developed a code of conduct specifically for knowledge management, which it calls knowledge sharing:

➤ Share what you know and do ... build and expand the company IQ.

➤ Discover what you don't know ... see if a solution already exists.

Know These

Codes of conduct, a code of ethics, or a credo are statements of organizational values and guidelines for employee behavior.

199

➤ Honor, respect, and credit sources ... build trust and reciprocity.

➤ When in doubt, err on the side of sharing ... protect what's private and confidential.

➤ Collaborate with customers, suppliers, and partners ... realize mutual learning and value.

Xerox's knowledge-sharing principles are part of a pocket-sized booklet titled *Gateway to Xerox Knowledge Sharing.* The inside cover features a quote by the then-president and CEO of Xerox, affirming the importance of knowledge. Other sections include a definition of knowledge, an explanation of Web communities and their benefits, a description of the corporate yellow pages, and Xerox technologies for knowledge sharing.

What else do I like besides the knowledge-sharing principles about this booklet? Well, it is

➤ Targeted for both external and internal audiences.

➤ Written in simple language with key definitions included.

➤ Has the equivalent of sound bites, with short, quickly read sections usually limited to two pages.

➤ Illustrated with arresting graphics also tied to the content.

➤ Small and easy to carry around.

➤ Loaded with examples and metaphors.

Producing a booklet like Xerox may not be the best choice for you, but the principles apply to any organization.

Know How

SAP America has a clear way to express the goal of its community of practice approach. Without a community, a person within SAP America has about 5,000 people he or she could contact, but with no idea of who to ask for help. The goal of a community is to help someone narrow that 5,000 down to 50, and then down to the five who can truly help.

Concept Visualization Video

Another option is a short video montage to communicate the concept of KM, which we discussed briefly in Chapter 5, "Developing a Strategy." A concept visualization video uses imagery, quotes, animation, and music to communicate a concept. It's short—generally less than three minutes. Its intent is to motivate people by enabling them to understand and relate to a concept quickly. By integrating media elements such as images and music, it touches the emotional, as well as intellectual, aspects of a person's thinking.

One example is the concept visualization video developed by Erick Thompson at the Saint Paul Companies.

Entitled "Knowledge in Action," it presents the story of knowledge and its use throughout history. Moving to contemporary times, it next communicates the vision of the Knowledge Exchange initiative within the Saint Paul Companies.

The goal is to motivate employees to participate in exchanging knowledge. It has proven to be a powerful tool in engaging employees and stirring their imaginations.

Your Press Kit

Put together items that would be the equivalent of a press kit. When people ask you about knowledge management, ask them if they wouldn't mind reading a few short articles. You can offer a written version of your elevator speech, a copy of the vision, and perhaps a few published articles. Put together what you think would be best for that person from the materials in the kit.

For those in your organization who might explore on their own by heading down to the library, ask your corporate librarians to stock some knowledge management titles, giving them a list of the ones you consider to be the most helpful. You want resources to be available when interested parties go looking.

You may be wondering when I'm going to shut up about the various types of media and set pieces you could use. A new fact of life for you is this: You can't overcommunicate. One rule of thumb is to estimate how much you need to communicate and then multiply that by 10. Better yet, multiply by a hundred. You have several barriers you are trying to overcome:

➤ **Breaking the threshold of awareness.** Think about the last time you bought a new car. Before you bought it you were marginally aware of the make and model. Now that you have one, you see it everywhere. You are now attuned to the model, but before you bought it you didn't notice if one was parked right next to you.

Expect that someone may have to hear about knowledge management many times before they start to pay attention. Getting through the awareness barrier takes repetition.

➤ **Breaking through cynicism.** People in organizations will look at you wearily and sigh. They'll ask you how this is any different from managing by objectives, total quality management, or, heaven help us, reengineering.

Know Nos

Don't go on the offensive when you're confronted by cynicism. It's to be expected. Sympathize a bit, but stand your ground, being as pleasant as you can. Continue to emphasize that there will be personal benefits for the naysayers, that knowledge management is important, and that it has to be done.

They may or may not believe you're sincere. They may or may not believe it is going to work. They may or may not believe there will be benefits. They're playing a waiting game. They're not about to be suckered in by another management fad that will go away if they wait long enough.

Know How

Be aware of your own preferences. These may unconsciously steer you to concentrate on the methods you prefer. You also may be less skilled in your nonpreferences. You can work around your natural tendencies—but first you must recognize them.

➤ **Reaching people in the way they prefer.** I prefer to hear someone speak about something. I learn best by listening. When a former colleague and I would be sitting in an auditorium for a presentation, I would stare off into space and listen. His eyes would be glued to the screen. He preferred to learn visually. A preference for audio or visual is one potential difference.

People also prefer different media. I, for one, tend to go for a well-designed Web site with good links to most documents or short articles by practitioners. I know some brains who like the well-researched, cross-referenced, academically-oriented paper. No one channel is better than the other. You have to use multiple channels so that you can reach people via the one they like best.

Putting Together a Communications Plan

The next step is to develop a running communications/marketing plan. At the least, it should last for one year so you can make sure you hit a full spectrum of media and audiences. You need to plan this out in the detail necessary for a project plan. Basics are:

➤ The things you plan to produce, like articles, Web sites, and so forth

➤ The schedule, to include due dates for drafts, revisions, final versions, production, and releases

➤ The intended audience

➤ Who is responsible for each phase

➤ Periodic reviews of the plan

You also need to coordinate your communications with your overall plans. For example, if you're going to launch a community of practice, begin introducing the concept before the launch. As you reach important milestones in your community effort, follow up with progress reports, tell stories of interim successes, and reiterate the concept. At the end of the project, report on the overall successes and explain what comes next.

Continuing to Listen

Communications aren't something you can set on autopilot and then go off for a cup of coffee. You can do your homework, craft wonderful messages, meet your planned deliverables, and still fail. You must build in feedback loops to monitor how things are working. Without those loops you will be clueless. You won't know …

➤ What people thought about the message.

➤ If the medium was appropriate.

➤ What other media needed to be used.

➤ If the timing was right.

➤ What groups have been missed.

➤ What questions still need to be answered.

Think of your goal as starting a dialogue. It takes more than one person to have a conversation. You must provide the mechanisms to have that conversation. Giving people a way to ask questions and argue also creates more buy-in. You want people to argue and ask for more information. It shows they are engaged, and it gives you the opportunity to tap their ideas. Knowledge management is a game that you need everyone to play.

The Least You Need to Know

➤ Your message should include a definition of knowledge management, what your strategies are, what is creating the need for action, and what will be different.

➤ It takes time and repetition to make people aware of your message, commit to changing their behavior, and develop a belief that it's right.

➤ Use a variety of media to communicate your message.

➤ Part of your project planning is developing a communications plan.

➤ Build in feedback loops for your communications.

Part 5
Keeping Score

As a young soldier I attended a training school located on an Air Force base in San Angelo, Texas. After 15 months at a military language institute I was more than used to taking tests—I had taken four a day for months. But I encountered a new wrinkle in Texas. One instructor was nicknamed Thumper, but the nickname baffled me. My conclusion was that he must thump a lectern hard when making a point. I had it all wrong. When Sergeant Thumper reached a point in the lecture that was going to be covered on the next test, he stomped his right foot hard. He quickly conditioned me and the rest of my class; whenever he thumped, we listened avidly, grabbed our pens, and wrote frantically.

Our behavior substantiates the dictum, "What gets measured gets done." However, hardly anyone measures knowledge management results well. The rest of the field has moved along rapidly, but measurement seems stuck in low gear.

In this part we'll look at the basics of KM measurement as well as some frameworks and measures that are being used. Additionally, we'll cover the one area of measurement and knowledge management that has gotten much attention since the early days: measurement of the intangible assets, the intellectual capital.

You Get What You Measure

Figuring out how to evaluate progress toward effective knowledge management requires both strategic thinking and an understanding of how to develop measures. Unfortunately, a valid measurement of knowledge management isn't easy. Look at most knowledge management programs and you'll find that the Achilles heel is measurement. Many rely on what has come to be called serious anecdote management, the careful collection of stories showing value. Anecdotes aren't systematic measurement, although they can give good insights and help explain things that numbers can't. Considering the ever-present imperative to justify resources, this can be a fatal flaw.

Besides fulfilling the dictatorial demands of budgetary pressures, failing to measure also means that many KM'ers do not have in-depth information to evaluate their programs. They don't know if they should keep on doing what they're doing or make adjustments. Given the amount of skull sweat that's involved, though, you have to decide if it's something you want to do. As a colleague of mine once said, "Anything can be measured. The question is whether or not you want to."

This chapter will help you to decide if you want to do the work needed for measures and provide some guidelines for developing useful measures of success.

Measure for a Purpose

All too often I've brought a group of people wrestling with measurement to a full stop in under a minute. I ask them, "What's the purpose of the measurement? What are you going to do with it? What action will you take? Tell me why you're doing this." By the time I reach the why, it's as though I've beamed a death ray upon the people in the room. Yet if those questions aren't answered, there's no point to developing measures in the first place.

Measurement for its own sake is a waste of time. This takes us back to our definition of knowledge: Knowledge is information in context to produce an actionable understanding. There are plenty of purposes for which we can produce measures that give information in context for specific reasons:

➤ The return on investment for their knowledge management projects, such as faster time to market, reduced costs, and higher customer satisfaction

➤ Barriers to sharing knowledge

➤ Success in gathering and using knowledge from customers

➤ How people feel about knowledge sharing

➤ The maturity level of their knowledge management effort

➤ Progress in reaching their goals and achieving their strategy

➤ The efficiency of the approaches being used

➤ Identifying gaps in the approaches being used

➤ An assessment of their intangible assets

➤ The continuing health of their knowledge management system

That purpose is the starting point. It drives the rest of your measurement development. If you can't spell out your purpose after lengthy discussion, stop right there. Now, that's not to say that you can't have multiple purposes. You can. Don't be surprised, though, if you find upon further reflection that what you really have are subdivisions of more general purposes. Whether you have related or independent purposes, you need to keep them distinct and separate. Clumping them together muddies the water, and for measurement you need fathoms of clear water.

Past *and* Future

When I read any financial prospectus, the part that invariably gives me pause is the standard disclaimer, "Past performance does not guarantee future performance." Sadly, past performance of stocks can give a false belief to many about their future performance.

Measures that give a sense of what was accomplished in the past without a clue as to what will happen in the future are *lagging indicators.* Dr. W. Edwards Deming said that such measures are like looking in your rearview mirror as you drive. They tell you where you've been, but not where you're going.

Such measures do have value and can give you some of the knowledge in context you need for an actionable understanding. For one thing, they tell you if what you did worked. That's good to know, particularly when you're trying something new. The danger is in relying solely upon these types of measures, no matter what your purpose in measuring is.

On the other hand, they don't tell you what to do next. If you have ever been through the persistent torture of driving young children to any destination, you flinch at the

Know These

A **leading indicator** is one that's predictive. Based on the results of the measure, you can either do nothing or make changes to affect the predicted outcome. Robert Kaplan and David Norton, authors of the Balanced Scorecard approach to measurement, term these "performance drivers," which I like as well. A **lagging indicator** is one that shows what happened, the outcome. It measures results, but not what may happen in the future.

People new to measurement usually concentrate heavily on lagging measures. Of the two types, lagging measures often are the easiest to develop. Knowing how well you did also is good to know. But force yourself to pay equal attention to the leading measures as well.

question, "When will we get there?" No matter how much it pains you, you could consider how many miles you have left to go (too many), the driving conditions (intolerable in the car), and how fast you're going (faster than your spouse approves of).

Your speedometer becomes a *leading indicator* of when the young child can no longer torment you with that question. Depending upon the miles left to travel and the speed you're going, you can predict how long it will take. Based on that prediction, you may take any number of actions: deciding where to stop for a meal, picking a location to stop for the night, changing to a different route, or resolving to go home before you tear your hair out.

Ideally, any set of measures should have a balance of both leading and lagging indicators. Identifying both the knowledge you need to guide your actions and also the knowledge that helps you judge your outcomes should be part of your purpose.

Too Many Measures Is Too Much

Once during a visit to an organization, I remarked with awe to an employee that they had a great measurement system. It had a simple three-part framework that could be sketched out on the back of a receipt or envelope. Its purpose in measuring things was also easy to understand. The person to whom I was talking groaned a bit and told me, "But we measure everything. You're only seeing the tip of the iceberg."

This put the measurement system in a different light, and I asked him which actions were the most important. His answer: "All of them and none of them."

One measurement pit into which I've seen that company and others fall into is the idea that they need to measure everything. Measures are good, so the more measures, the better. However, measuring everything bypasses a critical benefit of a well-developed measurement system: a focus on what's important.

As you develop measures, you need to look at your options. As you work through the requirements for defining and implementing effective measures, you'll discover that there are some things you just can't measure effectively. Sometimes you'll find it's too difficult to collect data. For others, it will turn out that the measures simply replicate the results of other activities. Finally, some will fail to measure what you want to measure.

As in any creative process—and never lose sight of the fact that developing measures is creative—you need to generate many options before you come up with something you can actually use. But you also need to practice convergent thinking, narrowing your choices of measures to a critical few.

I remember once that I was, unfortunately, the pivotal person in an Army team attempting to raise an antenna. I zigged when I should have zagged, and the partly raised antenna began to wobble. Frantic, the other team members and the onlookers began to shriek advice at me, some of which conflicted. Overwhelmed, I let go, dropping the antenna onto the shoulders of a senior officer passing by. (I must say he was quite a gentleman about the whole thing.)

Know How

So, how many measures are enough? The answer is the bare minimum needed to meet your purpose. To give you one example, the purpose of the balanced scorecard approach is to measure a single strategy and how well it's working. Although there are four perspectives in that framework, Kaplan and Norton (in their book *The Balanced Scorecard: Translating Strategy into Action*) state that there should be no more than two dozen measures.

That story makes me think about what it's like to have too many measures. You become uncertain of what you should pay attention to. The result can be that, overwhelmed by too much guidance for action, confusion reigns and disasters happen.

Ride the Wave of the Current System

One of the projects that British Petroleum applied its knowledge management program to was designed to reduce the costs of building new gas stations. The people in the unit responsible for building the gas stations already had their own *efficiency measures:* doing the job cheaper and faster while keeping the quality constant. They were used to those measures. The results were accepted without any questions.

The British Petroleum knowledge management team didn't attempt to impose any new measures. Its reasoning was that if the knowledge management methodology worked, it would show up in the current measures of improvement in other processes. And so it did, with significant improvements in what British Petroleum terms accountant-certified dollars. These are financial results documented using standard accounting methods—not just a reasonable guess. It's hard to argue with that.

Like the organization with too many measures I visited, you may have an organizational measurement system already in place. Lucky you. Someone else has gone through the arduous process of sweating out the measures and linking them to what's important for your business. That doesn't guarantee, though, that they have done a good job. At a high level, some questions you might want to ask about your organizational measurement system are as follows:

➤ Is it part of the strategic planning process?

➤ Are there key measures for each part of your business strategy?

➤ Do the measures focus on the vital few, the things that really matter for the success of your strategy?

➤ Do they flow from the top of your organization down to the lowest level, with modifications as needed for each level?

➤ Are they well understood throughout your organization?

➤ Are the measures taken often enough to provide a consistent guide for action?

➤ Are the results used to make decisions?

Know These

Efficiency measures assess how well you do some sort of process. They look at how much it costs in terms of resources, such as people, materials, and time, to complete the process. Typical efficiency measures are cycle time (how fast something is completed), cost, and rework. Using these measures helps a company reduce costs, improving efficiency while either holding the quality steady or improving it.

If the system works well to measure what's happening in your organization, it should be like a burglar alarm. It should warn you when things are starting to go wrong and allow you to do something about it quickly. It should also give you the information you need to make improvements.

Didn't Know

The twin of the efficiency measure is effectiveness. This type of measure addresses whether or not you delivered what you were supposed to. The key here is that the customer, not you, decides if you met their specifications for features, benefits, and value. If not, you're stuck with something you can't sell no matter how efficiently you produced it. As Peter Drucker puts it, efficiency is doing things right, while effectiveness is doing the right things.

Know How

Even if you have your doubts about how good an existing organizational measurement system is, you'd best hop on board if you can. It has the weight of being established and accepted. At the very least, link to it, emphasizing that what you're doing really isn't all that new, just a slight variation. Build on the foundation and understanding that people already have.

Coping with Skeptics

I guarantee you that in your organization there will be people who want just the facts. Give me the numbers, they tell you. The numbers will tell the story. To a certain extent, that's true. If the measurement system works well, the numbers should monitor how the business is performing and if your knowledge management program is working.

But I also guarantee you once you give them some facts they will question them. Any weakness is grist for their questions: old data, incomplete data, inconsistent data, how you aggregated the data, and how you collected it. And so on. Even if there is no weakness, these folks still may attack.

One defense is to be prepared to describe how you developed your measures in excruciating detail (not to mention having a rock-solid methodology). Document your approach, describe how it was carried out, and illustrate the pains you took to make sure the data you collect and analyze measure what they're supposed to.

No one may wind up reading your documentation, but you need it for yourself anyway. Also prepare a shorter, more communicable presentation to explain your methodology to the skeptics. Incorporate it into messages about your measurements.

Don't take skepticism personally. As Mark Twain said, there are lies, damned lies, and statistics. I'd add measurement to that list—at the end.

Combine Numbers with the Story Behind Them

I think that quantitative measures are often emotionally unsatisfying. No matter how dramatic a chart is that has profit figures skyrocketing, an anecdote has an emotional impact that is entirely different. From our viewpoint, stories also give us a superlative means of conveying complex meaning in a form people want to hear.

From a measurement viewpoint, qualitative data like stories, feedback, interviews, and focus groups can answer a question that quantitative data doesn't answer: Why? What caused us to get the numbers we got? What do they mean?

I remember working on an organizational survey on a sensitive issue for a large business unit. We carefully developed several pilot surveys, gave them to sample audiences, and worked hard to come up with the best final survey we could. A lot of questions got tossed out in that process, we reshaped the focus, and we refined the questions that had worked.

But when the results came back, one group of questions stumped us. The numbers didn't make any sense and we were clueless as to what had caused those results. Unfortunately, the group of questions covered an issue that was of prime importance to management.

What saved our bacon was a comment written in at the bottom of the survey. An employee asked us, "How can I tell you if our business unit is different on this from all of the others? I have never been in any of the other ones." We compared the data on how long the employees had been in that business unit as to how long they had been in the organization. It leaped out at us that the numbers showed that most employees had only been in that unit. No wonder the answers to questions about differences from other units were marked not applicable.

Know Nos

Don't assume that everyone will report honest results on measures. On the contrary, be prepared for people who'll doctor the results to make themselves look good. You can't solve this problem at the beginning. The way to deal with this is to prove over time that the purpose of the measures isn't to blame, but to assess performance and decide what to do in the future.

Didn't Know

Sometimes a sound bite can convey the meaning of pages of numbers. Once a colleague disappeared to help evaluate the implementation of a major program. He was supposed to be gone for two weeks, so I was surprised to see him back after a few days. I asked if the program was working out all right. He sighed, "If that program was a horse, I'd shoot it." He followed up with the hard, cold numbers that detailed the complete failure, but I already understood the reason why. I sprinkle sound bites throughout any report on measures to help explain the numbers, usually in a box offset from the text and the numbers.

You Are What You Present

During college, I once took what I called my walk on the wild side, a course on qualitative data methodology. I thought it would be a welcome diversion from a long round of statistics courses. It turned out to be one of the best courses I took on measurement. None of my previous courses ever considered the human beings who would need to understand and use the measures. They were aimed at producing people who could create the measures and do statistical analysis. Consequently, none of these courses prepared me for delivering results to people in the real world.

Know How

You might decide to do a survey of your employees. I know of several organizations that measure how employees feel about issues related to knowledge sharing. If so, get professional help, as developing and administering a survey requires considerable technical expertise. Those experts will give this advice.

The most important thing I learned in the qualitative data methodology course was the title of this section: You are what you present. No matter how sound your measurement methodology is, no matter how meticulous you analyze your data, no matter how brilliantly you draw your conclusions, none of it counts unless you can communicate it. You need to craft a communications strategy for your measures. What you tell your audience—that is, what you present—helps establish that understanding. A key here is giving the context, the purpose of your measures, and what you intend to do based on the results. The context must be crystal clear to your audience. Additionally, it should be tailored to different sections of your audience.

In general, follow the guidelines in Chapter 18, "Spreading the Word Far and Wide," for communications strategy. I've also given you some ideas in this chapter for improving how you communicate your measures: using words as well as facts, sprinkling sound bites throughout any report, and putting together short presentations. When crafting your communications strategy for your measures, go back to your pals in corporate communications and marketing for help on selling your measures. Also, you may want to talk to the people in your strategic planning section to find out how they sell measures. The bottom line is that you'll have to sell your measures, just as you do your vision, your strategy, and your approach.

In the next chapter, we'll go into a detailed look at a generic measurement process.

Know How

You know too much to be the best judge of how well your measures communicate an actionable understanding. Ask people in your target audience, preferably people who are unfamiliar with knowledge management, to review them for you.

The Least You Need to Know

➤ The goal of measurement is to produce information in context for an actionable understanding.

➤ Don't measure everything. Measure enough to give you the information you need for an actionable understanding.

➤ If your organization has a measurement system in place, consider linking to that, not growing your own.

➤ It's best to combine facts with words, like anecdotes and sound bites.

➤ Developing good measures is insufficient. You also have to communicate both the measures and the results.

➤ Craft a communications strategy for your measures.

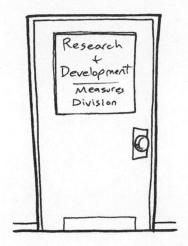

Chapter 20

Developing Measures

In This Chapter

➤ Determining your goals and your audience

➤ Developing an operational definition

➤ Specifying how and what data will be collected

➤ Graphically displaying your measures

➤ Evaluating your measures

I once needed to know what cities were adjacent to a town I planned to visit. I went to one of the travel Web sites to look up a map. At first, I looked at the largest map of the area, which gave me a relatively wide radius. I centered the map on the specific town, and then clicked down another level to zoom in closer. That narrowed the options considerably. I continued to work my way down the available levels until I was at the lowest level.

That experience of starting at a high level and gradually working down to a quite detailed level is similar to developing measures. At the highest level, you have your goals and the audience for your goals. At the next level, you zero in on defining your measures. You then move to specifying what data will be collected and how. At the lowest level, you determine how your measures will be displayed. In this chapter, we'll look at a generic process for developing measures.

Determining Your Goals

The generic process for developing measures has the following steps:

1. Determine your goals.
2. Describe the audience for the measures.
3. Define the measures.
4. Decide what data will be collected and how it will be collected.
5. Decide how to display the measures.
6. Examine the team of measures.

Know How

If you're tying into a measurement system that's already in place in your organization, your goal will be to make a positive impact on what that system measures. In the next chapter, we'll look at several standard measurement systems. However, regardless of the specific measurement approach, your task is to think through how you expect your knowledge management approach to affect the results.

Developing measures is a reality check for your goals. If they're not concrete and clear enough, this will show where the cracks are. For measures, you need goals that define the following:

➤ What success is in clear terms

➤ Success in terms that are measurable

➤ A measurable success that is doable

➤ A measurable success that matters to your organization

Expect to spend some time discussing and refining the goals you developed previously. It's one thing to put together goals for a program or approach. It's quite a different kettle of fish to put together goals concrete and clear enough to drive measures.

Also, expect to revisit your goals periodically throughout the process of developing measures. You may discover that a goal needs a bit more work, or even that a goal isn't realistic to measure.

At the same time, don't let yourself jump ahead to a much later step in the process, like what data will be needed. If you skip ahead to the tail end of the process, you'll find yourself slinking back to the goals. They are your foundation for the rest of the process.

Naming Your Audience

So who decides what success is? The second step in the process answers the question of what success means to certain groups. Those groups are the audiences for your measures. Since defining success is part of determining your goals, these two steps in the process are intertwined.

The level and scope of your effort helps name your audience for your measures. If you're involved in a global knowledge management effort that costs big bucks and spans your global organization, I'd suggest strongly that you consider your CEO and corporate board to be a potential audience, not to mention your external stakeholders. If, on the other hand, your effort is located within a specific business unit, your corporate board may be an option but not a necessity. At the same time, the senior managers in your business unit are an important audience.

Regardless of your level, some critical audiences you should consider are

➤ People who approve allocation of resources, such as funding.

➤ Management at all appropriate levels, to include middle management.

➤ The users, the people who implement and use the knowledge management approach or system.

➤ Others affected by the knowledge management approach, including other employees, customers, and suppliers.

➤ The people involved in running the knowledge management effort.

For example, in Chapter 8, "Communities of Practice—The Killer Application," we learned that you have three potential audiences for communities of practice measures:

➤ **Management.** You need their support to get resources for the community and thus, you need to show some return for their investment.

➤ **The community itself.** Does the community feel that it is receiving benefits for its investment, such as increasing access to expertise?

➤ **Individual community members.** They, too, must get a return on their time for participation.

There's no set answer for who the audience should be. However, there is one ironclad rule involving the audience: They are the ultimate judges of how good your measures are. No matter how good you may think they are, it must make sense to them.

Know How

Create a chart with three columns (a table of specifications in educational testing). In the first column on the left, list your goals. In the second column, enter the audience(s) for each goal. In the third column, enter each measure as you develop it. This table will track if you're developing measures for all of your goals and audiences and what the overall balance is.

Defining the Measures

As the proud parent of the measure, you have the right to give it a name. This doesn't give you free rein for your imagination; the name needs to be in simple, everyday language understandable by the audience for the measure. Resist any urge to give an overly long, detailed, and precise name. A good name is brief and gives a general idea of what is being measured.

You'll build on the name to develop an *operational definition*. An operational definition is your blueprint for the rest of your work developing the measure. It gives you the specifications in enough detail to guide the work. It also tells you what is and isn't included in the measure.

Know These

An **operational definition** is a working definition. It gives you a description of the measure that is detailed enough for the remainder of the development process. It also sets the boundaries for what is and isn't included in the measure.

It's another link in the long chain from your goals to your measures to the data collected and displayed to how the measures are used. While all links in the chain must be solid and tightly connected, the operational definition has a particular impact on the validity of the measure. Your operational definition is a critical step in moving from a more abstract goal to a concrete, measurable something.

It is also an important step for developing a good measure, one that actually measures what it is supposed to measure, not something else. This is called *validity,* a key concept in measurement. A valid measure is one that gives you the correct information you need for your intended actionable understanding.

Know These

Validity is a key measurement concept. Asking if a measure is valid forces the question of whether or not a measure actually measures what it is supposed to measure. Unfortunately, validity is impossible to prove conclusively, but you can collect proof that a measure is valid.

Validity for measures is contextual. It depends upon what question you are asking and what inference you will make from the measure. For example, if a goal defines success for a community of practice, a valid measure actually gives you the information you need to decide if the community of practice is successful. An invalid measure could lead you to assume that a community is successful when, in fact, it is not, or that a community has failed when it is, in fact, successful.

You have to take your best shot at validity. A measurement tenet is that validity is impossible to prove conclusively. You can collect proof of validity, but you can never prove it. Over time you may get unfortunate proof that your reasoning was faulty and that the measure doesn't give you the right information.

Or, you may get proof that your thinking was spot on. That's why, after you implement your measures, you need to evaluate and monitor how they're working, which we'll discuss later, in evaluating your team of measures.

However, one thing you can do immediately is to go back and look at your reasoning for the measure. Some of your conclusions may have been unvoiced, and thus unexamined. Force your reasoning out into the light of day. Think through your reasoning aloud, step-by-step. Ask yourself again:

➤ Are the goals clear and concrete?

➤ Are the goals attainable?

➤ Have the appropriate audiences been identified?

➤ How does the measure show that the goal has been reached?

➤ Could the results in fact be caused by something else?

➤ Are there other factors that could affect the results?

Measurement is an invasive procedure, like surgery. It changes the patient—in your case, your organization. It's also a good idea to think through the possible consequences of the invasion, the measure itself. What sort of actions could result from this measure? For example, if you only measure individual sales, what does that say to your salespeople about the importance of team sales? Will the measure encourage them to concentrate only on sales they can make alone, even though team sales might be more effective? What will happen if you push the amount of individual sales to the max?

Unintended and unwanted consequences also hurt the validity of any measure. They're certainly not what you wanted to measure.

However, validity is useless unless you will take action, if necessary, based on the results of the measures. Answering the following questions is the acid test for the ability to take action:

➤ What direction (up, down, or none) do you want the results of the measure to go?

➤ What will you do if the results of the measure go up?

➤ What will you do if the results of the measure go down?

➤ What will you do if the results of the measure stay flat?

If you can't answer any of those questions, your measure is useless. Stop. Think about what you can do to make the measure actionable. If you can't, drop this one and develop other measures.

Didn't Know

I once spent months working on a large organizational survey focusing on reliability, validity, and the other issues involved in good measurement and analysis. But I did not ask what actions could be taken based on the results; I did not ask what actions had been discussed or planned.

No actions were taken. The report was shelved. It was a waste of my time and the other organizational resources used. I learned the hard way to focus not only on good measurement, but the potential actions and the intent to take action. You can't guarantee that action will be taken, but you can increase the odds that it won't be.

Deciding What Data Will Be Collected and How

If you're a detail person, now's your time to shine. Specifying what data will be collected and how it will be collected is a process of spelling out necessarily excruciating detail. Expect to spend a lot of time on this. It's also hard to shift your mental gears from defining a measure, which is still fairly general, to a level of extreme detail.

Know How

This shift from definition to extreme detail can be a problem for a team working on the measures. Your big-picture thinkers may think you're getting lost in the grass and check out. Your more detail-oriented folks may lose sight of what you're trying to measure. Balance between the need for detail with the need to stay connected to the measure and the goal it's meant to measure.

To determine what data will be collected and how, you need to answer these questions:

➤ Who will collect it?

➤ What data will be collected?

➤ When it will be collected?

➤ Where will the data be collected?

➤ How it will be collected?

You need not only to be specific, but also be able to describe and communicate the specifications well enough so that the data collected is consistent. This brings us to another key concept for measurement—reliability. Reliability means consistency. For example, if every time I step on a scale I weigh 98 pounds, the results are reliable (and I will be heartbroken when I wake up).

The reliability of your measures will depend upon the consistency of the data collected. No matter how carefully you described the intended data and its collection, in practice, the actual data and its collection could vary widely from what you intended. For one thing, it may not be collected at the exact times you specify. While you can't control all of the variation that will happen (variation is inevitable), you do need to take special care when instituting new measures to give detailed descriptions for the data and to use effective communications. You'll also need to monitor how the data is collected over time.

Reliability and validity are related. To be valid, a measure must be reliable. A scale that gives different results every time isn't valid. However, a *reliable measure* isn't necessarily a valid one. A measure can give you a consistent but dead-wrong result.

The difficulty of collecting new data might tempt you to develop measures using existing data. However, just because reliable data already exists doesn't justify developing a measure using it. Every measure must provide important information, not nice-to-know stuff. Even though it may not cost anything additional to collect the data for the measure, you'll expend resources reporting and monitoring the measure in your effort. It still ain't free. It'll cost even more if it stunts your thinking and diverts you from developing more important measures.

Know How

When you look at collecting data, you also should consider the return on investment for any measure. If you have to build an expensive system to collect the data, it may not be worth it. Multiply the cost of collecting new data across more than one measure and the costs get even higher. What is the potential return on investment?

Know These

A **reliable measure** is one that gives consistent results. For example, if a person has a temperature of 98.6°F no matter how many times you take it using a thermometer, the results should be the same. A thermometer that gives unreliable results is useless.

Displaying and Analyzing Your Measures

As mentioned in Chapter 19, "You Get What You Measure," you are what you present. Think through how the measures will be presented graphically, preferably on

Know Nos

Never assume that existing data is reliable data. A common problem is that people within an organization use different definitions for the same data and collect it differently. What should be a basket of apples winds up being a fruit basket with everything from kiwis to pineapple. Check that the data is defined, collected, and reported in the same way across the entire organization before using it.

Know How

If you present your measures on your intranet, you must consider who should have access to the measures. You'll have to assess your corporate norms and also the political situation. Try to fit in with how measures are usually handled, if the political situation permits.

your intranet. If you're able to present using computerized graphics, you'll have many more options both for presenting and for dissemination.

Don't try to cram in too much information into a single display. The more things you try to present at one time, the harder it is to understand. Try to limit each graphic presentation to a key facet of the measure.

Determine how often the graphic displays will be updated. This may or may not dovetail with how often the measures are reported.

Looking at Your Team of Measures

Imagine what could happen if you went out and recruited star ballplayers for a baseball team without thinking what positions they played and what positions are needed to complete a team. You could come up with three pitchers, one shortstop, and five first basemen. That's not a winning team. Also, no matter how much money you had to play with, you'd be unable to get your dream team. You'd have to do the best you could with what money you had and what players were available.

Assembling a team of measures is similar to putting together a strong baseball team. You need to fill each position. For you, this means looking to see if you've developed measures for each of your goals. Unless you keep track, you can leave out some of your goals.

You also have to make sure that you don't have more than one player for the same position. Look to see if any measures are close enough to pass for duplicates. Also check to see if the measures are loaded up for a particular goal or a few goals, and thin for others.

Another important consideration for putting together a team is how the individual players complement each other. Each player has strengths and weaknesses. In the case of measures, you need to determine how the measures relate to each other. Using your chart, compare each measure to all of the others, one by one. Ask yourself these questions:

➤ If this measure improves, will this one improve as well?

➤ If this measure improves, will the other decline?

➤ Are the two measures unrelated?

Give enough context so that people understand the measures. Consider a glossary for your labels and various links, like links to define labels and measures. Also consider including a link to give more overall context. Overall, give people a point of contact for more information if they need it.

Don't drive yourself crazy. There may be no relationship at all, or the relationship may become clear over time. However, you do need to think about it up front.

Finally, ask yourself if this set of measures gives you a good team of measures. Will they do a good job of measuring your goals? Or are there still a few positions open on the team?

Know How

Go back to your completed chart of goals, audiences, and measures. If some measures supposedly measure the same goal, that's a good starting point for seeing if any measures are related to each other. Also, if certain goals are related to each other, that's another good starting point for looking at the associated measures. You may identify some that are almost duplicates and thus, redundant.

Reaching Retirement Age and Other Employment Rules

Consider your measures your employees. I invite you to hold them to the goals you have for them and to periodically have performance reviews.

Be prepared to send some measures off to the minor leagues. Having a set of measures requires adjustments to the roster just like a major league baseball team. As the season wears on, some measures will fail to perform and need to be replaced.

Developing measures is a difficult process of trial and error. You won't get it right the first time. Even if you do reach the point that you think you have a champion team, events can surprise you.

Even someone who has been a most valuable player and a member of the all-star team reaches a time when his or her playing days are over. You need to periodically evaluate your measures, looking to see if it's time for a well-deserved retirement. You can't be sentimental about old favorites. Nor can you keep on a measure because it is familiar and easy to keep using. Your answers to the following questions will tell you if it's time for a retirement dinner:

➤ Is the measure still needed?

➤ Is it still doing the job for which it was developed?

➤ Has the cost of collecting and reporting it become greater than the value obtained from it?

➤ Will anybody notice if you stop providing the measure?

➤ Has a better measure come along since you signed this one on?

The same questions apply for every measure in your team roster.

The Least You Need to Know

➤ For measurement, you need clear and measurable goals and an *identifiable* audience.

➤ Measures must be reliable and valid. Develop detailed specifications for what data will be collected and how it will be collected.

➤ Measures should be displayed in a variety of ways and with enough context to explain them.

➤ Monitor and evaluate how your measures are working.

➤ Developing a set of measures is a process of trial and error. You need to periodically reassess your measurement team, dropping some measures while adding others.

Chapter 21

A Sampler of Measurement Approaches

In This Chapter

➤ Calculating financial measurements

➤ Creating scorecards

➤ Valuing knowledge assets

➤ Measuring the maturity of your knowledge management effort

➤ Surveying your employees' opinions about knowledge management

---

As difficult as measurement is, it's not a barren wasteland out there. For one thing, there are a number of approaches used by organizations to measure their performance, although not all are friendly to knowledge management. As mentioned in the last chapter, the best long-term way to measure the effectiveness of knowledge management is to link it to your organization's performance-measurement system, if there is one. We'll look at two that are widely used in this chapter.

There are also approaches used specifically to measure knowledge management. In this chapter, we'll look at one methodology for calculating the return on investment and also knowledge management maturity models.

As many organizations also use employee surveys, we'll look at how employee surveys are used in relationship to knowledge management, as well.

Developing a Balanced Scorecard of Measures

In the mid-nineties, I spent several years researching performance measurement systems. Several cubic feet of research later, my pick of the bunch then available, my hands-down favorite, was *the balanced scorecard*, which has four perspectives: financial, customers, internal business processes, and learning and growth. This approach has many virtues:

➤ Of the four perspectives in the balanced scorecard, three are nonfinancial, the intangibles that drive success. (They, not coincidently, roughly equate to human, structural, and customer capital.) Creators Robert Kaplan and David Norton believe that intangible assets have become more important than tangible assets for an organization's success.

➤ It focuses on both leading and lagging measures (see Chapter 19, "You Get What You Measure").

➤ When used strategically, it links measurement to strategy and the business objectives. It gives feedback about how well the strategy is performing. It also helps to communicate strategy.

➤ It drives alignment with the business strategy and objectives, particularly as the approach is deployed from the top level to the bottom level of an organization.

➤ By identifying strategic initiatives, it helps to align all strategic initiatives for an organization.

➤ It emphasizes information in context for an actionable understanding. Kaplan and Norton state that the balanced scorecard has its greatest impact when it is used to drive organizational change.

The balanced scorecard addresses four perspectives for measurement:

➤ **Financial.** Although they do not stand alone, financial results still matter. Such measures usually center on profitability, to include such things as operating income, return on capital employed, and economic value added. However, financial measures are lagging measures.

➤ **Customer.** For this perspective, managers identify key customer and market segments. The goal is to identify desired outcomes of the business strategy and develop appropriate measures. Customer concerns normally involve price, quality, and time. Core measures of customer outcomes usually include things like customer satisfaction, retention, and market share. Also, targeted segments are identified. Unfortunately, most customer measures also are lagging measures.

Know How

For an organization, the four perspectives can be framed as four questions:

➤ How do we look to our shareholders?

➤ How do customers see us?

➤ What must we excel at?

➤ Can we continue to improve and create value?

➤ **Internal business process.** This perspective looks at what the company must do well to succeed. Those are the critical internal business processes that have the greatest impact on customer satisfaction and thus the financial objectives as well. (Measures for this perspective normally are developed after customer and financial objectives and measures.) Sometimes these processes don't exist at the start of a balanced scorecard effort, but are identified as being needed. This perspective also includes innovation processes, as innovation is a leading indicator of financial performance.

Kaplan and Norton suggest that although every organization has its own set of processes, a generic-value chain model can be customized to prepare an internal business-process perspective. This generic model focuses on three business processes: innovation, operations, and post-sale service. The innovation process has two parts itself: identifying the market segment and creating the product or service offering. Operations then picks up the ball, and includes building and delivering the products or services. Lastly, post-sale service focuses on serving the customer after the sale, to include such things as repairs, handling returns, and processing payments.

➤ **Learning and growth.** This perspective comes last because the ability to meet the objectives in the other perspectives depends on an organization's ability to learn and grow. Thus, these are leading measures. The three primary categories of the organizational infrastructure are employee capabilities, systems capabilities, and organizational alignment.

Determining a Return on Investment for Knowledge Assets

Face it. For most of us, showing a return on investment for knowledge management approaches is more than nice to have; it's a necessity. Unfortunately, knowledge management projects are bedeviled by two dilemmas. One is that many such projects dictate significant costs, perhaps involving investment in information technology, use of resources from across an organization, and challenges to an existing culture. At the same time the other dilemma, hard-to-measure benefits, worsens the picture. Outcomes like increased knowledge sharing, faster learning, and better decision making are hard to separate out and quantify.

In their book *Knowledge Assets: A Professional's Guide to Valuation and Financial Management*, authors Mark Clare and Arthur Detore of Lincoln Re, one of the world's leading life, health, and financial reinsurance organizations, detail a rigorous financial methodology for showing the return on knowledge assets. To give a context for their methodology, let's look at some of their key definitions.

First, though, I have a warning. This is an extremely detailed methodology involving complex concepts. A quick look will acquaint you with some of the fundamentals, but if you're interested I urge you to explore it in depth.

➤ Knowledge management is a set of management activities designed to leverage the knowledge your organization holds in order to create value for employees, customers, and shareholders.

➤ Knowledge is any system that has content, structure, and reasoning. It is organized content to get something done.

➤ A *knowledge asset* is any type of knowledge held or in use by an organization. It is related to but distinct from tangible assets, monetary assets, and the traditional accounting concept of intangible assets. Knowledge management is dedicated to understanding, leveraging, and protecting the knowledge assets of the organization.

➤ Knowledge management valuation is the process used to determine the value that will be created and protected by a proposed knowledge management strategy or project.

The knowledge management valuation process has six steps:

1. **Identify opportunities.** You set the agenda for your organization by answering three central questions:

   What do you know as an organization? Particularly, how does what you know distinguish you in the market place?

   How can you create more value from what you know?

   How can you get the knowledge needed to succeed in the future faster than your competitors?

   The output is a preliminary description of how to leverage the knowledge assets of your organization.

2. **Scope the project.** The goal of this step is to identify all of the areas of the organization that will be affected by the project, to include business processes. It also encompasses traditional scoping—what's in bounds and what's out of bounds for the project. The output is high-level models that frame the business and the knowledge management scope of the project.

3. **Develop an operational model.** The goal here is to create an organizational model of the operations that will be affected by the proposal, or to build a model of how the knowledge management strategy will be carried out. The outputs include a good operational model that is detailed enough to make a connection between the knowledge assets and the creation of economic value. They also include developing value drivers.

Know These

A **knowledge asset** is some sort of knowledge held by the organization. It has three components. Knowledge content contains what the knowledge is about and is often data or information. Knowledge structure is how the knowledge is organized. Knowledge reasoning is the active process that uses the content to complete a cognitive task, such as problem solving or decision making.

Know These

A **knowledge value tree** is a causal model visually linking the specific operational impacts of a knowledge management strategy or project to the creation of economic value.

4. **Discover value drivers.** This step focuses on the value drivers found in the previous step. The goal is to refine an understanding of the value drivers and use them to build causal models of how they work through the operational model. The outputs include a revised knowledge management proposal and a *knowledge value tree* for the project. A knowledge value tree is a visual means of linking the operational impacts to economic value.

5. **Develop valuation framework.** The goal of this step is to understand the value currently being created or destroyed by the operations within the project's scope. This provides a baseline for assessing the impact of the project. In some cases, this could lead to deciding not to make the proposal. The output for this step is a complete framework for valuation.

6. **Test and refine scenarios.** The purpose of this step is to develop a specific scenario for implementation. Despite all of the groundwork in the previous steps, there're still many questions to answer, such as implementation options, major risks, and how to maximize value. Outputs include a formal knowledge management project proposal.

Know How

In organizations implementing knowledge management, there will be variation across the organization, with knowledge management more firmly entrenched in some parts than others. This is normal; however, the long-term goal is to deploy knowledge management across the entire organization. Note that the HPC model starts with ad hoc, moves to core business processes, and ends by talking of the organization as a whole.

Even if you plan to link to an existing measurement system in your organization, I heartily recommend thinking through this methodology. In addition to providing a way to define a return on investment, it essentially gives a framework for managing knowledge management strategy for an organization.

Measuring If Knowledge Management Has Grown Up

A number of organizations, including Siemens and Hewlett-Packard Consulting, measure the maturity of their knowledge management effort. There's a lot to commend this approach. For one thing, it gives a framework for measuring progress and reaching goals. It helps you to plan your phases for a step-by-step implementation, with actions and measures needed at each stage. It also channels development of measures into actual measures that are appropriate for the organization's current stage.

One model for knowledge management maturity was developed by the American Productivity and Quality Center. This is their road map to knowledge management results: Stages of Implementation. Developed through years of benchmarking many organizations that successfully implemented knowledge management, this model has five stages:

1. Getting started
2. Explore and experiment
3. Pilots and knowledge management initiatives
4. Expand and support
5. Institutionalize knowledge management

There are measures associated with each stage. However, APQC points out that in the early stages, formal measurement is rarely used or required. Then, as an effort becomes more mature, there is more and more need to measure, particularly to show a return for the effort. In the last stages, however, the need to measure knowledge management decreases as the organization's standard performance measures should show the value of knowledge management.

Didn't Know

Although not designed to assess knowledge management, the evaluation criteria for the Malcolm Baldrige National Quality Award give three factors to think about for any maturity model: results, approach, and deployment:

➤ Approach looks at methods used to achieve results and includes appropriateness of method, alignment with business strategy, and evidence of beneficial innovation and change.

➤ Results focuses on outcomes and includes current performance along with rate and breadth of performance improvements.

➤ Deployment addresses the extent to which the approach is applied, both in application to the criteria and how broadly approaches are deployed across the organization.

If your organization uses the Baldrige criteria, it's a good idea to consider linking a knowledge management maturity model to it.

Hewlett-Packard Consulting adapted the people capability maturity model developed by Carnegie Mellon University in 1995. Their maturity model has five levels as well. An abbreviated version is given below:

Level	Attributes
5	The organization's knowledge, policies, practices, and optimized activities are improved continuously.
4	Managed processes include detailed quality measures of knowledge management. The organization adjusts its workforce practices to motivate and support the development of team-based knowledge competencies.
3	Defined knowledge requirements in core business processes are documented, standardized, and integrated into a standard process for the organization; gaps are identified.
2	Repeatable opportunities to create, leverage, and share knowledge are explicitly incorporated into business and development plans.
1	Ad Hoc is the process for knowledge capture and reuse.

Hewlett-Packard Consulting used an employee survey to measure where they stood on this model, the first one being conducted in March 2000. In addition to maturity, the survey also included an assessment of leadership, technology, and culture. Its goals for the survey process were to establish a baseline of its maturity, measure the trends, and give both the central and geographic teams the information they need for planning. The intent was to give the survey once a year.

Know These

An **attitude** is a tendency to respond in a certain way, either positively or negatively, to something. Strictly speaking, in testing parlance, an attitude survey measures the strength and the direction of attitudes. A single score for each attitude is reported. These require considerable technical expertise in testing to construct.

Asking Employees What They Think

You know the drill. You go through the questions, you tick off your answers, and then you drop the survey in the office mail or send it off electronically. Most of us have taken an employee survey at one time or the other. You may regard it as a waste of your time because nothing ever seems to happen afterward. You may think it at least gives the oppressed masses a chance to have their voice heard. However, in some organizations you know that the results will make a difference.

Employee surveys usually are one of two types. One type of survey measures the *attitudes* of employees. An attitude in testing is regarded as how someone feels about something, and whether he or she feels favorably or unfavorably about it. The something can vary considerably. Some examples are a policy, a group of people (such as management), or an organization itself. A set of questions is developed to measure an attitude, although a single score is reported.

Attitude surveys take a formidable amount of technical expertise in testing to construct. Some organizations hire out for such expertise. Some have the expertise in-house. Either way, some high-powered testing knowledge comes into play for attitude surveys.

Another type of employee survey is an *opinion survey.* In contrast to attitude surveys, an opinion survey's goal is to measure the answers to specific questions. Each question is important in its own right, and overall, the questions may not be related. I often see these questions reported separately, as issues deserving their own consideration. The report of one employee opinion survey I saw recently devoted some time to discussing the apparently hot topic of wearing business casual.

Know These

An **opinion survey,** in contrast to an attitude survey, focuses on specific answers to specific questions. Each of those questions is important in its own right and may be unrelated to others. Typical questions in employee surveys look at a person's relationship with his or her supervisor, for example.

Didn't Know

Most attitude or opinion surveys use a Likert scale (developed in 1932), the easiest of the three commonly used types of scales to develop. A Likert scale has a series of statements, each of which is either positive or negative. Responses are usually given in five categories: Strongly disagree, disagree, undecided, agree, and strongly agree. To make data analysis easier, responses are coded 5, 4, 3, 2, or 1.

To be reliable, a set of responses must have at least five choices. Any fewer than that and your results are invalid. You may have seen scales in customer satisfaction measures or marketing surveys that have as many as 11 choices. I usually prefer a smaller number.

235

You can use either approach, depending upon your goals for measurement. Either way, though, make sure you have adequate technical support for developing the survey.

Some organizations are surveying their employees about knowledge management. These surveys can be either attitude or opinion. One way to do this is to add some questions into the overall employee survey for the organization, as Xerox did. If the employee survey is actually used for action, adding knowledge management questions sends an important message internally about how management views KM.

Know How

Another benefit of tying into the organizational employee survey is that the measurement system is already developed. There is a supporting infrastructure in place, complete with development support, data collection and analysis procedures, and reporting processes. The tradeoff is that you probably won't get to ask as many questions as you may want.

Another way to survey employees on knowledge management is to develop your survey specifically for that. Johnson & Johnson, for example, developed a survey to measure how well the organizational culture enables knowledge sharing. I've also seen surveys intended to look broadly at the overall organizational environment, to include identifying barriers.

A key thing for you to remember is that you're measuring what people say about their attitudes, beliefs, or opinions. Don't be surprised if people's beliefs or opinions contradict the facts. If your employees feel that the promotion system rewards knowledge hoarding, you've got a problem regardless of whether or not you agree with that. With a survey you get a sense of their belief, attitude, or opinion.

As with other measurement approaches, the most important thing about employee surveys, either opinion and attitude, is to use the information for action. Such actions could include revamping a KM effort, developing a new KM strategy, or adjusting a communications strategy.

The approaches discussed in this chapter are a few options for you as the KM practitioner. While each approach has its benefits, any approach you choose must work best for you. Your overall goals for your KM effort and the goals you have for measures determine what is best for you. Ultimately, you will have to decide if you need to measure, what you need to measure, how you will measure, and how you will use the results.

The Least You Need to Know

➤ The balanced scorecard is a performance measurement approach that focuses on linking an organization's mission and strategy to the measures. It measures not only financials, but also three additional perspectives: customers, internal business processes, and learning and growth.

➤ The Lincoln Re knowledge management valuation approach developed by Clare and Detore gives a rigorous approach for measuring returns on investments in knowledge assets.

➤ This valuation approach also gives a framework for developing a knowledge management strategy.

➤ Some organizations base measures on models of maturity in their knowledge management efforts.

➤ Some organizations also use employee surveys to assess some aspects of knowledge management such as culture and barriers to knowledge management.

➤ Surveys measure people's perceptions, not necessarily reality.

Chapter 22

Measuring Intellectual Capital

In This Chapter

➤ How to measure intellectual capital

➤ Learning about the Intangible Assets Monitor

➤ Consider the Skandia Navigator

➤ Understanding the Intellectual Capital Index

➤ Changing the mental models

Knowledge management recognizes the value of knowledge; intellectual capital approaches attempt to give it a value. There are many approaches for measuring intellectual capital, that is, the valuable knowledge held as a shared asset among employees or the expertise of individual employees.

Perhaps the most widely recognized and easily understood indicator of intellectual capital is the difference between market value and book value. You've probably seen examples of how great a difference there is for firms like Microsoft—the market value of the company is much higher than its book value.

Another example is IBM's purchase of Lotus, for which they paid $3.5 billion dollars when the book worth of Lotus was $500 million. That kind of difference gets people's attention and clues them into the fact that's there's gold in those hills of intangible asset.

This difference is a measure of intellectual capital called market-to-book value. It's simple to calculate, it gives a better idea of the true worth of an organization than the traditional balance sheet, and it's easy to communicate. In this chapter, we'll look at a typology for intellectual capital approaches for measurement, some specific approaches for measuring intellectual capital, and some potential pitfalls in implementation. I'd like to point out, though, that I'm not advocating dropping financial measures in favor of intellectual capital measurement. The bottom line remains important. An organization needs both kinds of measures because an organization has both tangible and intangible assets.

Know These

Direct intellectual capital methods (DIC) estimate the value of intangible assets. To do this, the individual components must be identified and then evaluated.

Know These

Market capitalization methods (MCM) look at the difference between a company's market capitalization and its stockholder's equity. This type of approach thus focuses on the perceived value of an organization in the marketplace, which can be volatile.

A Typology for Measuring Intellectual Capital

In the 1990s, many people published approaches for measuring intangible assets. As measuring these assets gets more attention, professionals are doing even more work and sharing their findings. Classifying this range of measures is difficult. However, after an analysis of different approaches for measuring intangible assets, Karl-Erik Sveiby developed a typology I find extremely useful. This typology comes from a paper, "Measuring Models for Intangible Assets and Intellectual Capital," published on Sveiby's Web site (www.sveiby.com.au) in the library section. In the paper, he includes a chart of approaches, provides a classification scheme, and lists the advantages and disadvantages of each one. If you intend to measure intellectual capital, I refer you to that article (as well as the entire Web site) to learn more about these approaches. No one approach fits every situation. As always, you'll have to choose what is best for your organization.

The typology includes four types of measures:

➤ *Direct intellectual capital method* (DIC). These measures estimate the value of intangible assets by first identifying their various components. Then the components are evaluated, either singly or together.

➤ *Market capitalization method* (MCM). These are calculated by estimating the difference between a company's market capitalization and its stockholders' equity. Market-to-book value is one

MCM approach. Another is Tobin's q, the ratio of the stock market value of the firm divided by the replacement cost of its assets.

➤ *Return on Assets method (ROA).* The average pretax earnings of a company for a specific period of time are divided by the average tangible assets of the company. The result is compared to the industry average for the company, and then the difference is multiplied by the company's average tangible assets to calculate an average annual earning from the intangibles.

➤ *Scorecard method (SC).* In this method, you identify various components of intangible assets. You then generate indicators or indexes and report these on scorecards or as graphics. The balanced scorecard covered in Chapter 21, "A Sampler of Measurement Approaches," is a scorecard method, as are the methods we'll discuss in the rest of this chapter.

I'll admit to a bias for scorecard methods, as I think they provide better knowledge—more information in context for an actionable understanding. However, the fact that they're contextual is a disadvantage, as it makes them difficult to compare across organizations. They also have to be developed for each organization, although some measures are applicable across a range of organizations. One last drawback is that they can produce mountains of data, hampering analysis or producing total analysis paralysis. However, they still get my vote.

Know These

Return on assets (ROA) methods focus on an average earning from intangible assets. You calculate this by dividing the pretax earnings of a company by the average tangible assets. The result is compared to the industry average, and the difference is multiplied by the company's average tangible assets to get the average annual earning of intangibles.

Know These

Scorecard methods (SC) concentrate on identifying indicators or indexes for a range of intangible asset components. The indicators or indexes may be reported as numerical scores or graphically.

Intangible Assets Monitor

One method for measuring intellectual assets that has been in use since the early 1990s is the intangible assets monitor developed by Karl-Erik Sveiby.

Know How

Both ROA and MCM methods are one-dimensional, focusing as they do on financial terms. They also are of little use for the public and nonprofit sectors. In contrast, both the DIC and SC methods can apply to private, public, and nonprofit sectors. They also can be applied from the top of an organization down to the lowest level.

Know How

Customers provide more than revenue. Intangible revenues include learning and development for employees that a customer or supplier provides, spurred development of new human competence and internal structure to meet customer and supplier demands, and the enhancement of a company's image. To give an example of enhancing an image, have you ever seen a consultant's resume? It usually lists high-profile customers that enhance his or her image.

Three Categories

The intangible assets monitor has three categories: human competence, external structure, and internal structure.

➤ **Human competence.** Sveiby states that people are the profit generators for any organization. This category looks at people's capacity for action to generate value in various situations. This capacity includes values, experience, social skills, and educational background. People also create both external and internal structure. The caveat on human competence is that no organization "owns" it.

➤ **External structure.** This consists of how the organization is regarded externally and includes trademarks, brand names, and image. It also encompasses relationships with customers, suppliers, and partners.

➤ **Internal structure.** This is the structural capital we discussed earlier in Chapter 2, "More Models Than a Car Show." It's what's left at work when the people go home. Unlike human competence, it does belong to the organization. It includes databases, processes, models, and documentation. Intellectual property such as patents and trade secrets also are part of internal structure.

Some place social capital into internal structure. I think that it straddles both human competence and internal structure. From an organizational viewpoint, it does "own" the overall social capital. Such collective social capital can weather individuals leaving. It's part of the organizational culture.

However, all members of an organization also own their individual piece of the social capital pie through their reputation and connections in their networks and communities. When people leave, they take that piece of the social capital pie with them. People also vary in their skill and experience in building their own social capital. It's part of their individual competence.

Didn't Know

In his book *The New Organizational Wealth*, Sveiby identifies four types of people in any organization:

➤ Professional. These are the experts, the specialists who are the prime source of revenue for any organization.

➤ Managers. They're appointed to lead the organization to reach particular goals with specific resources.

➤ Support staff. Their job is to give the professionals and managers what they need to do their jobs.

➤ Leaders. The two tasks of organizational leaders are to provide vision and to persuade others to carry out that vision.

When an organization invests in building networks and communities in addition to building an internal structure capability, it's also building individual competence to function in networks and communities. An individual owns that personal capability. For example, if an organization creates documentation and training for the role of community coordinator, it has created internal structure from the organizational viewpoint. It also has increased human competence in the people who have been trained and act as coordinators.

These three categories are further subdivided along three more dimensions:

➤ **Growth and renewal.** How is this asset growing and renewing?

➤ **Efficiency and utilization.** How well is this asset being utilized?

➤ **Stability.** How stable is this asset? Is there a risk of losing it?

A Generic Example of Typical Indicators

Here is an example of some typical indicators in the intangible assets monitor:

	Human competence	External structure	Internal structure
Growth/ renewal	Number of years' education	Growth in market share	R&K investments
Efficiency	Value added per employee	Profit per customer	Percentage of support staff
Stability	Professional turnover	Repeat orders	Support staff turnover

The Celemi Intangible Assets Monitor

A consulting company with a long history of using the intellectual assets monitor is Celemi. Their 1999 intangible assets monitor has a section for both tangible and intangible assets, both of which are measured along the dimensions of growth/renewal, efficiency, and stability. Additionally, intangible assets are measured in the categories of external structure, internal structure, and competence.

A new addition to the monitor is Celemi's use of colors to indicate the status of each indicator. Individual cells in the monitor are red, green, or yellow. Green means that the indicator is equal to or greater than the strategic plan target. Red cells indicate values less than 80 percent of the target. Yellow cells indicate values in between. The monitor also gives the figures for three years (1999, 1998, and 1997), enabling a comparison at a glance.

Here is a sample of the measures of the intangible assets in the Celemi intangible assets monitor:

	Our Customers (external structure)	Our Organization (internal structure)	Our People (competence)
Growth/ Renewal	Image-enhancing customers	Revenues from new products	Average professional experience in years
Efficiency	Revenues per customer	Proportion of admin staff	Value added per expert
Stability	Customer satisfaction index	Admin staff turnover	Expert turnover

If you would like to see the complete report, you can order it from the Celemi Web site at www.celemi.com.

The *Skandia* Navigator

Skandia AFS, a financial-services firm based in Sweden, has been publicly reporting their intangibles via the Skandia Navigator. The measures themselves can be organized into five components:

➤ **Financial.** This includes traditional financial measures, although it also allows for the addition of new measures, such as ratios indicating performance and quality.

➤ **Customer.** The purpose of the customer component is to assess the relationships between the company and its customers. Issues for consideration include customer type, duration, role, support, and success.

➤ **Process.** This area focuses on how an organization uses its technology tools to create value. The goal is to avoid technology mistakes (an all-too-common phenomenon) and concentrate on picking the right tools to create value.

➤ **Renewal and development.** This looks at how the organization is preparing itself for the future. There are six strategic areas in which an organization can concentrate efforts for preparations: customers, attractiveness on the market, products and services, strategic partners, infrastructure, and employees.

➤ **Human.** This category is both the most important and the most difficult to measure. How do you measure the productivity of knowledge workers? How do you measure what they know? How do you measure their values and commitment? How do you assign a value to them?

This may seem like a lot of areas for measures to you. It gets better (or worse). Authors Leif Edvinsson and Michael Malone suggest 61 possible measures in just this one area. They argue that since it's so difficult to predict future trends, it's best to increase your odds of finding the right one by measuring many. Initially, the best way to determine the ones that matter is to ask a lot of different questions.

This Skandia approach is blessed with a plethora of associated and documented measures. In their book *Intellectual Capital*, Edvinsson and Malone give 112 measures in their overall standard model, which they consider to be universally applicable. Of these only 18 are financial. For each component, let's look at some examples of measures:

➤ **Financial.** Some are total assets, the ratio of profits to assets, market value, and return on net asset value.

Know How

The Skandia approach also has a time dimension. Financial measures indicate the past; customer, human, and process measure the current performance of a company; renewal and development predict future performance.

➤ **Customer.** Some are market share, customers lost, customer visits to the company, and customer IT literacy.

➤ **Process.** These measures include laptops per employee, the ratio of IT capacity to employee, and the ratio of administrative expenses to total revenues, the corporate quality goal.

➤ **Renewal and development.** These include the ratio of training expense to employees, share of training hours, the ratio of marketing expense to customers, R&D invested in basic research, R&D invested in product design, and patents pending.

➤ **Human.** These include percentage of women managers, average age of employees, annual turnover of full-time employees, percentage of company managers with advanced degrees, and annual turnover of full-time permanent employees.

Intellectual Capital Index

The Intellectual Capital Index was developed after an extensive program of research funded by government agencies in Scandinavia and Australia. The conceptual base was broad, including the balanced scorecard and the Skandia Navigator. The results of the research conducted by Goran Roos and Johan Roos concluded that the first generation of intellectual capital approaches to measurement failed to cover some critical areas:

➤ Showing the strategic impact of changes in intellectual capital

➤ Determining which categories were more important

➤ Giving a basis for comparison across different companies and business units

They came up with four high-level categories:

➤ Relationship capital index

➤ Human capital index

➤ Infrastructure index

➤ Innovation capital index

A key difference in this approach is that the individual indicators are consolidated into a single index. The authors claim that changes in the index are related to changes in a firm's market valuation. Thus, over time the index can indicate trends, although it doesn't give a direct financial evaluation of intellectual capital.

An index is apparently simple. It is one number and one number alone. From the news, you may be familiar with other indexes such as the Consumer Price Index.

However, that simplicity comes at a cost. Anytime you aggregate information, you lose some clarity in the process. That simplicity also dictates a need for greater communication to help people interpret the index. You also need to be sure that the index still provides actionable information, is valid, and gives the appropriate information for the level at which it will be used. In practice, I have invariably noticed that when an index is reported, a breaking out of the individual factors follows any change in the number.

In their book *Intellectual Capital: Navigating in the New Business Landscape*, Johan Roos and several coauthors lay out a process for developing an IC index:

1. Define the vision and business strategy for the enterprise.

2. Identify the critical success factors.

3. Choose the key performance indicators for each category.

4. Apply weightings to the indicators.

5. Consolidate the metrics.

6. Generate the IC index.

7. Use it to help determine management actions on the key factors.

Know Nos

If you're constructing an index, there are two ways to determine weights: statistically and using human judgment. Human judgment methods are completely subjective in nature. Multivariate statistical methods used to develop weights also require human judgment and aren't completely objective.

Possible Pitfalls

Let's get real for a moment. Measuring intangibles isn't what people are used to doing. Most managers have spent their careers tending the store of financial measures. Quarterly earnings, stock prices, and net profit have been the goals, not something as nebulous as measuring things that can't be seen and are hard to identify.

Furthermore, it's difficult to turn your back on what has meant success to you for your entire career. People have been promoted for good performance on financial measures. Others have been fired. Critical decisions for the future of the company are frequently based on such measures. And to turn your back on these for some newfangled, mysterious methods for counting stuff that can't be seen may seem like lunacy to some. Human judgment methods are completely subjective in nature.

Yet, these intangibles are real enough, and it does make sense to measure them and make decisions based on these measures. The fact is that accounting methods for evaluating intangibles have been around for only several decades and are still under intense development. In contrast, traditional financial accounting methods have been around for centuries. They are solid and time-honored to many, even though relying

Know How

Another important part of instituting a change in measures is your stakeholder analysis. Obviously, your financial people are one group who will be affected to a great degree. You also may find differences in acceptance among your subcultures, perhaps between functions and geographies, to name a few. As always, identify your critical stakeholders, how supportive or nonsupportive they are, and target them accordingly.

on them has become as out-of-date as the term "horseless carriage." In contrast, there's little scientific evidence that these new methods work or that one is demonstrably better than another. Although the same criticism can be leveled at more traditional measurement systems, since they're based on traditional accounting methods they seem more reasonable.

Expect resistance to change if you implement measures for intangible assets. You handle this resistance to change the same way you do other changes:

➤ Assess your organization's readiness to make the change, in this case to measure intangibles. For example, if your business goals already include nonfinancial performance indicators, you are building on a recognition that such things matter.

➤ Communicate the purpose and the goals.

➤ Get senior-level management support.

➤ Explain the models.

➤ Coach on the new behaviors, including teaching how to use the new metrics.

➤ Identify the strengths and barriers in the organizational culture.

Consider benchmarking. As relatively new as measuring intangibles is, there are a number of organizations that have been doing it for years and can attest to how well it works for them. Seeing is believing. Additionally, you'll have to develop a new infrastructure to collect and report data for your new measures as you would for any new measurement approach. The devil's in the details, so don't neglect those; a poor implementation can wreck the effort.

The Least You Need to Know

➤ The measurement of intellectual capital focuses on the intangible assets of an enterprise.

➤ A balanced scorecard method concentrates on producing indicators or indexes for a range of intangible asset components. The indicators or indexes may be reported as scorecards or graphics.

➤ Any index is an aggregation of information. Constructing an index requires careful consideration of how to weight the components, how to communicate the results, and how well the index actually measures what it measures.

➤ Scorecard approaches include the Intellectual Asset Monitor of Sveiby, the Skandia Navigator, and the Intellectual Capital Index.

➤ Implementing measurement of intellectual capital will require an understanding of your organizational readiness, cultural enablers and barriers, and the use of change management methodology.

Part 6

Settling In for the Long Haul

My parents like to tell a story about the birth of one grandchild. Part one of their story centers on the prospective father. Worn down by the months of problems associated with a difficult pregnancy dictating bed rest, he said earnestly to my parents, "I sure will be glad when the baby's born and we can get back to normal." (The mother didn't like it much, either.)

Part two is the day that they came home with the baby. Until that day the father retained his hope of a return to normalcy. However, after arriving home with their newborn, he and the new mother sat on their couch, looked at each other, and asked in complete bewilderment, "What do we do now?" The darned thing had come without an instruction manual.

You may feel like that after you conduct your knowledge management pilot. In this part we'll focus on what happens after the pilot baby has been brought home: the next steps after you implement your knowledge management approach, and how to avoid some common pitfalls. We'll also switch from concentrating on knowledge management for organizations to include a chapter looking at knowledge management for individuals.

Chapter 23

Where Did We Go Wrong?

In This Chapter

➤ Implementing IT for the right reasons

➤ Understanding the importance of critical differences

➤ Building broad support

➤ Recognizing unrealistic timelines

I hate it when I see the signs of certain failure. I struggle for something tactful to say. I frantically think of ways to change their minds. Above all, I tell myself, I must radiate calm, rationality, and hope. What I want to do is say as gently as I can, "Turn the ship around. You'll never reach port the way you are going. You need to change course." What I'd prefer to do is congratulate you on the soundness of your knowledge management approach, applaud your certain success, and ask you to tell your story to others. The world needs to learn from you. You're from a company that has used knowledge management to its fullest, another Hewlett-Packard Consulting or British Petroleum.

We've already discussed some potential pitfalls, such as failing to link knowledge management to business strategy, ignoring the importance of middle management, and bypassing users. But to increase the chances for the second scenario, this chapter will be devoted to other common pitfalls in implementing knowledge management initiatives. These are the things that drive me mad—and make knowledge management programs fail.

Build IT and They'll Come

We're doing knowledge management, they say to me. We're implementing

➤ A corporate portal—*one* corporate portal—for everybody.

➤ This fabulous database filled with every kind of data field we could think of.

➤ Groupware (fill in name).

No matter what the name or technology, the message is that implementing an information technology solution equates to "doing" knowledge management. Unfortunately, that's not how it works, folks.

I think the underlying belief here is that "people need more information." Forget that some surveys find that people are receiving upwards of 300 e-mails per day. Forget that there are vast hordes of dusty, unused databases. Forget that some intranets closely resemble a junkyard filled with rusting hulks.

Let's go back to our definition of knowledge: information in context to produce an actionable understanding. I'll agree that knowledge workers need information in context as they do their jobs. But information and technology for information doesn't necessarily give them what they need for action. What they need is something that gives context to information and makes it actionable.

Know How

People-based strategies do need supporting information technology. For example, communities of practice need a virtual workspace. This space should have areas for discussion, both private and public. There should be access to the documents and other tools the community develops. Other information sources used by the community should be available, such as Web sites and databases.

Sometimes there's no underlying thinking. No one has thought through how the information technology will help meet business strategies and goals. No one has thought through whether it is the only solution or only one part of what should be a combined solution involving clear management expectations, defined roles and responsibilities, and reward mechanisms. (To keep from falling into the pitfall of information technology gone wrong, use the following checklist:

❑ Stamp out solutions looking for problems. (Let them take out a personal ad.) Any information technology must serve a business purpose. It must help people to do real work, solve real problems, and support real strategies.

❑ Consider the wetware—the users. Even if a database application is the best solution for your business needs, it doesn't matter unless people use it. Design it to support the work process of actual people. Work on the design until the users can get excited about how much easier it made their jobs.

I spot a problem when someone talks on and on about the technology without ever mentioning the users (or what a darn nuisance they are). When confronted with this folly I ask, "Where are the people?"

❑ Use change management in the deployment. No matter how good the information technology is, it's a change.

Know How

In 1996, the editorial department at *CIO* magazine implemented Lotus Notes. Good folks on a cross-functional committee spent months considering programs and recommended implementing Notes. A project team including actual workers helped develop the applications. Then the technology was launched.

Unreasonable expectations had been set ... and went unmet. There were numerous technical problems. The pilot application was overloaded with features, obscuring the useful ones. Training was poor. There was no clear sponsorship of the change. Worst of all, the application was a solution in search of a problem. Outside experts in change management were brought in to make recommendations. Sadder but wiser, the group put the application on hold until the glitches could be fixed.

Ignoring Critical Differences

I used to be on a team with all of the other members coming from another part of the organization. I'd get in my car, drive 10 miles, meet with them, and drive back. In due course, the meeting notes would pop up in my e-mail. But I couldn't read them. Our information technology systems were different, and I couldn't open any attachments from their system. Information technology is one of the differences that make it difficult to scale up a knowledge management approach. Not everyone has the same information technology infrastructure across an entire organization. Starting over again and building one is a sizeable investment, one your organization may not be willing to make for something as new as knowledge management.

When planning an approach that incorporates an information technology application, be sure to analyze your current infrastructure. Also talk to the IT people about what changes are coming down the pike. What works today may not work in three months after the operating system has been upgraded to a new version.

Cultural differences are another potential stumbling block. Hewlett-Packard Consulting found that in the United States the sharing of tacit knowledge was weak. HPC therefore focused on communities of practice and the project snapshots. The goal was to accustom people to sharing their knowledge and experiences.

In contrast, in Japan the sharing of explicit knowledge was relatively weak, although the Japanese were quite skilled at sharing tacit knowledge. In Japan, the focus was on building a repository to share documents.

Another difference often tied to culture is language. Many global organizations solve this by declaring that corporate language is English. Indeed, the aviation industry decreed years ago that the language of the skies would be English.

But it's not that simple. Language skills and the opportunity to practice them vary from person to person. Some languages are much harder to learn, depending on what your native language is. There are also critical differences in the graphic representation of languages, ranging from different alphabets to different characters. Xerox dealt with this problem when it launched its Eureka system. Eureka was initiated in France, but once it was ramped up worldwide, it had to deal with input in eight different languages. Tips submitted by technicians can be in any language. Reviewers are bilingual. Approved tips are translated into English with the original language kept as an attachment. Another potential stumbling block is a difference in subcultures. This could be different functions, markets, product lines, geographies, or units. For example, in most organizations, marketing is different from research and development. Refining units in the oil companies are different from the discovery and exploration units. An office in the Boston area may be different from one based in the San Francisco area.

The bottom line is that one size doesn't fit all. Consider carefully the differences across your organization that could impact your knowledge management strategy and approaches. Then figure out how to take advantage of these differences and learn from each other to the benefit of all.

Be aware that the flip side of trying to accommodate differences is that you could wind up with a many-headed knowledge management monster that's difficult to implement and manage. That'll be one of the challenges you face as you scale up. One solution is to develop policies and procedures that are flexible enough to work across the organization, but specific enough to produce some consistency. In particular, you need to make sure that there are consistent information technology standards.

A Kinder, Gentler Place by Tomorrow

I sometimes think some organizations can be classified as either hares or tortoises. The hares I meet are harried (couldn't resist that one) and frantic. They tell me that their senior management or CEO has decided that they must do knowledge management. Their due date for delivering a plan is one month. They must implement within two months. Complete and overwhelming success is expected within three. World poverty is to be eradicated in four. I keep wondering when these folks will get around to reducing gestational time for a human baby from nine to three months.

Most organizations go through a gestational phase of discovery and exploration. The idea catches the imagination of someone within the organization. They find others who have the bug or are willing to catch it. Discussions start, but ignorance leads people to go outside to see what others are doing. They attend conferences, visit other organizations, and read voraciously. They join organizations and consortia.

As their understanding grows, they begin to flesh out a vision for their organization. They start preaching knowledge management, buttonholing any and everyone who will listen. They round up organizational support and find sponsors. They identify opportunities. They start locking down resources. The slow build to implementation is underway. I've done this myself, and it took more

Didn't Know

Aware of their cultural diversity, Hewlett-Packard Consulting hired a cross-cultural consultant. This consultant understood the differences in values and attitudes in the context of sharing and leveraging knowledge. You may want to consider this as well, because deliberately involving people from diverse cultures also helps you to identify and target differences.

Know Nos

Don't assume that having subcultures is bad. To the contrary, subcultures can be a sign of a healthy, well-functioning organization. Specialized subcultures can be more efficient, helping an organization to perform well in different environments.

Know How

A change agent must coldly analyze the odds for success. Some battles can't be won. Unrealistic timelines are a good clue that management lacks an adequate understanding, another portent of failure. I know it's hard to walk away when it's something you believe in. The first time you do it, you'll doubt yourself. But over time you'll have more confidence in your ability to pick your battles.

Know Nos

Sometimes people set themselves up to become hares. They convince a senior sponsor or CEO that there is no time to waste, and are told to get it done right away. Be careful what you wish for. Keep in the back of your mind that if you preach knowledge management, you may have to deliver someday. That day could come before you're ready.

than three months. In contrast, what I see from the hares is …

➤ Ill-defined vision and goals.

➤ Poorly thought-out links, if any, to business strategy and goals.

➤ Hastily chosen approaches.

➤ Inadequate organizational support from key leaders and other players.

➤ Lousy execution of approaches marked by major setbacks.

➤ Poorly demonstrated (if demonstrated at all) benefits and return on investment.

My answer to the ones giving the hares their orders is to ask if they want it done right or done on time. I do realize this is a bit hard to say to a CEO (I don't enjoy it, let me tell you). But, I prefer to do that instead of tap dancing my way around an utter failure later.

If you're implementing knowledge management, you want to prime for success. For that you need time. Resist the fear that this may be your only chance. I'll guarantee you that if you fail now, you'll increase the odds that it'll turn out to be your only chance.

The flip side of this quandary is the tortoise that never reaches the finish line. Organizations vary, but many tolerate only so much discovery and preparation.

I'll admit that one of my major lessons learned early as a change agent was that if I waited until I had something perfect, the opportunity was long gone. Besides, it's impossible to get something right the first time out of the gate no matter how long you study and plan. I've resigned myself to doing the best job I can within a reasonable amount of time.

Tortoises need to keep that lesson in mind, then develop a balance between the time they need and the time the organization will allow. One of the keys to success in any innovation or change is building momentum and finding a way to sustain it. It's hard to rekindle a fire that has gone out.

Betting the Farm on a CEO or Other Sponsor

Who wouldn't want the CEO passionately committed? Or the chief operating officer? Or the company president? Or the head of a strategic business unit? You're right, it's good to have high-level sponsors. The higher, the better. The more, the better.

The head of an organization, of course, has extraordinary power. With the CEO firmly behind your effort, it's like being on a superhighway in a Formula 1 racecar. Doors open, funds appear, barriers vanish. Even if your sponsor isn't the top dog, having someone at senior levels is also magical. In every successful knowledge management effort that the American Productivity and Quality Center has studied—and they've looked at a bunch—an important senior sponsor or sponsor group pushed for the initiative.

Didn't Know

Tom Young, formerly of British Petroleum and now of Knowledge Transformation International, tells of the day that he went to discuss the knowledge management program with a senior manager. As he came in, the manager asked him if he wanted a cup of coffee. Tom did, and someone scurried off to get it for him. When the coffee arrived the manager told him, "Drink your coffee, Tom. There's no need to talk to me. The top guy is behind it, so I am, too. That's enough for me." This baffled Tom, prepared for perhaps a lengthy back-and-forth discussion on the merits of the program. But he drank his coffee and left.

However, I wouldn't bet the farm on just one sponsor or sponsor group. That gives me the heebie-jeebies. Unless you foster wider organizational support, your lifeline is tethered to one person or group. A sad fact of organizational life is that people leave, sometimes of their own free will and sometimes not. I don't care if your sponsor is the CEO. What guarantee do you have the CEO will be there for the life of the program? What guarantee do you have that a replacement will have the same passion and commitment? The same holds true for any sponsor.

Granted, once the sponsor is on board, many people fall in line behind the effort. What worries me is their sincerity. There's a big difference between compliance and commitment. Hopefully the initial compliance will give knowledge management a chance to prove itself. The outward compliance will turn into inward belief.

259

Know Nos

A potential pitfall is having a program with no distinct business objectives. Goals like "change the culture to one of openness, foster collaboration, and become a knowledge-based organization" seem hard to argue with. But you need to have that clear link to business strategies, and for that you need business objectives. The World Bank's mission is to eradicate world poverty. Their knowledge management program has specific business objectives to achieve that mission.

This doesn't always happen, though. There will always be people who are KM believers in name only, and if the top-level sponsor leaves the organization, their outward compliance can change back into overt resistance. That's another reason betting the farm on a sole sponsor, no matter how heroic or charismatic, is risky.

The flip side of this is launching with what seems like adequate support from a sponsor or sponsor group, only to have the support eventually dry up. This can be hard to diagnose up front. An organization can assign a chief knowledge officer, create a budget, and sign up other resources. There are meetings at which high-flown rhetoric on the noble ambitions of the program fills the air. Approaches are identified. Sometimes outside consultants are brought in as well. Things appear to be going well.

But the backbone to confront knotty issues like the cultural assumptions needed for successful implementation isn't there. The people working on knowledge management, whether internal or external, can't seem to get any traction. When they ask management for support, management avoids taking any action. Instead, the KM people find themselves endlessly pushing a limp strand of spaghetti. This can even happen when a program shows success initially, just when you'd think that it's time to shift into high gear. In those situations, if an organization is brave, it'll face up to the fact that it wasn't ready after all. If not, my advice is to look for another job. Things aren't going to work where you are.

Luckily, some organizations select out. Unable to define knowledge management, the goals for it, and how it can enable their business strategy, they never get off the ground. I've seen some that can't even get their act together enough to hire a CKO. A potential flip side of this problem is sponsors who are committed to making knowledge management succeed but don't understand what their role needs to be. I call them absentee landlords. Sponsors and the rest of management need to be hands-on, from the beginning through implementation through scaling up and to maintaining the effort. My advice is to spell out what's expected of them. No matter what stage you're in, they'll need to

➤ Communicate constantly that knowledge management is critical for the organization's success.

➤ Interact frequently with the KM team.

➤ Enlist the support of other senior leaders.

➤ Buy the time needed to demonstrate the value.

➤ Press for defined and reachable goals.

➤ Monitor progress.

➤ Role model knowledge sharing activities.

Stopping Before You're Done

A successful pilot doesn't mean a successful program. It means there's been a good start, but there's still plenty of work left to do to embed knowledge management firmly in the organization. We'll discuss what's left to be done in the next chapter.

Didn't Know

To help its sponsors understand their role, Hewlett-Packard Consulting told the story of Moses leading the children of Israel to the Promised Land. Moses had a high-level sponsor who removed barriers for him. He led the decades-long journey, continuing a high level of involvement throughout. At the end of the story the new vice president and general manager of HPC volunteered to be Moses. He was a hands-on participant in the development of the KM initiative. He communicated the importance of KM to HPC. He worked on getting and keeping the support of the rest of his senior leadership team. He also worked closely with the KM team.

261

The Least You Need to Know

➤ Information technology, no matter how good, doesn't equate to knowledge management. Build it and they may yawn in your face.

➤ You'll have to consider potential differences in culture, organizational subcultures, and language. You may have to adjust to accommodate them.

➤ While accommodating differences you also need to worry about standardization.

➤ You need broad organizational support from leaders at multiple levels. Never bet the bank on just one sponsor.

➤ Spell out to your sponsors exactly what they should do. In particular, make sure they have enough time.

➤ Implementing knowledge management takes time. Unrealistic deadlines set you up for failure.

Moving to the Big Time

I remember all too well the end of a certain pilot for benchmarking I was involved in. Although there was some success, there also was more failure than I wanted to see. After we regrouped, our management decided the effort would continue, as it was part of a large initiative. I then moved to making benchmarking a permanent feature of the landscape. I figured it would be clear sailing from then on.

I was being naive again (well, I'll admit to stupid this time). Within a few weeks, I couldn't believe the change in my outlook. I couldn't believe how many new problems appeared, and how much harder it was to scale up. It was my first lesson in how having a successful pilot doesn't guarantee a successful program. A successful pilot doesn't even guarantee that you'll get a thumbs-up to proceed any further. You can bank on being much smarter than when you started. You'll be ready to do a better job than you would have without a pilot. But you're still under the gun. You can go from being the hero to being a goat. If anything, the pressure increases.

But this is the part that matters in the long run: embedding knowledge management into your organization. If you succeed, you'll have changed the way work is done. Permanently. In this chapter, we'll look at what's involved in embedding knowledge management into an organization.

How Long Will It Take?

If you were in the same room with me, you'd probably be tugging on my arm and demanding to know how many years you should plan on to embed knowledge management. I'm tempted to say "more than the sentence for a misdemeanor, closer to some felonies, but less than first-degree murder," but I'll resist. In practice, the answer is that it depends. We'll look at our two primary case studies, Hewlett-Packard Consulting and British Petroleum, to give you a rough idea.

Time Line at Hewlett-Packard Consulting

This abbreviated version of the time line later developed at Hewlett-Packard Consulting shows both the major activities and how long it took to implement their program.

1995	Recognized the need for and began exploring knowledge management. The HPC leadership was receptive to the concept.
May 1996	Initial discussion with SAP practice.
Fall 1996	Conducted pilot with SAP practice. Made the initial business case. Launched global KM initiative.
Spring 1997	Launched learning communities.
Fall 1997	Integrated project snapshots into project management methodology.
Summer 1998	Formed global KM team.
Fall 1998	Moved to Phase 2, systemic KM.
May 1999	Recognized knowledge management masters (special recognition program).

Fall 1999	HPC structure shifted to a regional mode. Consolidated and reorganized central KM team.
End of 1999	Knowledge managers hired in R&D and geographies.
2000	Moved to Phase 3, sustaining the KM effort.

Time Line for British Petroleum

This time line at BP, developed by Dr. Carol Gorelick, shows many similarities and also some differences.

August 1994	Team established to investigate emerging groupware technologies.
January 1995	Virtual teamwork pilot project team formed.
August 1995	First workstations for the virtual teamwork project installed.
June 1996	Knowledge management task force established.
November 1997	Development of knowledge management framework and methodology completed.
1998	Started to apply framework in significant value-adding projects
Fall 1998	Merger with AMOCO announced.
Late 1998–Early 1999	Restructuring of knowledge management in then BP AMOCO.
April 1999	Central knowledge management team greatly reduced in size.

Your time line could be entirely different. It'll depend upon many factors:

➤ The size, geographic dispersion, uniformity (or the diversity), and other factors relating to your organization.

➤ The amount of resources, funds, and time you have. For example, BP had a central KM staff of about 10 full-time people plus one part-time. HPC had about 20 for an organization of around 6,000 people during the initial phases and today about 30–35.

➤ The complexity of your approaches.

➤ The fit of your approaches with the organizational culture.

Tread the fine line between being a hare or a tortoise as gracefully as you can. I predict this'll necessitate much negotiation with your leadership and some adjustment as you go along.

Consolidating Lessons Learned

After the pilot it's time to forward all of your phones, hang a sign on the door (Skiing in the North Pole—back in a few months), and lock yourself in. Even though you should have been reviewing as you went along, now is the time to reflect at length.

Know How

An acid test for your framework is how simply you can describe it. Take a receipt or another scrap of paper no larger than the back of a small envelope. Can you sketch your framework in that small space?

You need to look back at the pilot from start to finish. It's also time to switch from recommendations on the day-to-day work of the pilot to recommendations for scaling up—or quitting.

To do this, I suggest that you use the learning-after process called a *retrospect* developed at British Petroleum and documented by Chris Collison and Geoff Parcell in *Learning to Fly*. Essentially, a retrospect is a review of a project or other major effort. The goal is to examine the lessons learned and to make recommendations for the future.

Preparation before the meeting is critical. First of all, the meeting should be scheduled as soon as possible after the project ends. Make sure that you invite the right people. Find yourself someone to facilitate, someone who wasn't involved in the pilot. The actual retrospect has several parts:

Know How

As part of an expansion you'll need to bring new people on board. Even if you keep the original KM team, it's hard to transfer all of what you've learned to new members. You may want to bring them in on your end–of–pilot review to help them come up to speed.

➤ Review of the project objectives and plans. Map out what happened, focusing on your tasks, deliverables, and decision points.

➤ Discussion of what worked well. Keep to the facts and insist on specific, repeatable advice.

➤ Discussion of what could have worked better. The purpose here isn't to assign blame. The purpose is to avoid mistakes in the future. Focus on what people would do differently if they had it to do all over again.

➤ Decision on whether to recommend continuing or stopping. Now's the time for brutal honesty. If you spent the pilot vainly begging for resources, arguing with leadership about the necessity for knowledge management, or losing to cultural issues no one's willing to face, it may be time to hang up your hat. The world may have changed, too: decline in revenues, unexpected losses, or other sad events. Internal or external events beyond your control such as a sudden economic downturn may change the organizational climate to one that's hostile.

Call it as you see it: continue or quit. If you continue, you'll need to evaluate your vision and strategy. You'll probably decide to recreate both. If you decide to stop there, at least try to make sure that the units using the approaches develop the supporting infrastructure they need to maintain them. Otherwise, if you just quit, you run the risk of losing all the ground you've gained. The organization will revert back to business as usual before you came along.

➤ Planning for the future. If you decide to recommend continuing, segue into planning. It's time to put together an expansion strategy.

Know These

A **retrospect** is an in-depth review held at the end of a project or other significant piece of work. It usually lasts about a few hours. The purpose is to capture lessons learned and make recommendations for future projects.

Expanding the Effort

Let's now look at how you expand beyond the pilot. There's a number of things you can do now.

Looking Again

Start with a clean slate on approaches. During the discussion of your expansion strategy, you may want to date around and marry some new approaches. If you had a single pilot with one approach, now's the time to play the field before you settle down. HPC began with one pilot and then expanded its approaches.

The Rush for Gold

This phase can resemble a gold rush, as everyone heads out to stake a claim and start panning for gold. No doubt about it, you want lots of enthusiasm and eager participants. What you don't want is folks going hog-wild and doing any darn fool thing they think of. Too much enthusiasm could lead to a big mess.

Know Nos

Don't allow anyone to sit silently in a corner. Make sure that everyone pipes up. A good way to start this rolling is to begin with a question that everyone has to answer, something simple like what was their role. Once people break the ice, they tend to keep contributing.

This is when you need some standards, policies, and procedures. You also need some enforcers (peaceful means only)—a central KM staff, an overseer group (such as the IT group at Hewlett-Packard Consulting), or some other group that can dance the dance of imposing as much order as is needed while still allowing people to exercise their creativity.

Ramping Up

You also have to decide how you will ramp up the effort. You have three options:

➤ Identifying specific projects and tailoring or developing approaches for them. Motorola does this well, always operating on a strict imperative to concentrate on projects that are linked to critical business objectives and also show a significant ROI. Projects often require fewer resources than an organization-wide approach and are easier to demonstrate concrete, specific results.

On the other hand, concentrating on specific projects can make it hard to embed knowledge management. For one thing, it creates an ongoing need for a central KM function, which can be more vulnerable to organizational shifts and stresses.

➤ Applying the approach(es) used in the pilot to other carefully selected areas of the organization. This middle strategy allows you to continue to target parts of your organization that are more receptive and, therefore, more likely to succeed. It also requires fewer resources than a global rollout.

This is another opportunity for brutal honesty. If you don't think you can pull off a global rollout, by all means go for a more limited scale up.

➤ Moving to a global rollout.

Now you need a whole bunch of resources. One of those that could be a showstopper is a knowledge management staff that can facilitate the rollout. During expansion, central KM teams tend to increase in size geometrically. You also may want to position such people within actual business units, close to the work and preferably with an in-depth knowledge of how the work is done there.

Know How

Valiantly try to time your recommendations so that any requests for resources match up with the proper time to submit budget requests. No matter how favorable your other circumstances may be, asking at the wrong time can put a hitch in your get-along.

Know How

You get what you pay for. If you decide against a global rollout, the amount of work and resources needed are less. The payoff for the organization is also less.

The larger the rollout, the higher level of management support you need. I wouldn't even dream of a global rollout without the CEO's support. For one thing, it's a matter of practicality. You just squared the resistance you will encounter.

Don't regard the CEO merely as a bank to be wooed for funds. A former CEO once asked me and my colleague to do something that I wish we'd thought of ourselves: conduct an assessment similar to what Hewlett-Packard Consulting did when they questioned their customers. The experience was as harshly illuminating as a theatrical spotlight. By golly, the CEO's some smart guy, I remember thinking. It changed the way I thought about him from being a semi-deity to just someone I worked with.

Paying for Your Sins

This is the time that mistakes you made way back when about scalability appear like the ghost of Christmas future to threaten you with a dismal end. Some could be:

➤ Poorly linking knowledge management to the business strategy

➤ Failing to consider cultural issues

➤ Picking supporting information technology that's not scalable across the organization (and other IT mistakes)

➤ Skimping on training

➤ Neglecting to build a broad base of organizational support

➤ Doing a poor job of building your repertoire of communications skills and strategies

➤ Failing to show proof that knowledge management delivers value and is thus worthwhile

And so on. Actually, no matter how carefully you planned to scale up, my bet is that you'll encounter some bumps along the road. Be prepared to deal with whatever problems pop up as you expand to the big time.

Know How

A supportive CEO can be one of your best partners. After all, this individual is in that position because of his or her abilities to formulate strategy, understand the business, and lead the culture. Regard your relationship as a collaboration. Of course, your culture may be more or less receptive to that concept and will help dictate how you handle it.

Know Nos

Never underestimate the disastrous effect of incompatible information technology, nor the determination of people to cling to their own systems. People sometimes claim their section is "special" and that without their particular information technology they can't do their jobs. Appeals to the greater good can fail. You may be pushed to enlisting the heavy hand of senior leadership. But this is a battle worth fighting.

Let me tell you that it's never too late to benchmark. Unless you compare yourself to external knowledge management programs, you have no way of knowing how good you are. Or how many gaps you have. You have no yardstick with which to measure yourself.

Sometimes you find out (to your immense surprise) that you're the benchmark. It turns out that the people you thought were such hot stuff are bowled over by what you're doing. Sometimes life is less kind, and you spend the exchange frantically taking notes and wondering if you'll ever catch up.

Usually the results fall somewhere in the middle. Some of what you're doing is great; some has room for improvement. But you'll never know until you go outside your own walls.

At the same time, you know your own organization best. You can best test the organizational waters to see how you're perceived internally. Don't discount your own knowledge, but combine it with a realistic view of what others are doing.

As you get further along in the expansion, both looking outside and relying on your own knowledge can help you to assess the strengths of your program, the weaknesses, and options for making it better. But this will only happen if, like you did during the pilot and initial expansion, you take the time to evaluate what you're doing.

Know Nos

Don't indulge yourself in what benchmarkers call industrial tourism. That is a benchmarking visit with no clear objectives and no resulting action. Define what it is you wish to learn, choose benchmarking partners who have the knowledge you need, and tailor any exchange so that you can get actionable information.

Part of the Establishment

Until the top dog joins the team, you aren't in the big time. You may have noticed (with envy) that both the top leader of Hewlett-Packard Consulting and British Petroleum were firmly committed to knowledge management. That's typical. The American Productivity and Quality Center notes that the best practice organizations come to rely on the CEO having a personal belief in the efforts and including effective knowledge management as part of the organization's vision.

However, depending upon your organizational scope you may be limited to embedding KM in a major business unit or division. In that case, you must have the support of the head of that unit or division, but not the CEO's. Never forget that it's extraordinarily difficult to embed KM across an entire large, global, and diversified organization in one fell swoop. Even with the CEO's support!

Didn't Know

In October 1996, the president of the World Bank, James D. Wolfensohn, announced the launching of an organization-wide strategy of knowledge sharing. He doesn't seem to have lessened his commitment over the years, either. In the annual report of 2000, Wolfensohn's message has a recurring thread of the importance of knowledge. He alludes to the important steps the World Bank has taken to advance the concept of a knowledge bank. He cites its experiences and lessons learned over the years. He writes of sharing knowledge with customers that is key to empowerment and progress.

Of course, even CEO's can leave. Another way to embed knowledge management is to make it a permanent part of the way business is done. This may be spelled out in the strategic plan. It may be part of policy. Or it may simply be an explicit part of the way your organization does business. Then even if the CEO does leave, it's more entrenched and harder to dislodge.

The time also has come to take on the reward and recognition system. If the current system fails to reinforce the behaviors needed for knowledge sharing, change it. I don't underestimate how difficult this may be. But what gets rewarded gets done. Some organizations have created separate rewards and recognition for knowledge sharing.

Know How

Performance evaluations feed promotions, another clear signal as to what's really important at a company. A former colleague of mine even claims that promotion recommendations are the best indicator of what matters in any organization. There's a lot to that.

You also could add new rewards and recognition to the existing system. That makes me a little uncomfortable, though. If other forms of rewards and recognition contradict knowledge sharing, I wonder which ones people will pay attention to.

Closely related and equally important is your performance evaluation system. A performance evaluation system should act as a coach, spelling out what behaviors are expected and giving suggestions, if needed, to steer someone back on track.

You also need to decide what sort of supporting personnel structure you want for knowledge management:

➤ One option, particularly if that's what you started with, is to maintain a centralized structure. You may want to move it, as the World Bank did by moving its KM staff from the CIO office to operations. Where it started life may not be the best place over the long run.

➤ Another is to reduce or eliminate the centralized support function and move roles to the local level. Hewlett-Packard Consulting did this and also increased the overall number of people in those roles. This puts the support folks closer to the actual work, as we discussed earlier.

➤ Another option is to eliminate the knowledge management function and outsource it. British Petroleum chose that option. In April 1999, it disbanded its central KM function.

Know Nos

Don't ignore new-hire orientations as a vehicle for maintaining cultural values and beliefs. An influx of new people destabilizes an organizational culture. Even though you may not have a large influx, over time even a slow influx can have an effect. Although they'll come in with their own cultural baggage, this is your chance to tell them what matters now in their new organization.

With knowledge management, in addition to retaining several people on a KM staff, British Petroleum also decided to allow some members of the team to leave with the intellectual property and form an independent company. That company, Knowledge Transformation International, now contracts to provide knowledge management support for British Petroleum and other clients. The ties are so close that the majority of their people have BP e-mail accounts. You may think it was foolish to make that decision, but it is consistent with the BP way of doing business. It also ensures that they still get additional support as and when they require it.

Know How

Although few companies are happy with the way they measure knowledge management, I do believe that as part of embedding it, you should consider measurement. I refer you back to Part 5, "Keeping Score."

Even if you dislike how BP handled it, it beats the heck of out declaring victory and sending all the troops home. That leaves no one to monitor how things are going and take action if necessary. Some believe that the hallmark of a truly successful knowledge management program is that a knowledge management staff disappears. I think that mind-set begs the question: If knowledge was so important that you launched an effort to better manage it, isn't it worth a continuing effort and attention?

That mind-set also ignores organizational entropy, the tendency to regress to old habits. If no one remains to sound the clarion call to value knowledge, an organization might revert back to the bad old habits.

Whether or not a knowledge management function does the work, do establish a means for assessing and monitoring continuing knowledge management efforts.

The Least You Need to Know

➤ Developing, implementing, and embedding a knowledge management program usually takes years.

➤ After you complete your pilot, assess what you learned and decide whether or not to continue.

➤ If you decide to continue, map out an expansion strategy.

➤ To embed knowledge management in an organization, you must gain the support of the CEO, become part of the way business is done, and align rewards, recognition, and the performance evaluation system. You also must decide what sort of supporting knowledge management function you wish to have.

Chapter 25

Lagniappe: The Thirteenth Doughnut

In This Chapter

➤ Managing your personal knowledge with IT

➤ Assessing your personal capital

➤ Importance and rewards of networking

➤ Finding mentors

In 1996, the American Productivity and Quality Center conducted its first consortium study on knowledge management. One of the six strategies discovered for knowledge management was *personal responsibility for knowledge.* Between that time and the year 2000, I saw practically nothing on the topic. It was as if the notion had dropped off the face of the KM earth.

Unbelievable, you might say. How could all of these people devote so much effort to improving the knowledge management of organizations and not think about applying it to individuals (not to mention themselves)? However, this issue has surfaced again in the field with the publication of several books and articles.

You may not be able to implement knowledge management within your organization, or at least not yet. But you as a knowledge worker and thus, a capitalist, can and must manage your own knowledge. We can no longer count on lifetime employment. We can no longer count on staying in one career field. Much like the sports figure making much more money than most of us, we're free agents, like it or not.

Know These

One definition of **peer-to-peer computing (P2P)** is computers communicating directly with each other. Another way to look at it is computers communicating and sharing resources with each other, often without an intermediary such as a server. One example is SETI@home, a group that looks for extraterrestrial intelligence by tapping the resources of personal computers whose owners install SETI@home's software.

Know Nos

Don't ignore the basic need for security. You may not have a firewall on your PC. The person with whom you're swapping files may not have virus software or have updated their software. Additionally, think about the potential burden on your PC. Many P2P applications require a lot of bandwidth. Can your PC handle the potential demands?

I titled this chapter lagniappe, a term used in Louisiana to indicate a little something extra, like the thirteenth doughnut in a baker's dozen. Until now, we've focused on the organization. In this chapter, the something extra is a focus on you, looking at some techniques for taking responsibility for, or managing, your personal knowledge. We'll also look at some of the rapidly emerging technology for supporting personal knowledge management.

IT Support for Personal Knowledge Management

My favorite definition of personal knowledge management comes from Steve Barth: taking responsibility for what you know, who you know, and what they know. It includes acquiring, creating, and sharing knowledge, developing personal networks, and collaborating with others.

Like an organization, individuals also need information technology support, and a new type of IT geared for individuals is becoming better known and more popular. This is peer-to-peer computing. For some, Napster has given *peer-to-peer computing (P2P)* a bad name. Forget that, because P2P is an option you need to consider for managing your personal knowledge. Peer-to-peer computing is computing that involves sharing resources and communicating between individual computers. That can include the sharing of files, work on shared documents, and communicating via instant messaging. Another form of P2P is the development of communities. These communities have shared spaces where they interact directly, doing such things as searching each other's computers, working together, and sending instant messages.

P2P is one way you can use technology to manage your knowledge. There are also applications that can help. For example, one application focuses on managing information. It indexes, finds, and views files in multiple formats. This may seem trivial, but think about how many files and how many formats you may have on your PC, all of which represent an inventory of your personal codified knowledge. How many megs or gigs do you have? How much time do you spend searching for files? It's something to think about, although the market for such applications is still relatively undeveloped.

Managing Your Personal Capital

Mick Cope, a writer and consultant in this field, has developed a methodology for assessing and managing what he calls *personal capital*. Personal capital has three dimensions:

➤ **Knowledge stock.** This refers to our store of tacit and explicit knowledge.

➤ **Knowledge currency.** This focuses on the ways we acquire or sell our knowledge.

➤ **Knowledge flow.** This involves the choices we make about processing knowledge.

All of these factors can be combined into a single framework that you can use to develop a visual display of your knowledge, which Cope calls a knowledge profile or K-Profile. This also helps you to assess and consciously manage your knowledge.

Knowledge Stock

Knowledge stock focuses on how your knowledge is stored, and whether it is explicit or tacit. As Cope points out, tacit knowledge also can be physical knowledge. For example, riding a bicycle is tacit knowledge of the physical skill needed to ride one.

Knowledge Currency

Knowledge is acquired and offered via one of three routes: head, heart, or hand.

The head is our thinking ability, often referred to as our intelligence. It includes our capability to learn, and use what we've learned.

The heart refers to the emotions that we use to manage ourselves and our relationships with

Know These

Personal capital is your own knowledge. It has three components: Your stock of knowledge, knowledge currency, and knowledge flow. You can assess and manage personal capital, just like other forms of capital.

Didn't Know

Another thing to think about is *implicit knowledge*, knowledge that can be articulated but hasn't been used yet. You can find it by looking at observable behavior and performance and then asking someone to explain what they've done. Or you can attempt to say out loud how you did something. From this perspective, implicit can be an intermediate stage between explicit and tacit.

others. We've talked about the importance of connecting people to people, but this hones in on the abilities needed to work with others. Not everyone has the emotional skills needed for collaboration, unfortunately, or the skills to resolve conflict, build trust, or wheel and deal politically.

The hand covers what we do. That can include our observable behaviors, our responses, our reactions, and so on. It can range from something like Pele's genius at playing soccer to a leader's ability to direct a team.

Knowledge Flow

Knowledge flow focuses on various processes for knowledge. There are five "d" words to describe it:

➤ **Discovery** is the process for enhancing the quality and quantity of knowledge stock. It includes reading, writing, collaboration, and even conference presentations.

➤ **Delay** encompasses knowledge that's stored for later use.

➤ **Dispose** is the often-neglected but necessary process of getting rid of old knowledge. The ability to unlearn is as important as the ability to learn. For example, in the chapters on corporate culture we discussed that many times what an organization learned in the past can cause it to fail in the present. What was once true is no longer true. Yet, the gorillas continue to keep other gorillas from getting the bananas.

➤ **Diffuse** concentrates on the process of sharing knowledge with others. The goal is to improve the value and quality of the knowledge being shared.

➤ **Deliver** refers to the process of capitalizing on your knowledge and getting a payback on it.

Taken together, these components can be put into a table, as seen below. You then can use it to do many things, including the following:

➤ Map out your future goals.

➤ Determine what knowledge you need to acquire.

➤ Develop strategies to acquire new knowledge.

➤ Identify new career options.

Know How

You more than likely will need more than one K-Profile. All of us have different roles. You're best off mapping the knowledge you need for each major role you play. This gives you a personal knowledge portfolio. Additionally, you may want to map out a role you want to have in the future. CIO.com has a research center called Future CIO, to give you an example.

➤ Manage your portfolio of knowledge. This includes making sure that your profiles complement each other, not act as a liability for each other.

➤ Use all of the above to help guide personal coaching.

Summary of the Explicit and Tacit Aspects of Knowledge Flow

Personal K-Profile	Discovery	Delay	Dispose	Diffuse	Deliver
Explicit (head)	Acquire new codified knowledge	Store codified knowledge	Discard old codified knowledge	Share codified knowledge	Sell codified knowledge in the market place
Tacit (Heart or Hand)	Acquire new intuitive knowledge	Store intuitive knowledge for later use	Discard old intuitive knowledge	Share intuitive knowledge	Sell intuitive knowledge in the market

If you want to read more about this framework and use it, read Cope's book, *Know Your Value? Value What You Know.*

Connecting Yourself to People

Take your own medicine. In Chapter 5, "Developing a Strategy," the advice was that if you have a choice between connecting people to people or connecting people to information, go with the people-to-people option. That's just as true for you as it is for your organization.

Giving to Get

You must learn to develop your own connections through networking. Networking will bring you many benefits:

➤ Information

➤ New ideas

➤ Answers to problems

➤ New business and social relationships

➤ Support in hard times

➤ Encouragement

➤ New opportunities

One benefit that may be important to you is influence. When you connect people to other people or information they need, you become a trusted source. At the same time, you begin to wield some influence. The people or information you refer gain value. Likewise, the people you choose not to refer (or the sources) lose the opportunity to gain value. That can give you enormous influence.

Another potential benefit is access to new work. As your network grows, you may find that some of the thought leaders in your field may share their new work with you or even invite you to help them develop it. This puts you on the leading edge of your field. What you give in return is careful thought, helpful suggestions, and an honest critique. Most people don't want a blanket endorsement or flattery of their work in progress. They want you to help them improve it. To get benefits from networking, you must give in order to get. It may seem like an unrealistic view of human nature; you may believe that people are inherently selfish and those that give get nothing in return.

Actually, the reverse is true. Most of us also have a need to give and this leads to reciprocation. Think about some of the shows you may have seen on TV where people publicly ask for help in finding someone who assisted them in a time of great need. Years later, they're driven by the need to find and thank that person.

In networking, don't think about what you'll get. Concentrate on helping people. Never forget that what may seem like a small thing to you could have an enormous impact on the person you help.

Know How

You may want to assess your personal networks. In his book *Achieving Success Through Social Capital*, Wayne Baker gives a simple methodology using social network analysis. I did it myself and was shocked to realize that despite years of devoting much effort to networking, I had some serious gaps. Even if you don't want to assess your networks, it's a great guide on how to network.

This brings me to one of the most important characteristics of the good networker—concern for the other person, not for your own gain. You undoubtedly will run into situations where it's in your best interest not to help someone. Perhaps it's a situation where your product or service is not the best solution for a customer. Perhaps it's something more personal, like a job opportunity for which you're not the ideal choice, but a friend of yours is. What should you do then?

As much as possible, do what's best for the other person. This also goes to the heart of another hallmark of the good networker—honesty. The foundation of any relationship is trust, the reasonable expectation of how another person will behave. If people perceive you as dishonest and untrustworthy, you'll never develop a good network.

Wait a minute, you may be saying at this point. Being a nice person is all well and good, but it's still reasonable to expect a return on all of that work. Don't worry, you will get a return. Again, the paradox is that the less you think about what return you'll get, the more you will receive in the long run. This is one investment with a guaranteed profit.

Granted, some people you help may not come through for you in tough times. Some may even betray you. But you have to look at the overall picture. And overall, the best way to help yourself is to help others.

Making Connections

There are many ready-made groups to tap for your personal network:

➤ Professional associations

➤ Alumni groups

➤ Communities of practice, both internal and external

➤ Internet communities

➤ Clubs

➤ Religious organizations

➤ Local interest groups

However, don't concentrate on only one or even a few. An important key to building effective personal networks is diversity. For both an organization and an individual, it's not just ignorance that's dangerous; it's what you don't know that you don't know that's potentially the worst situation. Having diversity in your networks, points out social network analysis expert Valdis Krebs, helps you to cross boundaries and discover what you didn't realize you didn't know—and needed to know. Some potential sources of diversity in networks are

➤ **Geography.** How international are your networks? Or within your own country, are you limited to one region?

➤ **Functionality.** Within your organization do your networks span different functions?

Crossing boundaries also can spark creativity and give you other opportunities you otherwise wouldn't have found. Make sure you build diversity into your networks.

> **Know How**
>
> Although it's far from ideal, you may find yourself contacting people for the first time by phone. Ask if there would be a better time to call them. They may not have time to talk. If so, set up a time to call back.

Tips on Networking

Once you find people, you need to connect personally with them. Usually, the best way to do this is face-to-face. What I look for is for the moment when someone lights up. This happens when someone talks about something they care about deeply. This may be a spouse, children, home, hobby, or some aspect of his or her profession. At that moment, there is a spark that is immensely attractive. You are seeing some of the very best of that person. I look for that because I respond to it genuinely. At that moment, I feel connected to that person.

For example, the next time you're at an airport, watch the other people who are waiting for someone to arrive. When that person walks through the gate, you can see it on their faces. Sometimes it's blatantly obvious how glad they are. Sometimes it's a quiet glow. But if you pay attention, you'll see it.

That's another key to connecting to people. You have to pay attention. People will tell you a lot about themselves, verbally and nonverbally, if you listen. The best networkers are great listeners.

Once you've connected, you need to provide value to that person. I view this much like being a personal shopper. For people in your network, build your knowledge of what their needs and wants are. The best way to find out is to ask them, but you also should be familiar with their work and professional and personal interests. Again, they'll tell you if you listen.

Know How

There are some generic needs and wants. For example, people are interested in information on competitors. If you discover that someone has a new competitor, tell him or her about it. Or you may notice something in the news and share that. Another example is a major new publication in someone's primary field.

One of the most important ways to provide value to people is to help them find information they need. The source may be another person. If so, introduce them to each other, provide some context, and gracefully step out of the way. In addition to making the connection, you're also providing another service: verification. You're vouching for the trustworthiness and knowledge of both parties. Take this responsibility as seriously as any doctor who refers a patient to a specialist.

One wonderful way to connect to people is to pass on a genuine compliment about their work. It seems to me that not only are we shy about accepting personal compliments, but we're shy about passing on compliments about someone. In addition to the personal recognition such a compliment provides, it also implies an interest in the work complimented and thus an opportunity to connect two people with common interests.

Know Nos

Don't refer people without asking their permission first. Some people don't want to be bothered under any circumstances. Some may want to be bothered, but want to be able to decide by whom and when.

Keep in touch with the people in your networks. Every so often touch bases to see how they're doing. Tell them what's going on with you. You put some effort into establishing the connection. Keep the investment going.

Another way to network is to act as the host. For example, at a meeting of your professional association, offer to set up a dinner for a small group. This takes a small amount of time to find and contact the restaurant, as well as acting as social co-ordinator. My preference is to keep this type of gathering relatively small so that people get a chance to talk one on one at length. I also suggest, just as with a personal dinner party, that you invite people who have common interests or who can help each other. To increase the potential networking value, you may even want to have people change places in the middle of the gathering so they sit next to someone new.

You also may want to host formal meetings. Again, you may volunteer to be the host for your professional association or other groups to whom you belong.

Both those informal and formal meetings can even take place electronically. The Internet offers many opportunities to host groups for free.

Know How

You might want to develop an informal agreement with your mentor that covers such topics as what is expected from both parties, how often you'll interact, and how you want to interact. The better you can set the expectations up front, the better both parties can meet those expectations.

Forming a Network of Mentors

One of the best things about this field is how quickly many move from the eager and earnest newcomer stage to old pro. However, during that initial stage, I suggest that you develop a network of mentors. You can ask people you meet to help you out. A professional or other association might be able to suggest people and connect you. There may be people locally who'd be willing to help a neighbor. You also may be able to find groups on the Internet.

The golden rule of networking is to give. However, at first you'll feel as though you're only taking, never giving. Do the best that you can. If you find something you can offer, do so. If you can't, keep in mind that your mentor undoubtedly loves this field and does enjoy helping others to learn about it. You can give your appreciation for that help. One way you can do that is by giving back details of how specific advice has helped you and other specific results.

Know Nos

Don't be shy with your mentor. If you don't understand something, say so. If a technique suggested to you didn't work, say so. If there's something about the way you work together that you want to change, say so. Your mentor needs feedback to give you what you need.

Most of all, you can give to your mentor the satisfaction of seeing the protégé transform into a peer. I remember the day that my first mentor in benchmarking came into town for a business trip and set up a lunch appointment with me. When I arrived, he told me that he had a perplexing problem and he wanted my help. I was startled. Ask me for help? It had always been the other way round. I then realized that I had become a peer in his eyes. It made all of the time that he'd invested in me worthwhile.

I also look forward to the day we can meet as peers, sit over a cup of coffee (or non-caffeinated beverage), and you can teach me some things about this field. In the meantime, welcome to the club.

The Least You Need to Know

➤ Personal knowledge management is taking responsibility for what you know, who you know, and what they know. It includes acquiring, creating and sharing knowledge, developing personal networks, and collaborating with others.

➤ Consider what information technology you could use to help you manage your own knowledge, such as peer-to-peer computing.

➤ Use networking skills and approaches to connect yourself to other people.

➤ Develop a network of mentors.

Glossary

artifacts   The visible aspects of an organizational culture.

attitude   Tendency to respond in a certain way, either positively or negatively, to something. In testing parlance, an attitude survey measures the strength and the direction of attitudes, with a single score for each attitude. Such surveys require considerable technical expertise to construct.

balanced scorecard   A measurement approach that focuses on linking an organization's mission and strategy to performance. It measures not only financials, but also customers, internal business processes, and learning and growth.

benchmarking   A systematic process of learning from the best that originated in the quality movement. It focuses on learning to improve performance. It implies humility, a willingness to acknowledge that others are better and to learn from them.

best practice   Best practices, processes, and techniques are those that have produced outstanding results in another situation and that could be adapted for your situation. Like all knowledge, it is contextual. A best practice is what is best for you.

browser   A piece of software that searches large amounts of information. A Web browser is software that interfaces with the World Wide Web, making it easier to locate Web pages, download files, play video, etc.

burning platform   In organizations, a burning platform is an issue that dictates change because not changing is unthinkable.

change agent   Someone who is responsible for planning and implementing a change. Knowledge of the basics of organizational culture, knowledge of the specific culture, and knowledge about the discipline of change management are critical. Experience, as always, is even better.

change management   This field focuses on ways to implement change within an organization despite resistance. Most CKOs regard their ability to master change management as a critical success factor.

chief information officer   An executive who is responsible for both IT strategy and the IT infrastructure. He or she must plan to meet business needs and to implement, and must have the same people skills that a CKO needs.

chief knowledge officer   A senior corporate executive whose role is to leverage knowledge, usually by leading a knowledge management program. The level is equal to that of the chief information officer, head of Human Resources, and other functional roles.

chief learning officer   A senior corporate executive. In contrast to a CKO, though, the role usually focuses more on leveraging learning and on education and training.

code of conduct   Also called a code of ethics or a credo, it is a statement of organizational values and guidelines for employee behavior.

corporate culture   The unspoken but shared assumptions that guide the daily behavior of people in organizations. It is not only what we do; it is the beliefs that underlie what we do—the whys. It is complex and hard to puzzle out.

corporate yellow pages   A mechanism to help people locate others with expertise, often utilizing individual Web pages.

creative abrasion   The purpose of diversity in team settings is to bring about creative abrasion. A team designed to be diverse has differences meant to rub together to produce friction. The result is not placid, but it does generate options.

critical success factor   Something that has to work so that the intended goal can be met.

current state   In change management, the current state is the ways things are right now. It's the "what is."

direct intellectual capital methods of measurement   Such methods estimate the value of intangible assets. To do this, the individual components must be identified and then evaluated.

Economic Value Added   A financial measure of an organization's performance. It is calculated by deducting the cost of capital from the net operating profit. Additionally, the balance sheet is adjusted to add back in costs often ignored, such as the cost of research and development, certain marketing costs, and also goodwill that has been written off.

effectiveness measure   This type of measure addresses whether or not you delivered what you were supposed to. The customer, not you, decides if you met their specifications for features and value.

efficiency measures   This type of measure assesses how well you do some sort of process. They look at how much it cost in terms of resources like people, materials, and time to complete the process. Typical efficiency measures are cycle time, cost, and rework.

employee competence   The capabilities of people in an organization are the employee competence.

explicit knowledge   Things we know that we can write down, share with others, and put into a database. One example is the steps used to perform CPR. Those steps can be described in a detailed, exact sequence of actions you can teach to someone.

extensible markup language (XML)   An important technology for content management. It is a set of rules for defining data structures that makes it possible for key elements in a document to be categorized by their meaning. A search engine then can find those elements.

external structure   The component of intellectual capital that is the value of your relationships with the people with whom you do business.

extranet   An extension of an organization's intranet that has been opened to selected outsiders, such as customers, suppliers, partners, vendors, or even members of the organization itself. An extranet uses Internet protocols and a public telecommunications system.

facilitation   Skills used to improve group interactions. These include conducting meetings, reaching consensus, resolving conflicts, improving relationships, and managing group tasks. In a team environment, the facilitator only addresses the group interactions, not the actual content.

firewall   A combination of hardware and software that protects a private network from unwanted intrusion. A firewall filters predetermined types of information from the Internet in an attempt to stop hackers from using the Internet as a means of entry.

future state   In change management, a future state is the finish line. It is what "done" looks like.

information richness   Information richness is a characteristic of a collaborative tool that indicates how much information and how many types of information it has. The more information-rich a collaborative tool is, the more context it provides.

instant messaging   Instant messaging is short-text e-mail messages that are sent and received immediately. Some applications have the capability to see who else is online. Others enable the messages to be stored and re-sent.

intangible assets   Assets that have value to a company, but no physical existence. Some intangible assets have been recognized for years: patents, copyright, and trademarks. In contrast, physical assets (such as land, buildings, and equipment) can be sold, used, and depreciated.

intellectual capital   This term includes everything an organization knows. That can be ideas, different kinds of knowledge, and innovations. The bottom line, though, is that it's knowledge that an organization can turn into profit.

internal structure   That part of intellectual capital that belongs to the organization. It includes patents, documented processes, and information carried on computer systems. Leadership produces much of internal structure, such as vision, strategy, and policies.

Internet   The global network of individual networks that are interconnected through public links. All of these networks use the TCP/IP protocol for communication. Anytime you connect two networks together, you have an Internet.

intranet   A private Internet. Most use the TCP/IP protocols that help provide a number of services.

knowledge   Information in context to produce an actionable understanding.

knowledge asset   Some sort of knowledge held by the organization. It has three components: Knowledge content contains what the knowledge is about and is often data or information; knowledge structure is how the knowledge is organized; knowledge reasoning is the active process that uses the content to complete a cognitive task such as problem solving or decision-making.

knowledge management   How an organization identifies, creates, captures, acquires, shares, and leverages knowledge. Systematic processes support these activities, also enabling replication of successes.

knowledge mapping   A process for identifying knowledge and skills.

knowledge spiral   A model proposed by Ikujiro Nonaka to represent how tacit knowledge and explicit knowledge interact to create knowledge in an organization, through four conversion processes or patterns: socialization (tacit to tacit), externalization (tacit to explicit), combination (explicit to explicit), and internalization (explicit to tacit).

knowledge worker   Knowledge workers are educated and have experience. They're hired for what they know. At work, they need information and knowledge as they apply theoretical and analytical knowledge. They see work as a source of satisfaction, a place to create and produce.

lagging indicator   A measurement term. It shows the outcome. It measures results, but not what may happen in the future.

leading indicator   A measurement term, a leading indicator is one that's predictive. Based on the results of the measure, you can either do nothing or make changes to affect the predicted outcome.

learning community   Hewlett-Packard Consulting defines a learning community as informal groups of people that cross organizational boundaries and come together to discuss best practices, issues, or skills that the group wants to learn about.

learning organization   An organization that creates, acquires, transfers, and retains knowledge. It's particularly good at changing its behavior to reflect new knowledge and insights.

local area network (LAN)   A local group of computers that are linked together physically by network cables. In contrast, a wide area network (WAN) covers more than a single building or area. WANs usually rely on leased communications lines.

market capitalization methods of measurement   Such methods look at the difference between a company's market capitalization and its stockholders' equity. This type of approach thus focuses on the perceived value of an organization in the marketplace, which can be volatile.

Moore's law   Gordon Moore, one of the founders of Intel, predicted that the computer power available on a chip would double approximately every 18 months—which accounts for computers becoming obsolete so fast.

network   A network is a loosely and voluntarily connected group of people who know each other and do things for each other. However, it isn't a team, which has a fixed task and is usually appointed by management. It also isn't cohesive enough or focused enough on a practice to be a community of practice.

operational definition   A description of any measure that is detailed enough for the remainder of the development process. It also sets the boundaries for what is and isn't included in the measure.

opinion survey   In contrast to an attitude survey, an opinion survey focuses on specific answers to specific questions. Each of those questions is important in its own right, although they may be unrelated to one another.

Pareto principle   Alfredo Pareto, an Italian economist, discovered a few people (20 percent) owned a large share of wealth (80 percent). In process improvement, the Pareto principle is applied to identify and prioritize problems. The goal is to categorize problems until the vital few (20 percent) of the causes can be identified, thereby addressing 80 percent of the problems.

peer-to-peer computing (P2P)   One definition of peer-to-peer computing (P2P) is computers communicating directly with each other. Another way to look at it is computers communicating and sharing resources with each other, often without an intermediary such as a server.

personal knowledge capital   Your own knowledge that can be assessed and managed, just like other forms of capital.

personal knowledge management (PKM)   Personal knowledge management involves a range of relatively simple and inexpensive techniques and tools that anyone can use to acquire, create, and share knowledge; extend personal networks; and collaborate with colleagues without having to rely on the technical or financial resources of the employer.

289

project snapshot   Hewlett-Packard Consulting defines a project snapshot as a session designed to collect lessons learned and materials from a project team that can be reused by future project teams.

prototype   In new-product development, a prototype is usually a physical model of the concept designed to get an idea of whether or not the concept is doable.

reliability   A key measurement concept. A reliable measure is one that gives consistent results.

retrospect   A retrospect is an in-depth review held at the end of a project or other significant piece of work. The purpose is to capture lessons learned and make recommendations for future projects.

return on assets methods of measurement   Such methods focus on an average earning from intangible assets. This is calculated by dividing the pretax earnings of a company by the average tangible assets. The result is compared to the industry average and the difference is multiplied by the company's average tangible assets to get the average annual earning of intangibles.

scorecard methods of measurement   Such methods concentrate on producing indicators or indexes for a range of intangible asset components. The indicators or indexes may be reported as scorecards or graphics.

search engine   A piece of software that carries out searches for information. Searches usually focus on finding content from multiple sources, such as all of the content on an intranet or the resources of the Internet.

serial discussion   Message boards and chat rooms can have serial discussions, where all messages are listed as they are received.

server   A computer that shares resources with other computers on a network. A Web server is a specialized server that is the lynchpin of an intranet. It includes the computer itself, the specialized software, and content.

social capital   Social capital is the connections between people and the associated norms of trust and behavior that create social cohesion. In an organization, it is a vital enabler to collaboration and knowledge sharing, as it provides a basis for cooperation and coordination.

social presence   Social presence indicates how a collaborative tool helps people to connect to each other. When a tool has high social presence, such as videoconferencing, the interactions are more social and warm. In contrast, tools with low social presence can seem distant and impersonal.

spam   A term used for junk e-mail. As with junk snail mail, your e-mail address may have been put on a list, and now you're getting unwanted e-mails.

springboard story   A springboard story enables a leap in understanding by the audience so as to grasp how an organization or community or complex system may change.

tacit knowledge   What we do not know that we know. It includes know-how, rules of thumb, experience, insights, and intuition.

taxonomy   A hierarchical structure for a body of knowledge. This framework gives an understanding of how the knowledge can be grouped and how the groups relate to each other. It also gives a way to classify a particular thing. In content management, a taxonomy is a classification scheme for the content in a system or interface. It organizes and helps users navigate through the content.

threaded discussion   In a threaded discussion on a message board or chat room, all of the replies to a message are grouped and indented under that message. This makes it easy to see what the replies are and to follow the discussion.

transition state   In change management, the transition state is the stage in between the current state and the future state. It is the journey of reaching your goals and vision.

Transmission Control Protocol (TCP)/Internet Protocol (IP)   Transmission Control Protocol routes and transfers data. It does so by breaking data into smaller units, which are stamped with the size and the sequence number. Internet Protocol (IP) handles the addressing and routing of the data to specific computers. Together, the TCP/IP protocols are the key protocol for Internet communications, and also for intranets.

trust   Trust is an expectation of how someone else will behave. It may be grounded in experience or it may be granted immediately.

validity   A key measurement concept. Asking if a measure is valid forces the question of whether or not a measure actually measures what it is supposed to measure. Unfortunately, validity is impossible to prove conclusively, but you can collect proof that a measure is valid.

value network   In the work of Verna Allee, a value network is a web of relationships that generates economic value through complex changes of both tangibles and intangibles.

vision   An idealized view of a desirable and achievable future state—where or what an organization would like to be in the future.

workflow   A group of tools that help automate business processes, leading to better quality work.

Web Sites

The range of topics covered in this book was broad, so the range of topics covered by the Web sites is equally broad. Web sites appear and disappear quickly, so there is no guarantee that a particular site will be operational when you attempt to access it.

The American Productivity and Quality Center

Many free sources are listed, as well as APQC publications. Bookmark this one. APQC also offers a knowledge management certification program.

www.apqc.org

The Balanced Scorecard Collaborative

Includes an online community center.

www.bscol.com

Brint, the BizTech Network

An extensive site on knowledge management as well as other topics.

www.brint.com

The Know Network

Includes a news section, a resources list, and links to other sites. Updated regularly.

www.knowledgebusiness.com

Celemi homepage

Includes articles and also information about the Celemi measurement report, as well as descriptions of its products supporting knowledge management and intellectual capital.

www.celemi.com

Web site for CIO.com

Includes current and past issues of *CIO* magazine, which is a top resource for both technical and nontechnical readers. Also has a knowledge management resource center.

www.cio.com

Web site for Collaborative Strategies

This Web site includes a number of well-written references by David Coleman, including many case studies.

www.collaborate.com

Web site for Community Intelligence Labs

Provides a wonderful resources page for communities of practice.

www.co-i-l.com/coil/knowledge-garden/cop/index.shtml

Web site for the Delphi Group

Includes a number of studies on knowledge management.

www.delphigroup.com

Web site for *Fast Company* magazine

Includes a reference section on change management.

www.fastcompany.com

Web site for Knowledge Management Consortium International

Gives information on this nonprofit organization, includes a news section, and has an online bookstore. KMCI also offers a certification program.

www.kmci.org

Web site for Lincoln Re

Here Mark Clare and Arthur W. DeTore, the authors of *Knowledge Assets: Professional's Guide to Valuation and Financial Management,* explain the methodology in their book.

www.lincolnre.com

Web site of Stern Stewart and Company

Includes information on Economic Value Added.

www.sternstewart.com

A number of journals are published electronically, or have a significant Web presence.

Knowledge Management Magazine (published monthly on the Web for free on the eighth of each month). This journal focuses, to a large extent, on information technology, but there are some insightful articles, particularly those by Steve Barth.

www.kmmag.com

Knowledge Management World, which focuses on information technology.

www.kmworld.com

Knowledge Management Review has a number of articles that can be downloaded, many for a fee. This is the best journal for the practitioner.

www.melcrum.com

A number of the KM leaders cited in this book have their own Web sites.

Web site of Verna Allee

Includes many downloadable articles and a library section with ratings assigned to the books.

www.vernaallee.com

Web site of Karl-Erik Sveiby

The Web site easily has the content of another book but is organized well into topic areas and individual sections. Dr. Sveiby also publishes work by others.

www.sveiby.com.au

The Peter Drucker Foundation

This includes several articles from each issue of their journal, *Leader to Leader,* which has articles by top thinkers.

www.pfdf.org/index.html

Web site of Etienne Wenger

Includes a list of publications.

www.ewenger.com

Web site of Richard McDermott

Includes a list of publications.

www.mcdermottconsulting.com

For more information on some of the information technology discussed in this book, I recommend the following Web sites.

Glossaries of information technology terms can be found at

www.2400hrs.com/glossary

www.trinity.edu/rjensen/245gloss.htm

To see a sample intranet, go to

www.wiley.com/compbooks/bernard

Additional Resources

Here is a list of nonprofit organizations:

The American Productivity and Quality Center

This non-profit organization has been a long-time leader in this field. APQC helps enterprises manage change, improve processes, leverage knowledge and increase performance by becoming more agile, creative, and competitive by providing information, strategies, skills, knowledge experience, contacts and best practices. They also have an informative website with many free resources that I recommend bookmarking. APQC also offers a KM certification program.

www.apqc.org

IBM Institute For Knowledge Management

This is a global consortium of about 40 organizations that participate in knowledge management projects. Research projects include such topics as communities of practice, social network analysis, and customer knowledge.

www.vistacompass.com/ikm_public/index.htm

International Corporate Learning Association

Founded in 1990, InterClass is a knowledge community, or consortium, of companies in different industries seeking to understand and implement the ever-changing concept of corporate learning. This concept includes—but is not limited to—ideas such as e-learning, organizational learning, communities of practice, instant and on-demand learning, intellectual capital, new management practices in the E-conomy, knowledge sharing, and new leadership styles.

www.interclass.com

Knowledge Management Consortium International

The KMCI is a non-profit organization devoted to developing a balanced view of knowledge management from the context of an organization, defining knowledge management as a part of a complex adaptive system involving people, processes and tools. The Web site gives information on the organization, includes a news section, and also has an on-line bookstore. KMCI also offers a certification program.

www.kmci.org

Queen's University Research Centre for Knowledge-Based Enterprises/Queen's KM Forum

The vision is that the Centre will be a global leader in the production, transmission, and diffusion of a better understanding of the management of knowledge-based enterprises through sustained partnerships with business, government, and academics. Their Web site includes research papers.

www.business.queensu.ca/kbe (Click on industry forums tab.)

Books and Articles

Books

Allee, Verna. *The Knowledge Evolution: Expanding Organizational Intelligence*. Boston: Butterworth Heinemann, 1997.

Baker, Wayne. *Achieving Success Through Social Capital*. New York: John Wiley & Sons, 2000.

Beckhard, Richard, and Reuben T. Harris. *Organizational Transitions*. Second Edition. Reading, MA: Addison-Wesley, 1987.

Bernard, Ryan. *The Corporate Intranet*. New York: John Wiley & Sons, 1998.

Bridges, William. *Managing Transitions*. Reading, MA: Addison-Wesley, 1991.

Bukowitz, Wendi, and Ruth Williams. *The Knowledge Management Fieldbook*. Harlow, UK: Prentice Hall, 1999.

Clare, Mark, and Arthur W. Detore. *Knowledge Assets: Professional's Guide to Valuation and Financial Management*. San Diego: Harcourt Professional Publishing, 2000.

Cohen, Don, and Laurence Prusak. *In Good Company*. Boston: Harvard Business Press, 2001.

Collison, Chris, and Geoff Parcell. *Learning to Fly*. New Milford, CT: Capstone, 2001.

Conner, Daryl R. *Managing at the Speed of Change.* New York: Villard Books, 1993.

Cope, Mick. *Know Your Value: Manage Your Knowledge and Make It Pay.* London: Prentice Hall, 2000.

Cortada, James, and John Woods. *The Knowledge Management Yearbook 1999–2000.* Boston: Butterworth Heinemann, 1999.

———. *The Knowledge Management Yearbook.* Boston: Butterworth Heinemann, 2000.

Davenport, Thomas H., and Laurence Prusak. *Working Knowledge.* Boston: Harvard Business School Press, 1998.

Deal, Terrence E., and Allan A. Kennedy. *Corporate Cultures: The Rites and Rituals of Corporate Life.* Cambridge, MA: Perseus Publishing, 1982.

The Delphi Group. *Knowledge Leadership Study.* Boston: The Delphi Group, 1998.

Denning, Stephen. *The Springboard: How Storytelling Ignites Action in Knowledge-Era Organizations.* Boston: Butterworth Heinemann, 2000.

Dixon, Nancy M. *Common Knowledge: How Companies Thrive by Sharing What They Know.* Boston: Harvard Business School Press, 2000.

Garvin, David A. *Learning in Action.* Boston: Harvard Business School Press, 2000.

Gonzalez, Jennifer Stone. *The 21st Century Intranet.* Upper Saddle River, NJ: Prentice Hall Computer Books, 1998.

Kaplan, Robert S., and David P. Norton. *The Balanced Scorecard.* Boston: Harvard Business School Press, 1996.

———. *The Strategy Focus Organization: How Balanced Scorecard Companies Thrive in the New Business Environment.* Boston: Harvard Business School Press, 2000.

Kotter, John P. *Leading Change.* Boston: Harvard Business Press, 1996.

Lesser, Eric, ed. *Knowledge and Social Capital.* Boston: Butterworth Heinemann, 2000.

Lesser, Eric, Michael A. Fontaine, and Jason A. Slusher, eds. *Knowledge and Communities.* Boston: Butterworth Heinemann, 2000.

Nadler, David A. *Champions of Change*. San Francisco: Jossey Bass, 1998.

Nonaka, Ikujiro, and Hirotaka Takeuchi. *The Knowledge Creating Company*. New York: Oxford University Press, 1995.

O'Dell, Carla, and C. Jackson Grayson Jr. with Nilly Essaides. *If Only We Knew What We Know*. New York: Simon and Schuster, 1998.

O'Dell, Carla, Susan Elliot, and Cindy Hubert. *APQC's Passport to Success Series: Knowledge Management*. Houston: American Productivity and Quality Center, 2000.

O'Dell, Carla, Farida Hasanali, Cindy Hubert, Kimberly Lopez, Peggy Odem, and Cynthia Raybourn. *APQC's Passport to Success Series: Stages of Implementation*. Houston: American Productivity and Quality Center, 2000.

Schein, Edgar H. *The Corporate Culture Survival Guide*. San Francisco: Jossey-Bass, 1999.

————. *Organizational Culture and Leadership*. San Francisco: Jossey-Bass, 1992.

Senge, Peter M. *The Fifth Discipline*. New York: Doubleday, 1990.

Simmons, Annette. *The Story Factor*. Cambridge, MA: Perseus Publishing, 2001.

Skyrme, David. *Measuring the Value of Knowledge*. London: Business Intelligence, 1998.

Stern, Joel, and John Shiely with Irwin Ross. *The EVA Challenge: Implementing Value Added Change in an Organization*. New York: John Wiley & Sons, 2001.

Stewart, Thomas. *Intellectual Capital*. New York: Doubleday. 1997.

Sveiby, Karl-Erik. *The New Organizational Wealth*. Williston, VT: Berrett-Koehler, 1997.

Tenner, Arthur R., and Irving J. DeToro. *Process Redesign*. Reading, MA: Addison-Wesley, 1997.

Tirwana, Amrit. *Knowledge Management Toolkit, The Practical Techniques for Building a Knowledge Management System*. Upper Saddle River, NJ: Putnam, 1999.

Von Krogh, Georg, Ikujiro Nonaka, and Kazuo Ichijo. *Enabling Knowledge Creation*. New York: Oxford University Press, 2000.

Articles

Allee, Verna. "The Value Evolution." *Journal of Intellectual Capital* 1, no. 1 (November 2000): 17–32.

———. "Reconfiguring the Value Network." *Journal of Business Strategy* 21, no. 4 (July–Aug 2000): On the web www.vernaallee.com/reconfiguring_val_net_html

———. "Knowledge Networks and Communities of Practice." *OD Practitioner* 32, no. 4(Fall–Winter 2000): vol 32, no. 4.

———. "A Delightful Dozen Principles of Knowledge Management." on the Web at www.vernaallee.com/12principles.html

Botkin, Jim, and Chuck Seeley. "The Knowledge Management Manifesto." *Knowledge Management Review* 3, no. 6 (January–February 2001): 16–21.

Carrozza, Tony. "From Hyperlinks to Human Links at Hewlett-Packard." *Knowledge Management Review* 3, no. 3 (July–August 2000): 28–33.

Collison, Chris and Geoff Parcell. "Embedding KM Into Business Practices at BP." *Knowledge Management Review*, 4, no. 2 (May–June 2001): 30-33.

Dale, Adrian. "Designing Taxonomies at Unilever." *Knowledge Management Review* 3, no. 6 (January–February 2001): 30–34.

Drucker, Peter F. "Managing Knowledge Means Managing Oneself." *Leader to Leader* (Spring 2000): On the web at www.pfdf.org/leaderbooks/121/spring2000/drucker.html

———. "The Age of Social Transformation." *Atlantic Monthly* (November 1994): On the web at www.theatlantic.com/politics/ecbig/soctrans.htm

Edmundson, Henry. "Technical Communities of Practice at Schlumberger." *Knowledge Management Review*, 4, no. 2 (May–June 2001): 20–23.

Fahey, Liam, and Laurence Prusak. "The Eleven Deadliest Sins of Knowledge Management." *California Management Review* 4, no. 3 (Spring 1993): 265–272.

McDermott, Richard. "Community Development as a Natural Step." *Knowledge Management Review* 3, no. 5 (November–December 2000): 16–19.

McDermott, Richard. "Nurturing Three-Dimensional Communities of Practice." *Knowledge Management Review* (November–December 1999): no. 11, 26–29.

———. "Public and Private Community Spaces." *Knowledge Management Review*, 4, no. 2 (May–June 2001): 5.

Parker, Andrew and Rob Cross and Dean Walsh. "Improving Collaboration with Social Network Analysis." *Knowledge Management Review*, 4, no. 2 (May–June 2001): 24–29.

Seeley, Chuck, and Bill Dietrick. "Crafting a Knowledge Management Strategy, Part 1." *Knowledge Management Review* no. 9 (November–December 1999): 18–21.

———. "Crafting a Knowledge Management Strategy, Part 2." *Knowledge Management Review* no. 10 (January–February 2000): 20–23.

———. "Crafting a Knowledge Management Strategy, Part 3." *Knowledge Management Review* no. 12 (January–February 2000): 20–23.

Seeley, Charles P. "Change Management: A Base For Sharing." *Knowledge Management Review* 3, no. 4 (September–October 2000): 24–29.

Sharon, Joyce, Lisa Sasson, Andrew Parker, Joseph Horvath, and Eric Mosbrooker. "Identifying the Key People in Your KM Effort." *Knowledge Management Review* 3, no. 5 (November–December 2000): 26–29.

Snowden, David. "Three Metaphors, Two Stories, and a Picture." *Knowledge Management Review*, no. 7 (March–April 1999): 30–33.

———. "Storytelling: An Old Skill in a New Context." *Business Information Review* (March 1999): 30–37.

———. "The Art and Science of Story or 'Are You Sitting Uncomfortably?' Part 1: Gathering and Harvesting the Raw Material." *Business Information Review* (September 2000): 147–156.

———. "The Art and Science of Story or 'Are You Sitting Uncomfortably?' Part 2: The Weft and the Warp of Purposeful Story." *Business Information Review* (December 2000).

Wenger, Etienne, and William Snyder. "Communities of Practice: The New Organizational Frontier." *Harvard Business Review* 78, no. 1 (January–February 2000): 139–145.

303

Index

Q-R

A Little Knowledge Goes a Long Way ...

Check Out These
Best-Selling
COMPLETE IDIOT'S GUIDES®

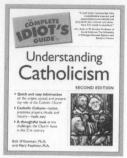

1-59257-085-2
$18.95

0-02-864451-4
$18.95

0-02-864382-8
$18.95

1-59257-115-8
$16.95

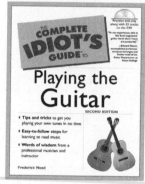

0-02-864244-9
$21.95 w/CD

0-02-864374-7
$19.95

0-02-864440-9
$14.95

1-59257-120-4
$18.95

0-02-864232-5
$19.95

More than *400 titles* in *30 different categories*
Available at booksellers everywhere

ALPHA